D1760320

(continued)

Children, Language, and Literacy
CELIA GENISHI & ANNE HAAS DYSON

Children's Language
JUDITH WELLS LINDFORS

The Administration and Supervision of Reading Programs, Fourth Edition
SHELLEY B. WEPNER & DOROTHY S. STRICKLAND, EDS.

"You Gotta BE the Book," Second Edition
JEFFREY D. WILHELM

No Quick Fix
RICHARD L. ALLINGTON & SEAN A. WALMSLEY, EDS.

Children's Literature and Learning
BARBARA A. LEHMAN

Storytime
LARWRENCE R. SIPE

Effective Instruction for Struggling Readers, K–6
BARBARA M. TAYLOR & JAMES E. YSSELDYKE, EDS.

The Effective Literacy Coach
ADRIAN RODGERS & EMILY M. RODGERS

Writing in Rhythm
MAISHA T. FISHER

Reading the Media
RENEE HOBBS

teaching**media***literacy*.com
RICHARD BEACH

What Was It Like?
LINDA J. RICE

Research on Composition
PETER SMAGORINSKY, ED.

The Vocabulary Book
MICHAEL F. GRAVES

Powerful Magic
NINA MIKKELSEN

New Literacies in Action
WILLIAM KIST

Teaching English Today
BARRIE R.C. BARRELL ET AL., EDS.

Bridging the Literacy Achievement Gap, 4–12
DOROTHY S. STRICKLAND & DONNA E. ALVERMANN, EDS.

Out of This World
HOLLY VIRGINIA BLACKFORD

Critical Passages
KRISTIN DOMBEK & SCOTT HERNDON

Making Race Visible
STUART GREENE & DAWN ABT-PERKINS, EDS.

The Child as Critic, Fourth Edition
GLENNA SLOAN

Room for Talk
REBEKAH FASSLER

Give Them Poetry!
GLENNA SLOAN

The Brothers and Sisters Learn to Write
ANNE HAAS DYSON

"Just Playing the Part"
CHRISTOPHER WORTHMAN

The Testing Trap
GEORGE HILLOCKS, JR.

Inquiry Into Meaning
EDWARD CHITTENDEN & TERRY SALINGER, WITH ANNE M. BUSSIS

"Why Don't They Learn English?"
LUCY TSE

Conversational Borderlands
BETSY RYMES

Inquiry-Based English Instruction
RICHARD BEACH & JAMIE MYERS

The Best for Our Children
MARÍA DE LA LUZ REYES & JOHN J. HALCÓN, EDS.

Language Crossings
KAREN L. OGULNICK, ED.

What Counts as Literacy?
MARGARET GALLEGO & SANDRA HOLLINGSWORTH, EDS.

Beginning Reading and Writing
DOROTHY S. STRICKLAND & LESLEY M. MORROW, EDS.

Reading for Meaning
BARBARA M. TAYLOR, MICHAEL F. GRAVES,
& PAUL VAN DEN BROEK, EDS.

Young Adult Literature and the New Literary Theories
ANNA O. SOTER

Literacy Matters
ROBERT P. YAGELSKI

Children's Inquiry
JUDITH WELLS LINDFORS

Close to Home
JUAN C. GUERRA

Life at the Margins
JULIET MERRIFIELD ET AL.

Literacy for Life
HANNA ARLENE FINGERET & CASSANDRA DRENNON

The Book Club Connection
SUSAN I. MCMAHON & TAFFY E. RAPHAEL, EDS., ET AL.

Until We Are Strong Together
CAROLINE E. HELLER

Writing Superheroes
ANNE HAAS DYSON

Writing Instruction That Works

Proven Methods for Middle and High School Classrooms

Arthur N. Applebee
Judith A. Langer

with Kristen Campbell Wilcox, Marc Nachowitz,
Michael P. Mastroianni, and Christine Dawson

National Writing Project
Berkeley, California

Teachers College, Columbia University
New York and London

Published simultaneously by Teachers College Press, 1234 Amsterdam Avenue, New York, NY 10027 and the National Writing Project, 2105 Bancroft Way, Berkeley, CA 94720-1042

Chapter 2 and the section "Uses of Technology for Writing at School" in Chapter 7 contain reworkings of material originally published in "A Snapshot of Writing Instruction in Middle Schools and High Schools," by Arthur N. Applebee and Judith A. Langer, 2011, *English Journal, 100*(6), 14–27. Copyright 2011 by the National Council of Teachers of English. Used by permission.

The National Writing Project (NWP) is a nationwide network of educators working together to improve the teaching of writing in the nation's schools and in other settings. NWP provides high-quality professional development programs to teachers in a variety of disciplines and at all levels, from early childhood through university. Through its network of nearly 200 university-based sites, NWP develops the leadership, programs and research needed for teachers to help students become successful writers and learners.

This project was supported by grants from the Spencer Foundation, the National Writing Project, and the College Board. The views expressed, however, are those of the authors and do not necessarily reflect the views of the funding agencies.

Library of Congress Cataloging-in-Publication Data

Applebee, Arthur N.
    Writing instruction that works : proven methods for middle and high school classrooms / Arthur N. Applebee, Judith A. Langer ; with Kristen Campbell Wilcox, Marc Nachowitz, Michael P. Mastroianni, and Christine Dawson.
        pages cm—(Language and literacy series)
    Includes bibliographical references and index.
    ISBN 978-0-8077-5436-8 (pbk.)—ISBN 978-0-8077-5437-5 (hardcover)
    1. English language—Study and teaching. 2. Report writing—Study and teaching. I. Langer, Judith A. II. Wilcox, Kristen C. III. Title.
    LB1576.A635 2013
    808'.0420712—dc23   2012051314

ISBN 978-0-8077-5436-8 (paper)
ISBN 978-0-8077-5437-5 (hardcover)

Printed on acid-free paper

Manufactured in the United States of America

20 19 18 17 16 15 14 13   8 7 6 5 4 3 2 1

For Richard Sterling,
who wanted us to do this study and kept after us until we did

◇◇◇◇◇◇◇

Contents

◇◇◇◇◇◇◇

Preface

You are reading this book thanks to the perseverance, hard work, networking, and persuasive skills of Richard Sterling, past director of the National Writing Project. It must have been in the year 2000 or 2001 that he first contacted Arthur about replicating the study he had done in 1979–80, published in 1981 as *Writing in the Secondary School: English and the Content Areas*. Richard felt the field needed an update on the state of writing instruction in American schools as a basis for making informed decisions about what was needed—in research and in practice. This first invitation met with a resounding "No." Arthur felt that too much had changed in the field, in educational policy, and in technology. Thus a replication of the first study did not make sense. But Richard persisted and also invited Judith to become involved. Finally, in 2005, with funds from the National Writing Project and the College Board, and a very much updated research agenda and research design, the National Study of Writing Instruction (NSWI) was born. In all, it involved 4 years of data collection interspersed with 2 additional years of analysis and synthesis of results. The final 3 years of work were funded by the Spencer Foundation as well as the National Writing Project.

Why did we do the study? Why did Arthur change his mind and say "Yes"? Why did Judith become involved? For both, the answer was in the timing. The No Child Left Behind Act was passed in 2002, legislation that carried higher stakes than ever, with immediate implications for teachers, students, and schools based on the test results. The rhetoric of the time demanded an improvement in literacy achievement, but in practice *literacy* meant reading, not writing. By the year 2005 our questions had become:

- What *is* happening in writing?
- What kinds of writing are students doing in English, social studies/history, mathematics, and science on a typical day?
- What kinds of instruction are they receiving?
- Has writing been sidelined in daily practice as teachers respond to the calls for a focus on reading?

- What about English language learners and students in poverty: What are their writing experiences like in comparison to their age-mates?
- And finally, what does writing look like given the rapid changes in the technologies for both creating and presenting information and ideas?

These questions were strongly related to the work each of us had been doing for most of our professional careers. They promised to move us, as well as the field, to new understandings about the interplay of broad educational policies, school and district emphases in curriculum and instruction, changes in social resources such as technology, and students' opportunities to learn to write well. They also promised to tell us, "What is writing literacy today and what can it be tomorrow?"

We describe the various parts of the new NSWI study in Chapter 1, with additional details available online (Applebee & Langer, 2011a). But the meat of the book is in the findings about current practice as well as the many examples of exemplary instruction; these are found in Chapters 2 through 9. Chapter 10 is both our reprise of *what is* and our vision of *what can be*—of the critical role writing can play in each of the major subject areas, across the middle and high school years, for all students.

◇◇◇◇◇◇◇

Acknowledgments

This study, and thus this book, result from the extraordinary cooperation of many colleagues with an interest in writing. First, we owe deep thanks to the National Writing Project, to the College Board, and to the Spencer Foundation for having supported our work. Without that support, the underlying research could not have been done. Our studies also could never have been completed without the hard work and dedication of Kristen Wilcox, Marc Nachowitz, Mike Mastroianni, and Christine Dawson, authors of individual chapters, as well as our other hard-working project staff at the Center on English Learning and Achievement. Whether helping us think through issues of design and analysis, carrying out case studies of schools and districts, or focusing on the laborious work of organizing databases and coding data, the talents of our research team played a critical role in the success of NSWI. We are also indebted to the 16 National Writing Project consultants who served as field researchers (and the site directors who supported them) during our five-state study of schools with reputations for excellence in the teaching of writing. They endured our training sessions, as well as frequent e-mails and phone calls, and met with us at national conventions to keep everything on track. Once we had selected the schools we wanted to study in their states, they arranged and made the school visits, kept careful records of what they saw, and sent all of the data they had collected to Albany to become part of our project databases. All of them, as well as research staff at the National Writing Project, were critical contributors to the success of the project. With deep thanks, we have listed their names, together with those of our staff at Albany and those at the National Writing Project who were most directly involved, in Appendix A of this book.

And, of course, we send our unreserved gratitude to each of the teachers, students, and administrators with whom we worked, and who allowed us to gather our data. Their names, when mentioned in this book, are pseudonyms; their contributions to us and to the field are real and gratefully appreciated. Most of the schools we studied asked to be recognized for their achievements, and their names are used throughout; a few others asked to remain anonymous. Appendix B lists the 20 schools chosen for their reputations for excellence in the teaching of writing, and provides additional information on their characteristics.

We would like to add our warm thanks to Emily Spangler, our editor at Teachers College Press. She has been a delight to work with.

—ANA, JAL

Vly Creek Farm

CHAPTER 1

◇◇◇◇◇◇◇

Writing Today

This book addresses a seemingly simple question: What and how are students in U.S. middle and high schools learning to write?

What seems like a straightforward question, however, masks a number of complex issues in literacy instruction. Three in particular shape the chapters that follow:

- To what extent does present-day writing instruction reflect "good practice" as indicated by research and policy statements on learning to write?
- How do content-area teachers outside of the English language arts, as well as English teachers, address the disciplinary demands of writing in their subject areas?
- How does the larger context for instruction, including the standards and assessments in individual subject areas, alter the writing experiences that students have?

To address these questions, we will be looking closely at students and teachers in schools across the country—some struggling with the many demands being placed upon our schools, others offering new visions of the role that writing can play when students are engaged in challenging subject matter across their core academic subjects. There are several themes that run through our discussion, including the following:

- The story of considerable progress in the teaching of writing over the past 30 years
- Some serious obstacles that constrain attention to writing in many schools and classrooms
- The opportunity and challenge to realign curriculum and instruction around the reading and writing skills that are central to each discipline

Together, they move us toward a vision of what writing at school can be like in the 21st century.

CONSIDERABLE PROGRESS:
RECENT HISTORY OF SCHOOL WRITING

Since the late 1990s there has been a renewed and very public effort to improve the literacy performance of the nation's children and adolescents. This has included direct attempts to improve practice through new standards and assessments, enshrined in the No Child Left Behind (NCLB) legislation of 2002. There also has been an emphasis on research (and research syntheses) with a focus on "what works." At first, these efforts targeted reading at the primary grade levels, including the Reading First initiative and the National Reading Panel report (Langenberg, 2000), commissioned jointly by the U.S. Department of Education and the National Institute of Child Health and Human Development. Later, the effort broadened to include writing, both as an ancillary skill and as a "comprehension strategy" that contributes to general literacy development (Pressley, Allington, Wharton-McDonald, Block, & Morrow, 2001; Torgesen et al., 2007). The focus also expanded from the initial stages of literacy development to the higher level skills that emerge in the middle and high school years (Biancarosa & Snow, 2006).

Focus on the "Second R"

Although these syntheses mentioned both reading and writing, their major focus was on reading and the instruction needed to improve it. Pushing back against this limited view of literacy, the National Commission on Writing in America's Schools and Colleges (2003), sponsored by the College Board, called writing the *"Neglected R"* in American classrooms and emphasized the importance of writing ability as a tool both for learning and for economic growth and social advancement. The commission's report included a broad list of needed reforms, including calls for teacher professional development, changes in curriculum, and significant increases in the amount of writing that students are required to do. Graham and Perin's (2007) report, *Writing Next*, took the process further, synthesizing research on effective writing instruction in order to better foster "evidence-based" practice. Taken together, these and related reports began to reinstate writing as a domain that needed specific attention in any effort to help adolescents gain the literacy skills and knowledge needed for their present schooling and future success.

The Common Core State Standards

Building on this work, writing is also featured in the *Common Core State Standards* (Council of Chief State School Officers [CCSSO] & National

Governors Association [NGA], 2010) as a major component of literacy in English as well as in the other core academic subjects. As the introduction to the standards describes it,

> Literacy standards for grade 6 and above are predicated on teachers of ELA, history/social studies, science and technical subjects using their content-area expertise to help students meet particular challenges of reading, writing, speaking, listening, and language in their respective fields. (p. 3)

The college and career ready standards that anchor the document identify ten specific standards for writing in English and other subjects. In slightly abbreviated form, the standards state that, across subject areas, students should be able to do the following tasks:

1. Write arguments to support claims in an analysis of substantive topics or texts
2. Write informative/explanatory texts to examine and convey complex ideas and information clearly and accurately
3. Write narratives to develop real or imagined experiences or events
4. Produce clear and coherent writing in which the development, organization, and style are appropriate to task, purpose, and audience
5. Develop and strengthen writing as needed by planning, revising, editing, rewriting, or trying a new approach
6. Use technology, including the Internet, to produce and publish writing
7. Conduct short as well as more sustained research projects
8. Gather relevant information from multiple print and digital sources, assess the credibility and accuracy of each source, and integrate the information while avoiding plagiarism
9. Draw evidence from literary or informational texts to support analysis, reflection, and research
10. Write routinely over extended time frames (time for research, reflection, and revision) and shorter time frames (a single sitting or a day or two) for a range of tasks, purposes, and audiences (p. 18)

Elaborated further to suggest appropriate goals by grade level, K–12, the standards outline an ambitious agenda for the teaching of discipline-specific writing in the next generation of curriculum and instruction. The writing standards for English language arts Grades 6 through 12 (pp. 42–47) are modified slightly for history/social studies, science, and technical subjects (pp. 64–66) by emphasizing the importance of discipline-specific content, norms, and conventions.

Two consortia of states have been developing sets of assessment instruments based on the Common Core State Standards (also called simply "the Common Core"): the Partnership for Assessment of Readiness for College and Careers (http://www.parcconline.org) and the Smarter Balanced Assessment Consortium (http://www.smarterbalanced.org). Both groups are committed to having new systems ready for implementation in the 2014–15 academic year. Each consortium will produce both formative and summative assessments designed to engage students in deeper understandings or to tap what they know, including at least some tasks that will require students to write. Thus these assessments inevitably will have a strong impact on both curriculum and instruction.

IMPROVED WRITING INSTRUCTION AND OBSTACLES TO GOOD PRACTICE

For at least the last 25 years the improvement of writing instruction has emphasized teaching students the skills and strategies needed to write effectively in a variety of contexts and disciplines. Such instruction has typically been called process-oriented and has emphasized teaching students to engage in extensive prewriting activities, sharing work with partners or small groups, sometimes writing more than one draft, and paying careful attention to the conventions of Standard English before final presentation to others.

Increases in Process Instruction and Technology Use

Graham and Perin's (2007) meta-analysis of research on writing instruction found that such approaches had a significantly positive effect on student achievement, whether considering "process writing" as a whole or focusing on its separate components, including teaching strategies for planning, revising, and editing; working collaboratively with peers; engaging in prewriting activities; or focusing on inquiry. They also found empirical support for setting specific product goals, the use of word processing to facilitate writing, the study of models, sentence-combining activities, summarization, and writing to support content learning. These findings are largely consistent with earlier syntheses, including Hillocks's *Research on Written Composition* (1986).

Of these approaches, reports from teachers as part of the National Assessment of Educational Progress (NAEP) in writing indicate that process instruction has been widely adopted for at least the past 20 years. In 1992 over 71% of eighth-grade students were in classrooms emphasizing process instruction, and another 26% were in classrooms where instruction was supplemented by process approaches. Results in 1998 (when the question was last addressed) were essentially identical. Students report similar emphases. In 2002, for example, 68% of students at Grades 8 and 12 reported that they almost always made changes to fix mistakes, and 39% reported that they almost always wrote more than one draft in their English language arts classes (Applebee & Langer, 2009). Less encouraging, NAEP results from 2002 to 2005 show there was a small but consistent drop in the amount of time devoted to writing in the other academic subjects, as well as in English. And many students reported they did not write very much for any of their classes.

The NAEP results also suggest major increases over the past 2 decades in the use of word processing. By 1996, over 90% of 11th-grade students were reporting that they used word processors for their writing, compared with only 20% in 1984. During the same period, the Internet was becoming a major resource for student writing; by 2002, over two thirds of Grade 12 students reported regular use of the Internet for information to support their writing.

The 2011 assessment asked about these issues in slightly different ways. On this assessment, 43% of eighth graders and 60% of 12th graders reported using the computer at least once or twice a week for school writing assignments. And 47% of eighth graders and 84% of 12th graders reported they used the Internet very often to look for information to include in their writing assignments. (Results from the NAEP Data Explorer [NCES, n.d.].)

How Are New Techniques Implemented?

The NAEP data on technology use and on teachers' reported approaches, combined with Graham and Perin's results, would seem to imply that the nation's teachers are using effective approaches to writing instruction, but achievement levels would suggest otherwise. NAEP achievement levels in both reading and writing have shown almost no change since 1969, when the first assessments were introduced, in spite of successive waves of instructional reform. Other studies that have looked more closely at classrooms raise a different possibility: It is relatively easy for teachers to assimilate new techniques into their practice, and that may be what is happening with process-oriented instruction. But it is much more difficult to change the underlying epistemology that shapes teaching and learning, and such changes may be necessary for instruction to work well (Applebee, 1986; Marshall, 1984).

One plausible explanation would be that teachers think their instruction is process-oriented, even though it isn't. Another would be that despite their best intentions, teachers who are not part of a professional community providing ongoing professional development and support find it difficult to teach as they wish or to maintain a needed level of consistency in their instruction (Langer, 2000). Effects of word processing, on the other hand, may not have shown up because the assessment was done with paper and pencil until 2011.

> *   Thus an important goal of the discussions in this book is to understand how and whether research-based practices like those enumerated by Graham and Perin (2007) and Hillocks (1986) are being implemented in the nation's schools.

Writing in the Academic Disciplines

A related problem in writing performance focuses on the kinds of writing students are asked to do at school, as well as the frequency with which they are asked to write—throughout the school day and across their academic classes. Early work on the development of writing ability (e.g., Britton, Burgess, Martin, McLeod, & Rosen, 1975; Kinneavy, 1980; Moffett, 1968) treated writing as involving a relatively small number of aims or purposes that subsumed a wide variety of more specific genres. Britton et al. (1975), for example, proposed that a simple taxonomy of transactional, expressive, and poetic techniques was sufficient to describe writing across all of the school disciplines, treating "report" (one of his categories for transactional writing) in science as in some fundamental way akin to "report" in literature or in history.

More recent research in writing has tended to emphasize the extent to which writing genres are socially situated and context specific. This is true whether one begins with Miller's (1984) emphasis on genre as social action, or the systemic linguistics approach of the Australian genre theorists (Cope & Kalantzis, 1993). These perspectives pose a challenge to the earlier emphasis on writing as a generic skill, taught primarily in English language arts or composition classes, and transferable directly to other disciplinary or socially constituted contexts. They suggest that what counts as effective argument and persuasive evidence varies greatly in moving from one context (or discipline) to another, so that what counts as "good writing" is itself socially constructed and context specific. As Halliday and Martin (1993) demonstrate, for example, science writing has many features such as reliance on technical vocabulary, use of the passive voice, and nominalization (use of verbs and adjectives as nouns) that English teachers find objectionable—though these features have evolved in science and other technical fields to serve particular communicative needs. Bazerman (1988), Bazerman and Paradis (1991), Russell (1991), and others have produced a substantial body of research on the disciplinary differences in writing that exist across the academic subjects.

This research suggests that a significant part of learning to write is subject specific: The skills and strategies that work well for writing in an English class may not lead to effective writing in other subjects. Or put another way, learning to write effectively within a discipline is part of that discipline's knowledge base—not simply another context to practice English language arts. One learns the content in a subject not merely by reading it but also by writing with it and about it in ways that are discipline specific; together with reading, writing is a literate behavior that underlies disciplinary "knowing" (cf. Langer, 2011a). This is quite a different perspective than that which has motivated a long history of efforts to encourage writing "across the curriculum," which have typically been treated as an English add-on rather than as an integral part of the various disciplines themselves (on the long history, see Applebee, 1974).

Graham and Perin's (2007) meta-analysis suggests another value for writing in the content areas: When students write about new concepts and ideas, they learn them better. In this way writing becomes in effect a cognitively engaging comprehension strategy (Guthrie & Alvermann, 1998) that can be used instructionally to activate what students know, consolidate new learning, or extend what they have learned (Langer & Applebee, 1987). In this sense, different kinds of writing can be used by teachers to help students deal with the material they are learning in different ways, sometimes extending and sometimes focusing student reasoning about the content (Langer, 1986).

> *   Thus a second goal of this book is to examine the ways in which writing is incorporated into the core academic disciplines, including what counts as writing well in these contexts, and whether and how students are learning discipline-specific writing skills.

AN OPPORTUNITY AND A CHALLENGE:
THE CONTEXT OF SCHOOLING AND ITS EFFECT ON WRITING

Although much research has highlighted the variability in teachers' approaches even within the same schools, other studies have made it clear that there are also powerful schoolwide contexts at work. Langer (2001, 2004), for example, found that it was elements of the larger professional context that distinguished middle and high schools whose literacy

achievement was consistently higher than that of demographically similar peers. The lone teacher struggling against the odds was not enough to
make a significant difference.

In the teaching of writing there have been a number of initiatives
over the past decades designed to improve student performance, including reduction of class size in English to allow more writing instruction,
efforts to institutionalize writing across the curriculum, development and
use of sheltered practices for English language learners (cf. Echevarria,
Vogt, & Short, 2004) and professional development projects such as the
National Writing Project. Such initiatives have uneven effects, taking hold
and becoming fully institutionalized in some schools, fading in others as
teachers and administrators shift their focus to other concerns.

Instruction is also shaped by initiatives or policies at a district or state
level. Writing, perhaps more than any other school subject, lacks a widely
accepted framework for discussing what students should know and be
able to do. The National Assessment of Educational Progress has used a
simple taxonomy based on purposes for writing: to inform, to persuade,
and to narrate (a category set that derives in large part from the work of
Britton, Moffett, and Kinneavy). Understanding that effective writing is
bound by the language, content, and uses to which it is put within specific
disciplines, the Common Core uses a similar set of three types of writing:
narrative, informative/explanatory text, and argument (CCSSO & NGA,
2010). These may be overly simplistic, but as presented in the standards
document they do provide space for each subject area to integrate its own
disciplinary norms of appropriate argument, evidence, and uses of language within the three broad types of writing.

When a particular approach to defining writing is in turn incorporated into high-stakes assessments, the influence on curriculum and instruction can be significant. Even the choice of scoring rubrics and anchor
papers can have unexpected and unintended consequences on what students learn (Hillocks, 2002).

> *   Thus a third goal of the present book is to relate the instruction
>   that students receive both to schoolwide initiatives and to stan-
>   dards and assessments of writing.

A CLOSER LOOK AT THIS BOOK AND THE RESEARCH BEHIND IT

In the chapters that follow we will draw from four studies to develop as
full an understanding as possible of writing instruction in U.S. middle and
high schools: what changes have occurred over the past several decades,

what instruction looks like now, and what the future may hold. These studies are all part of the National Study of Writing Instruction (NSWI) mentioned in the preface: a collaboration between the Center on English Learning and Achievement at the University at Albany, State University of New York, and the National Writing Project at the University of California, Berkeley, with additional support from the College Board and the Spencer Foundation.

The Research

The NSWI began in the recognition that there has been no systematic, large-scale examination of writing and writing instruction in the middle and high school years since Applebee's *Writing in the Secondary School* (1981) which gathered data in 1979–80. Because so much has changed in the 30 years since that study, NSWI did not attempt a direct replication of the earlier study. Rather, it sought to understand the impact of the variety of changes that have taken place through a series of studies that provide different perspectives on writing and learning in U.S. middle and high schools. We describe these studies in brief here, with a fuller discussion of the methodologies underlying the four studies available online (Applebee & Langer, 2011a). There were 4 phases to the study, each taking 1 year:

1. We began with analyses of data drawn from the National Assessment of Educational Progress to provide a first look at changes in the teaching of writing over the past 30 years (Applebee & Langer, 2009).
2. We followed this with yearlong case studies of six middle and high schools that reflected relatively typical practice in the teaching of writing in urban, suburban, and rural communities in upstate New York. These studies helped us understand the issues that teachers were facing in the teaching of writing across subject areas, as well as the historical and institutional contexts that were shaping instruction.
3. In order to understand what writing instruction looked like in contexts that were most likely to be supportive of it, we next studied writing and writing instruction in 20 middle and high schools chosen for local reputations for excellence in the teaching of writing. We selected these schools across five states that differed in their state-level approaches to curriculum and assessment in writing (California, Kentucky, Michigan, New York, and Texas). These studies included visits to 260 English, math, social studies/ history, and science classrooms; interviews with

220 teachers and administrators; and a semester's worth of written work from 138 students in these schools. The 20 schools and their characteristics are listed in Appendix B.

4. Finally, to put the individual schools in our studies into a larger context, we conducted a national survey of 1,520 randomly selected middle and high school teachers of English, social studies/history, science, and math.

The Chapters to Come

Chapter 2 provides a general overview of the state of writing instruction across levels and schools, including a discussion of changes that have taken place in the past 30 years.

Chapters 3 through 6 then consider the core subject areas. Each chapter begins with an overview of current practice, followed by examples of schools and classrooms that offer models for the future.

Chapters 7, 8, and 9 focus on three issues that cut across subjects and grades: the role that technology might play in supporting instruction; writing instruction for English language learners; and writing instruction in schools serving students in poverty.

Chapter 10 brings the book to a close by examining major themes and issues that emerge across all of the previous discussions, highlighting the problems, and envisioning the possibilities for the future of writing instruction in all subject areas.

Portraits of Success. In the various phases of the National Study of Writing Instruction, we saw examples of teachers and schools that were very successful in creating rich and engaging programs. In Chapters 3–9, within sections entitled "Portraits of Success," we will describe the models these programs provide. The challenge for the profession is how to ensure that such programs can continue to flourish and spread to other schools in spite of the constraints and pressures that are generated by the demands of high-stakes tests.

Writing in the 21st Century. One of the recurring themes we bring out in Chapter 10 is the importance of skills driving 21st-century productivity, including collaboration, creativity, cognitive agility, and knowledge generation, production, and transformation. Underlying these are the critical thinking and analytical skills—the ability to synthesize, evaluate, and connect to new contexts—that mark the innovators and intellectuals of any generation. But to make them work in the 21st century, students need to become active participants in their own learning, with a sense of agency for their ideas and opportunity to explore contexts and perspectives, to develop interpretations, to use what they know in order to formulate new connections, and to write about the possibilities they see, formulating careful arguments and explanations supported with evidence that is appropriate to audience and task. They also need to learn that knowledge in the 21st-century workplace does not rest within an individual, but in the collaborative cognition of a group.

The Common Core stresses the reading, writing, speaking and listening, and language skills of the individual, but the larger challenge will be to structure schools and classrooms where students learn to use their developing skills to become the innovators and leaders who can excel within the work environments of the next generation.

CHAPTER 2

Writing Instruction in Schools Today

Writing instruction 30 years ago was a relatively simple affair: The typical assignment consisted of a few sentences setting out a topic, given in class and finished up for homework. Students were expected to write a page or less, to be graded by the teacher. Almost no class time was given over to writing instruction, or even to introducing the assignment. When students were asked to write, the teacher took an average of just over 3 minutes to introduce the assignment, answer the inevitable procedural questions (How many pages? Single or double spaced? Can it be in pencil?), and ask the students to start writing (Applebee, 1981).

The teaching of writing was generally the domain of the English language arts class. Although teachers of other subjects did ask their students to write, this was usually done to "show what you know," not because the act of writing itself might have a special role in the acquisition of disciplinary knowledge and skill.

This portrait of writing instruction as it was over a quarter century ago, drawn from data collected in 1979–80 for Applebee's *Writing in the Secondary School* (1981), provides the backdrop and points of comparison for the current study. At the time of the earlier study, the profession was just beginning to develop a systematic research base on learning to write and writing to learn, building from the work of Braddock, Lloyd-Jones, and Schoer (1963), Britton (1970; Britton et al., 1975), Emig (1971), and others (e.g., Gregg & Steinberg, 1980). Since then, a concentrated period of research on writing development, teaching, and learning has ensued, accompanied by active engagement with teachers through collaborations such as the National Writing Project. This burst of research led to the development of new approaches, which were in turn shared in workshops and conference sessions, and taken up by many teachers across the country.

As we explained in Chapter 1, much has changed since 1980: in our understanding of effective practice, in the institutional context that shapes instruction, and in the technologies available for students to use. But how have these changes influenced the writing and writing instruction that students experience? That is the focus of this chapter, in which we provide an overview of current practice in the teaching of writing. Major topics include the amount of writing currently required, the audiences for student work, the impact of high-stakes tests, and the approaches to writing instruction in the core subject areas in middle and high schools across the United States.

HOW MUCH EXTENDED WRITING DO STUDENTS DO?

We asked teachers in the national survey how much extended writing (a paragraph or more) students were asked to do in a typical 9-week grading period, for each of the four core academic subjects: English, social studies/history, science, and math. Their responses indicated that, while students were asked to write more for their English classes than for any other subject, they wrote more for all their other subjects combined than they did for English. For papers of a page or less, for example, teachers reported requiring 5.5 papers for English during a 9-week grading period, 4.3 for social studies/history, 3.5 for science, and 1.1 for math. This adds up to 8.9 papers for the other subjects in comparison to 5.5 for English. The differences were smaller for papers of 1 or 2 pages (2.6 for English versus 3.5 for the other subjects combined) or 3 or more pages (1.1 for English as well as for the other subjects combined), but the pattern held. Clearly, students' experiences across the curriculum are likely to have an important impact on how they write and the qualities that they consider important in their writing.

Further, these figures suggest that even in English class students, on average, were not writing a great deal at the time of the national survey. Combining all three types of papers, the typical student was expected to produce approximately 1.6 pages a week of extended prose for English and another 2.1 pages for the other three subjects combined. When the National Assessment of Educational Progress asked a similar set of questions 15 years ago, results were quite similar: 40% of Grade 12 students reported hardly ever being asked to write a paper of three or more pages (Applebee & Langer, 2009). More recently, in the 2011 assessment, 10% of Grade 8 students and 14% of Grade 12 students reported they did no writing for homework for their English language arts classes in a typical week; another 31% at Grade 8 and 26% at Grade 12 reported a page or less of writing (results from the NAEP Data Explorer [NCES, n.d.]).

What is an appropriate length and frequency of writing may, of course, differ from subject to subject and from task to task; that is, what may be an appropriate length for a particular type of writing in one subject may differ in another subject. However, as Writing Standard 10 of the *Common Core State Standards* (CCSSO & NGA, 2010) asserts, it is still important for students to write "routinely over extended time frames . . . and shorter time frames . . . for a range of tasks, purposes, and audiences" (p. 18) appropriate to each discipline.

The amount of extended writing—a paragraph or more—seems particularly limited when viewed against how students spend the rest of their time. Of the 8,542 separate assignments that we gathered from 138 case study students in the 20 schools in the five-state study (a sampling of all of their written work in the four core content areas during a semester), only 19% of assignments represented extended writing of a paragraph or more; all the rest consisted of fill-in-the-blank and short-answer exercises, and copying of information directly from the teacher's presentations— activities that are best described as writing without composing. (Results were similar for middle and high school students, with 21% and 18% of their work, respectively, involving extended writing.)

Classroom observations found a similar emphasis, with students having pencil-on-paper (or, less often, fingers on keyboards) much of the time, but very little of it involving extended writing. In the middle school classes only 4% of observed class time was devoted to writing of a paragraph or more, rising to 8% in high school. Although low, this is a significant increase over results from 1979–80, when only 4% of observed class time in high school classes involved extended writing. (Middle school classes were not observed in the earlier study, so comparable data are not available.)

Even in the schools from the five-state study, selected for their emphasis on writing instruction, some of the teachers commented that there was less writing going on than might be expected:

> I don't do it [use writing] as much as I would want to do it. Most is done through notes, summarizing. Sometimes I have students do comic strips. I try to make it fun. (Grade 6 social studies teacher)

After a visit to a semiurban middle school in the study, the field researchers hinted at some of the constraints that limit the amount of writing assigned:

> While the current administration would like more writing, at present it's not a major focus. . . . All of the teachers agreed that writing and writing across the curriculum are important to student success.

However, they also stated that the current cuts in funding and pressure to teach a certain amount of specified content before state tests come around have drastically limited writing in their classes.

Teachers who have long-term institutional memory point to a time (about 15 years ago) when there was ongoing, excellent professional development in writing from both outside (a National Writing Project affiliate) and inside the district (writing project fellow who worked in the district). The district at that time had good funding and used it for professional development. (Field researchers' summary and interpretation of school visit)

Overall, in comparison to the 1979–80 study, students in our study were writing more in all subjects, but that writing tended to be short and often did not provide students with opportunities to use composing as a way to think through the issues, to show the depth or breadth of their knowledge, or to make new connections or raise new issues.

WHO READS WHAT STUDENTS WRITE?

Much of the emphasis in improving writing instruction over the past several decades has focused on providing authentic tasks that would be read by responsive audiences, including the teacher interacting with students about the growth of the ideas and understandings they have expressed in writing. This differs qualitatively from show-you-know writing where the teacher wants students to include particular information and students must figure out what is wanted. In the first case, the student and teacher are thinking about the student's understanding and how it can be refined and further developed; the student is an active agent in meaning development. In the second case the student is engaged in guessing what the teacher wants rather than what the ideas mean.

Teachers in 1979–80 and again in the present study were asked directly about who would read the writing from a typical class. Their responses show a noticeable shift over time, with students today being considerably more likely to have teachers respond to their work as part of what James Britton and his colleagues (1975) called a "teacher-learner dialogue" in which teachers react without necessarily assigning a grade. The percent of high school teachers in the four core subjects who reported reacting to students' writing without grading rose from 12% to 20% across these 30 years, and was even higher in middle school (35%). Similarly, the percent of high school teachers who frequently reacted as well as graded rose from 52% in the earlier study to 80% in the present study. Both sets of responses are evidence of a heightened concern with engaging with the content of student work.

Students today also are considerably more likely to be asked to share their work with other students. Over half of middle school and 44% of high school English teachers reported frequently asking students to share work with other students; in the earlier study, only 16% reported regularly asking students to share their work. Similar increases were apparent in responses from science and social studies teachers (increasing from 1% to 15% and from 3% to 7%, respectively), though they were clearly less enthusiastic than their peers in the English department.

WHAT IS THE EFFECT OF HIGH-STAKES TESTS?

That we teach in an era of high-stakes tests is more than obvious, but what can we say about the effects of such testing on the teaching of writing? At the middle school level, 81% of the teachers of English and 79% of teachers of math reported that the students in a typical class would take a high-stakes test *this year*; the comparable figures were 40% for science and 36% for social studies/history. At the high school level, 48% of the English teachers and 70% of the math teachers reported a high-stakes test *this year*, compared with 56% in science and 41% in social studies/history classes. For most subjects, three quarters or more of the teachers at both levels reported their students would face a high-stakes test in their subject *in this or a later* year. The only exception was for social studies/history, where only 58% at middle school and 50% at high school expected their students to have to take a high-stakes exam in their subject.

When asked about the importance of various external exams in shaping curriculum and instruction, the state exam was rated as important by 86% of the teachers at middle school, followed by district exams (64%). At the high school level, state exams again topped the list, rated as important by 66%, followed by district exams (48%), SAT and ACT exams (46%), and Advanced Placement or International Baccalaureate exams (30%). Unfortunately, as we will see, responses to other questions on the survey suggest that the importance placed on these exams does not auger well for the teaching of writing. Another series of questions asked what percent of the grade on the high-stakes test would be based on open-ended responses of any sort. The responses make it clear that relatively little writing was required even in English (an average of 30% of the high-stakes grade in high school, only 17% in middle school). Comparable figures for other subjects at the high school level were 26% for social studies/history, 12% for science, and 11% for math. These numbers are of particular concern because they included *any* open-ended responses, from single sentences to whole essays, as well as show-your-work and explain-your-problem-solving tasks in math and science. Even including these abbreviated tasks, the use of writing as a way to demonstrate content knowledge or disciplinary thinking was minimal.

English end-of-course exams, in contrast to high-stakes external exams, gave slightly more emphasis to extended writing. Teachers reported that 24% of the total grade in middle school, and 41% in high school, would be based on writing of at least paragraph length. But even these somewhat higher numbers mean that writing on average mattered less than multiple-choice or short-answer questions in assessing performance in English. (Percentages for the other three subjects did not differ noticeably from those for the high-stakes exams.)

Some teachers and administrators, in fact, were quite explicit about aligning their own testing with the high-stakes exams their students would face:

> I think our school gives significant emphasis [to writing]. One of the things that acts as a limiting factor on that emphasis is the TAKS [Texas Assessment of Knowledge and Skills] test, and only in English are students required to write in order to pass the exit level TAKS. In social studies, science, and math there are only multiple-choice components. I think the pressure to do well on TAKS sometimes takes away from the time that teachers feel that they have available and the energy they are willing to commit to [writing]. We spend a lot of time on TAKS preparation and, unfortunately, I think teachers would be nonsensical not to prepare kids for TAKS. (High school principal)

When asked how they prepare students for the high-stakes tests they face, teachers reported heavy emphasis on some familiar types of test preparation, including frequent "test prep" on the particular types of question that appear on the exam (76%), and using sample questions from old exams or commercial practice materials that present similar items (63%). They also reported making frequent use of rubrics or scoring systems similar to those that would be used on the exam (68%), and of incorporating the types of writing from the exam in the regular curriculum rather than providing "test prep" (71%). Although the provision of rubrics and the use of curriculum standards and assessments to align the curriculum can both be valuable strategies (see Langer, 2004), on balance the teachers' responses suggest that high-stakes tests were having a very direct and limiting effect on classroom emphases. And given the dearth of writing required on most tests, this created a powerful momentum away from the teaching of writing.

On another question, some 55% of English teachers reported frequent practice in timed, on-demand writing, another seeming response to the writing tasks that are included on some high-stakes tests. Such tasks were less frequent in subjects that were less likely to have on-demand essay questions: 24% for social studies/history, 17% in science, and 12% in math.

One teacher described the effects of the tests on the curriculum in her school:

> I teach sixth-grade social studies. They do a lot of writing in my class. We try to get them to echo the questions in their answers. And first, we probably start with basic sentence-building skills and eventually expand into writing paragraphs. Then, in eighth grade, they have their DBQs [document-based essays]. So getting them used to writing sentences, then paragraphs, then into essays. (Middle school social studies teacher)

Others described how what counts on the exam influenced, perhaps unintentionally, curriculum and instruction. The following comments are typical:

> Everybody's willing and enthusiastic every time we talk about [writing across the curriculum], and we get really excited. . . . But how often do you really get a chance to do something like that? . . . [We benchmark in math] four times a year, plus the state test, plus the practice state test. To give you an idea, we had a practice test middle of February and here it is the second week in March and we're doing another benchmark assessment. So we're losing another 2 days of work, and I could write a paragraph about that, but you couldn't publish it. (Middle school math chair)

> I used to do a research project but don't do it anymore because of the emphasis on tests. Research projects are so much more time intensive—go to bare bones to prepare for tests. (Eighth-grade history teacher)

> Writing is essential as it promotes higher order thinking, and it demonstrates to a teacher the extent to which students are understanding or making sense of the content. Currently high-stakes testing is at odds, at least in history, because there is mostly multiple-choice testing. (High school history teacher)

In the attempt to focus on what is most essential for later success, many state standards and their accompanying assessments have limited the range of purposes for writing. One eighth-grade language arts teacher described how writing instruction today compared with instruction at an earlier stage of her career:

> We don't do the fun things anymore. You can't give them a picture with a maze and ask them to write the adventure of what happened. You can't give them creative things; it helps with their fluency but it doesn't help with "business." It's all business now. It's all about standards-based teaching and teaching the standards.

The effects of examinations were not all bad, however; schools that focused on the International Baccalaureate or certain Advanced Placement examinations found that the exams increased their attention to writing:

> Because we're an IB school, there is a big emphasis on students being able to reflect on their learning; to reflect in some type of way that they have learned something. So there is a big emphasis on writing that reflection. So they're getting writing in all their classes; not just in the language arts class. (Sixth-grade language arts teacher)

> I guess 15 years ago, I would never have asked my kids to justify anything; it was just an answer, and I graded it. And now, I am trying to get them to be able to validate what their answer is and be able to put it into words so that they can support it. . . . I think one of the main influences in that has been the AP test, probably. (High school math chair)

And some changes in state exams do seem to be reinforcing the place of writing in the curriculum. A middle school math teacher in New York State explained the value she saw:

> When kids are writing, I can get a sense of what they understand, like taking a picture of what they understand—for assessment. Writing is a study skill for them. When they write in their own words, they understand the content better. It's a translation of sorts of what the book is saying. [It's] also a form of communication.

In the earlier study, carried out during 1979–80, pressure from external exams was nonexistent. Norm-referenced standardized tests were used to assess the progress of individual students, but they were not tied to the curriculum and did not carry high stakes for schools and teachers. In the current study, for better or for worse, external examinations are driving many aspects of curriculum and instruction.

WHAT KINDS OF WRITING INSTRUCTION DO TEACHERS EMPHASIZE?

For classes that were asked to do any writing of at least paragraph length, teachers were asked about their typical approaches to the teaching of writing. Teachers of all subjects reflected a concern with being clear about what was expected in particular types of writing assignments. The most frequent emphasis in all four subject areas was to clearly specify the specific parts (depending on type of writing, such things as introduction, body paragraphs, hypotheses, evidence, citations from passages, summary, or conclusions) that must be included (ranging from 94% of English teachers to 69% of math teachers); this was paralleled with an across-subject emphasis on providing rubrics that highlighted the characteristics of a good response (ranging from 82% of English teachers to 52% of math teachers).

Process-oriented approaches to writing instruction were widespread and easily identified in English classes (91% frequently spending class time on generating and organizing ideas before writing, and 90% teaching specific strategies for planning, drafting, revising, and organizing), and to a lesser extent in social studies/history (61% reporting class time on generating and organizing ideas before writing, and 41% teaching specific writing strategies). Also popular was providing models of effective responses for students to read, analyze, and emulate (85% in English, 43% in other subjects). This can be useful in helping students develop a clearer understanding of what is expected in different kinds of writing tasks.

Collaborative work remains less popular than teacher-led activities. Some 60% of English teachers reported frequently having students work together on their writing, and 44% reported organizing a workshop environment. Both approaches were less popular in other subject areas: Some 41% of teachers of the other subjects reported asking students to work together, and only 13% reported organizing a workshop environment for student work.

The following notes from a classroom observation illustrate how some of these emphases came together in a 12th-grade social studies class to support students' revisions of their work:

Teacher opened class explaining that their "Privacy Project Portfolios" were due next week. Today they'd have the opportunity to do a Gallery Walk . . . and give feedback (using feedback forms and rubrics) on portfolios before they're turned in.

Teacher outlined what the 1–5 scale meant in more specific terms. Rubrics clearly defining 1–5 are posted in the back of the room and also distributed for reference during the Gallery Walk. After expectations have been clearly outlined, students begin their Gallery Walk with their small groups, evaluating all projects except their own. Groups will then receive the feedback from the rest of the class in order to make revisions before the project is due.

Students are heard intensively (but quietly) reviewing the criteria rubric, trying to come to consensus on what an appropriate score will be for each section. Students are clearly actively engaged in the process, and the discussions and process seem familiar to them. The teacher was left free to monitor small groups, and have one-on-one discussions as needed regarding the evaluation/feedback process. Students were comfortable and familiar with the rubric, so much of Ms. H's time was spent observing and "listening in." She would occasionally step in and ask some pointed questions in order to elicit thinking about the rubric and the process.

At the end of class they were able to briefly discuss, when they gave a 1, why they gave a 1. Ms H: "Hopefully this will create a sense of urgency, that even if you thought you were done, you're not." Revision was encouraged.

As a set, these activities reflect a much more sophisticated understanding of effective writing instruction than was evident in 1979–80. In the earlier study, instruction took place mostly as a response to completed work, rather than as a systematic attempt to clarify the task and to provide strategies and collaborative activities that would help students learn to complete the task successfully. Only 32% of English teachers in the earlier survey, for example, reported making regular use of model responses, compared with 85% in the present study; only 37% reported brainstorming activities before writing, compared with 91% spending time on generating and organizing ideas in classrooms today.

The complication is that although teachers seemed to have a better understanding of appropriate techniques to use when they assign writing, they still did not assign much of it. Competing priorities, such as test preparation, constrained the amount of time given to writing instruction. Classroom observations in the 20 schools selected for local reputations for excellence in the teaching of writing represent "best case" scenarios, both in the selection of the schools, and in the fact that teachers were aware that our teams of observers were interested in the teaching of writing.

Even so, the percent of class time focused on any aspect of writing instruction was very small. In the English classes observed, 6% of time was focused on the teaching of explicit writing strategies; 6% on the study of models; 4% on evaluating writing, including discussion of rubrics or standards; 4% on vocabulary; 3% on structure and organization; 1% on grammar or usage; and 1% on spelling. (Since multiple things were often going on at once, summing these percentages would overestimate the time devoted to writing instruction.) To put the numbers in perspective, in a 50-minute period, students would have had on average just over 3 minutes of instruction related to explicit writing strategies (the most frequent emphasis observed), or a total of 2 hours and 22 minutes in a 9-week grading period.

Writing-related instruction was observed most often in English classes, but the other subjects had their own particular emphases. Science classes put most emphasis on the development of vocabulary (9% of observed time), coupled with the study of models (5%) and a focus on explicit writing strategies (3%), both typically in the context of the ubiquitous lab report. Math classes also emphasized the study of models (10%) demonstrating appropriate steps in solving mathematical problems, and vocabulary (4%). Social studies/history classes had the least emphasis on writing-related instruction, with most attention to the study of models (3% of class time) and to rubrics or standards for evaluation (2%).

Comparable data are not available from the earlier study, which found that most writing instruction came after the fact, in teacher comments and suggestions on completed work.

WRITING THEN AND NOW

The snapshot of writing instruction presented here looks quite different from the picture that emerged in 1979–80. In 1979–80 students were typically provided with a question to be answered in a page or less, with instruction taking place after the fact, in the comments and responses that teachers offered on completed work. In contrast, teachers today reported emphasizing a variety of research-based instructional practices (Graham & Perrin, 2007), including clearly specifying what is required in a particular type of writing; teaching specific strategies for prewriting, writing, and revision; and using models of successful responses for students to analyze, critique, and emulate.

If notions of good instruction have changed, for a variety of reasons the typical classroom still did not pay much attention to extended writing. In 1979–80 the majority of the writing that students completed was writing without composing—short-answer or fill-in-the-blank tasks, or copying from the board, where the resulting "text" was completely structured by the teacher or textbook. In the current study that picture looked much the same, with students completing many more pages of exercises and copying than they did of original writing of even a paragraph in length. And even some of the extended writing that students did complete was constrained in the current study as practice for on-demand, timed assessments. The instruction that occurred in such cases was limited to the skills necessary for successful performance on the specific types of writing included in the assessment, rather than on the development of the skills and strategies that would serve a student well in the varied tasks that make up the much larger domain of writing that students will encounter in higher education and the workplace.

For Example: Two Social Studies Tasks, Then and Now

We can illustrate the changes that have taken place with two examples, one drawn from the earlier study, and the other from the present one. Both are social studies tasks that ask students to deal with broad historical questions.

Then. The question from the earlier study given in Figure 2.1, on the changes that occurred during the Reformation, is in many ways an impossible task, requiring book-length treatment to be handled well. It becomes a possible task only when it is seen as a request for a summary of material that has already been covered by the teacher or textbook. To do well, the students have to have learned a series of generalizations about the Reformation, and must be able to repeat them in their own words; the task does not ask for original analysis or synthesis.

Now. Now consider the task in Figure 2.2, on the causes of the French Revolution. Like the question from the earlier study, this is essentially a test of what students know about a particular historical period. Indeed, the instructions begin by asking them how they would answer the ques-

FIGURE 2.1. A Typical Writing Task from 1979–80

Western Europe on the eve of the Reformation was a civilization going through great changes. In a well-written essay describe the political, economic, social, and cultural changes Europe was going through at the time of the Reformation. (25 points) (Ninth-grade social studies)

Note. From Applebee 1981, p. 74.

tion based on what they have already learned. The task continues, however, providing them with a set of new source materials to analyze in light of their knowledge of the historical period and in light of the question that is posed. This is a considerably more difficult task than the earlier example, and its structure provides a variety of supports to help students complete it successfully (including some comprehension questions that are not presented here, following each of the documents).

Such document-based questions are typically accompanied by a rubric that explains how the essay will be graded, providing a tool for revision and self-evaluation. New York State, where this question originated, offers a generic rubric for such document-based questions (New York State Education Department, Office of State Assessment, 2007). A superior paper (scoring 5 on a 0 to 5 scale):

- Thoroughly develops all aspects of the task evenly and in depth
- Is more analytical than descriptive (analyzes, evaluates, and/or creates information)
- Incorporates relevant information from at least xxx documents [xxx varies by item]
- Incorporates substantial relevant outside information
- Richly supports the theme with many relevant facts, examples, and details
- Demonstrates a logical and clear plan of organization; includes an introduction and a conclusion that are beyond a restatement of the theme

A minimally scoring paper (score of 1), on the other hand:

- Minimally develops some aspects of the task
- Is descriptive; may lack understanding, application, or analysis
- Makes vague, unclear references to the documents or consists primarily of relevant and irrelevant information copied from the documents
- Presents little or no relevant outside information
- May demonstrate a weakness in organization; may lack focus; may contain digressions; may not clearly identify which aspect of the task is being addressed; may lack an introduction and/or conclusion

This task is typical of many that we have seen across subject areas, with built-in scaffolding and an obvious attempt to be clear about what success will require. Many of the tasks we have seen exhibit the prob-

FIGURE 2.2. A Typical Writing Task Now

CAUSES OF THE FRENCH REVOLUTION

Historical Context: The French Revolution of 1789 had many long-range causes. Political, social, and economic conditions in France contributed to the discontent felt by many French people—especially those of the third estate. The ideas of the intellectuals of the Enlightenment brought new views of government and society. The American Revolution also influenced the coming of the French Revolution.

Directions: The following question is based on the accompanying documents in Part A. As you analyze the documents, take into account both the source of the document and the author's point of view. Be sure to:

1. Carefully read the document-based question. Consider what you already know about this topic. How would you answer the question if you had no documents to examine?
2. Now, read each document carefully, underlining key phrases and words that address the document-based question. You may also wish to use the margin to make brief notes. Answer the questions which follow each document.
3. Based on your own knowledge and the information found in the documents, formulate a thesis that directly answers the question.
4. Organize supportive and relevant information into a brief outline.
5. Write a well-organized essay proving your thesis. The essay should be logically presented and should include information both from the documents and from your own knowledge outside of the documents.

Question: What were the most important causes of the French Revolution? (Discuss three.) (10th-grade social studies)

---

lems that are buried even in this example, however. Although the task requires students to work with new material, the underlying task remains one that begins with a restatement or summary of points that have been developed in previous classes or in the textbook, and then asks students to use the new documents to illustrate (or "richly support") those points rather than to generate new understandings. There is also a tendency in tasks of this type to generate formulaic writing. In this particular case, the admonition to "discuss three" causes of the French Revolution points strongly toward a five-paragraph theme, albeit one to be elaborated with new details drawn from the accompanying primary source documents.

Hillocks (2002) noted this tendency toward formulaic writing in his critique of state writing assessments, and teachers in the schools we studied were quite aware of the dangers, if resigned to the necessity. As one teacher put it,

I think we become repetitive, but it's the nature of the beast—same things with TAKS (Texas Assessment of Knowledge and Skills); this is what you have to write, this is what has to be included, you have to include this number of quotes, you have to respond to your quote, so I think our essays become the same thing. We are able to use different literature, but the essays tend to have the same process. Same outline.

I think we need to move away from TAKS and move more into extended writing. Begin with this idea, add to it, add to it, add to it, rather than just little chunks. Our students now have a hard time finding a focus and staying with it with anything long enough to have extended-writing assignments. (12th-grade English teacher)

On the brighter side, some teachers have been successful in revising their curriculum and instruction in response to new knowledge about effective instruction, resulting in students who do well on high-stakes tests because they are immersed in a rich and engaging curriculum (Langer, 2004). At the end of their visit, one of our teams of field researchers described such a high school program, warts and all:

From the teachers observed and interviewed, it seemed the majority of teachers had an in-depth understanding of how writing can propel thinking, how writing can help students understand content, and how writing can help teachers understand what students come away with. They draw on a wide repertoire of approaches and strategies. Most impressive is that teachers have specific intentions and are very reflective about the writing strategies they teach. Some of the strategies observed were: deconstructing prompts, how to pose questions, how to anticipate readers' questions, strategies for paraphrasing, Socratic Seminars, use of criteria charts, writing on "Classroom Graffiti Walls." (Field researchers' summary and interpretation of school visit)

THE BOTTOM LINE

Clearly the 30 years since the previous national study have seen a great deal of development in teachers' conceptions of writing and its importance in learning. Across subject areas, teachers voice an understanding of the ways in which writing can contribute to learning, see writing as a valuable tool for assessing students' understanding, and in many cases see unique and particular roles that writing could play within their own disciplines.

At the same time, the actual writing that goes on in typical classrooms across the United States remains dominated by tasks in which the teacher does all the composing, and students are left only to fill in missing information, whether copying directly from a teacher's presentation, completing worksheets and chapter summaries, replicating highly formulaic essay structures keyed to high-stakes tests, or writing to "show they know" the particular information the teacher is seeking. Writing as a way to study, learn, and go beyond—as a way to construct knowledge or generate new networks of understandings (Langer, 2011a, 2011b)—is rare.

CHAPTER 3

◇◇◇◇◇◇◇

Writing in the English Language Arts

Christine Dawson

The teaching of writing has long been an integral part of the English curriculum. It is implicit in 6 of the 12 Standards for the English Language Arts promulgated by the National Council of Teachers of English and the International Reading Association (1996), and it has a similar role in the *Common Core State Standards* (CCSSO & NGA, 2010). Yet there are many debates about the best approaches to writing instruction and about the amounts and types of writing that students should do.

Indeed, the very nature of writing curricula in English classes is complex. English teachers are urged to prepare students to use writing to inquire, to communicate, to learn, to demonstrate knowledge or understanding, and to participate in disciplinary conversations. These varied purposes can make it challenging for English teachers to create a writing curriculum that supports the development of skills and knowledge across the broad domain of writing, while at the same time attending to other major components of the English curriculum, including literature and language study. For our purposes, it may be useful to consider the overarching goal of writing instruction in English language arts classrooms as rhetorical in nature: to prepare students to consider context, purpose, and audience in making their choices about genre, organization, and language.

EFFECTIVE WRITING INSTRUCTION IN ENGLISH LANGUAGE ARTS

Researchers have explored these curricular and instructional challenges, asking questions about what features of writing instruction result in what types of learning. Research has shown that writing instruction that focuses on clear instructional objectives, that is inquiry-based, and that supports students as they interact with peers around complex tasks results in the most significant gains in student writing (Hillocks, 1995). A more recent study also demonstrates the significance of a cohesive curriculum, high academic expectations, and authentic, discussion-based, instructional approaches in increasing students' abilities to perform well on challenging literacy tasks, including writing (Applebee, Langer, Nystrand, & Gamoran, 2003).

Looking across these and other studies, we can identify several characteristics of effective writing instruction that position students and teachers to best meet the complex writing demands implied in English language arts curricula. These characteristics include the following:

- Curricular cohesion (Applebee, 1996; Smagorinsky, 2008)
- An emphasis on authentic discussion practices promoting student inquiry (Nystrand, 1997)
- Opportunities for students to collaborate around complex tasks (Langer, 2001)
- Explicit instruction in writing strategies (Graham & Perin, 2007; Hillocks, 1995)

Since the 1970s recommendations for the teaching of writing have focused on one or another version of process-oriented approaches to instruction as a means to implement these types of instructional practices and to help students develop as writers. While the term *process writing* has been used in wide and varied ways (Pritchard & Honeycutt, 2006), in these pages we have particular interest in classroom examples where teachers understand writing as recursive and rhetorical in nature (Hairston, 1982), in which an author moves between gathering ideas, drafting language, and revising and reenvisioning writing decisions, attending to a clear purpose and desired effect upon an audience (even if that primary audience is the self). Paul Prior (2004) explains:

> Situated acts of *composing/inscription* are themselves complex composites. Writers are not only *inscribing text*. They are also repeatedly *rereading* text that they've written, *revising* text as they write as well [as] going back later to revise, pausing *to read other texts* (their own notes, texts they have written, source materials, inspirations), pausing *to think and plan*. (p. 172; italics in the original)

As process-oriented writing instruction has evolved over the past several decades, and especially with the advent of "post-process" or "structured process" approaches, we can see a shift in the teacher's role

(Applebee, 1986; Smagorinsky, Johannessen, Kahn, & McCann, 2010). Rather than being primarily the assigner and assessor of writing as in so-called traditional or product-focused writing instruction (historically with little emphasis on the instruction of writing itself; see Applebee, 1981), the teacher essentially is responsible for leading students' inquiry into writing practices and processes (Hillocks, 1995; Ray, 2006). Teachers in these writing classrooms teach students specific strategies for generating content, determining writing purpose and desired effect on an audience, considering questions of form and genre, analyzing and emulating models, conferring with other writers about their writing, and revising their writing based on feedback from self and others (Atwell, 1998; Calkins, 1986; Dawson, 2009; Ray & Laminack, 2001).

At the same time, process-oriented approaches to writing instruction stand in tension with some trends in curriculum and instruction, particularly the emphasis on high-stakes tests. Typically, to the extent writing is included at all in high-stakes assessment, it is on-demand writing with little time for recursive processes of reflection and revision. According to critics, these limitations on writing tasks lead to narrow definitions of "good" writing and formulaic approaches to instruction (Hillocks, 2002).

THE WRITING STUDENTS ARE ASKED TO DO IN ENGLISH

Taken as a whole, the results from the national survey presented in Chapter 2 suggest that while students write more in English classrooms than they do in any other subject, they still have relatively limited opportunities to engage in extended-writing projects—and the nature of these writing experiences may be further limited by constraints associated with high-stakes testing.

Overall, teachers' reports in the national survey indicate that only 12% of the extended writing assignments for English were three pages or more in length. By comparison, in our study of schools with local reputations for excellence in the teaching of writing, 25% of the extended writing assignments completed by case study students were at least three pages in length. There was also an appropriate progression by grade level, with the more extended compositions rising from 22% of the total work at Grade 6 to some 40% by Grade 12. (It is important to remember, of course, that fully 54% of the assignments that students completed for English required only short-answer or fill-in-the-blank responses.)

While English teachers reported valuing most those writing assignments identified with essential disciplinary knowledge (e.g., literary analysis), they also valued other genres and types of writing. The five types of writing that were rated as important by the most teachers were the following:

- Critical analysis of issues or a text (96%)
- Student response or interpretation (94%)
- Explanations of subject-area concepts (89%)
- Persuasive writing (85%)
- Personal essays or personal narratives (85%)

Not surprisingly, very few English teachers rated any type of writing as unimportant, yet two traditional staples of the English curriculum were not rated as important by 29% of the English teachers: Imaginative writing and research papers. These responses demonstrate one of the challenges associated with creating a coherent writing curriculum in English language arts, where teachers must balance the demands of teaching students to participate in conversations within the disciplines of English while preparing them to write for broader audiences and purposes beyond those disciplines.

As we pointed out in Chapter 2, English teachers reported frequently using instructional strategies designed to support students in completing particular assignments (e.g., clearly specifying the parts of assignments, studying models and rubrics), as well as strategies designed to help students engage in the processes associated with effective writing across contexts. Taken together, these responses indicate that much of the process-oriented instruction that teachers described was likely implemented in the context of helping students produce successful responses to specific writing tasks, especially those that mimicked tasks on high-stakes tests.

In contrast, fewer teachers reported emphasizing problem solving and inquiry in their writing instruction, and peer interaction around the content, organization, form, and language of student writing also received inconsistent attention. Only about 58% of English teachers reported frequently using collaborative approaches to writing instruction (peer conferences and revision), and less than half reported frequently using workshop approaches or inquiry-based instruction.

Overall, typical practice in the teaching of writing in English language arts seems constrained by the pressures to prepare students for the limited genres of writing featured on high-stakes tests, on the one hand, and the wide range of potential audiences and purposes for writing, on the other. The result in many classrooms is an overemphasis on formulaic approaches and a movement away from writing tasks that extend over days or weeks, as well as from imaginative writing, that might otherwise play a more important role.

PORTRAITS OF SUCCESS

We now turn to exploring effective lessons and schoolwide initiatives from our five-state study of schools with reputations for excellence in the teaching of writing. We selected these examples to illustrate effective, research-supported writing instruction, including cohesive and intentional writing curricula; an emphasis on authentic, inquiry-based discussion practices; opportunities for students to collaborate around complex tasks; and explicit instruction in writing strategies and practices. Additionally, the examples that follow show students developing, using, and assessing their own writing strategies across contexts.

Instruction for On-Demand Writing

Because English language arts teachers are tasked both to prepare students to write about disciplinary content (in particular, about literature) and also to write across other contexts, preparing students to take high-stakes tests can present a particular challenge. In Santa Monica, California, eighth-grade teachers at John Adams Middle School navigated these issues by helping students attend to the writing context and audience of high-stakes tests, treating test essays as a genre that can be studied and practiced through attention to process-oriented writing strategies.

Ms. Bridges, the principal, was a former English teacher and a strong advocate of writing. She routinely provided time for teachers to write at faculty meetings, and she invited the teachers to share writing they did outside of meetings. Ms. Bridges described her practice of regularly writing back to each teacher (approximately 50) as "a labor of love for me." She also took a keen interest in writing instruction schoolwide. At the semester break, for example, she asked every teacher to provide samples of student writing (taken from three different ability levels), which she used to determine staff development priorities for the coming year.

Part of Ms. Bridges's commitment to writing instruction came from her own professional development experiences. She had taken workshops with Lucy Calkins and Katie Wood Ray (two leading advocates for writing workshop pedagogies; see Calkins, 1986; Ray, 2006), and she purchased many writing books for the teachers' professional library (including those by Nancie Atwell, Lucy Calkins, Ralph Fletcher, and many others). Teachers reported that Ms. Bridges emphasized workshop approaches to writing instruction, and that she encouraged teachers to model writing practices by writing alongside their students. Additionally, she ensured that English teachers at each grade level shared a common planning period, and she provided an on-site coach once a month to support them in implementing Lucy Calkins's approach to reading and writing workshops.

Regarding high-stakes tests, Ms. Bridges described John Adams Middle School as focusing "on the standards and how students are meeting the standards rather than focusing narrowly on state and local assessments." Despite the fact that students in the eighth grade took a high-stakes test, Ms. Bridges believed that strong teaching would prepare students for the most part for those assessments. Consequently, the emphasis at John Adams was on effective writing and writing instruction, as opposed to out-of-context test preparation.

Using Process Approaches to Plan On-Demand Writing. We gathered several examples of writing instruction by eighth-grade English teachers at John Adams Middle School, in which teachers adapted process-oriented writing pedagogies to prepare students both to write about literature and to take on-demand writing tests. For example, once a month eighth graders chose independent reading books from a focal genre or category of literature (e.g., award-winning novels, biographies, or historical fiction). After finishing their books, students responded to a prompt during a timed, in-class writing task modeled after the district writing assessment. In December students independently read award-winning novels and then received the following writing task and instructions: "In 4 paragraphs, analyze the personality of one of the characters from your December award winner. Refer to two specific events from the text." This prompt (like all monthly book responses) followed the district writing assessment's focus on characterization in literature, and students' essays were assessed using a rubric that was essentially the same as that for the district test. The three components of the rubric focused on thesis and content/evidence; organization, structure, and style; and conventions and syntax.

This practice of modeling in-class writing assessments after high-stakes test questions is not in itself unusual. Rather, what stood out at John Adams was the emphasis on the students' writing processes as they tackled the writing task. Before beginning their essays, students were asked to "unpack" the prompt. Questions below the prompt asked students to identify a "cue word" from the prompt (for the essay on the award-winning novel, for example, the cue word was "analyze"), to restate the question in their own words, to identify the rules for this type of essay (in this example one student responded, "3rd person, present tense"), and to locate any additional instructions in the prompt (in this example, to write four paragraphs and refer to two specific events). After unpacking the prompt, students had additional space on the same page to plan their essays. In some cases the teacher suggested a particular method for this planning work (e.g., lists, outlines, or bubble clusters), and in other cases the students were free to choose their own planning approach.

For some essays students also received a worksheet on indirect characterization, which had a blank outline of a person surrounded by a thought bubble, a speech bubble, and other boxes where students could write. Directions told students to "Look for characterization clues [in the story] and fill in the bubbles with passages/quotes from the text of the story. Then, on the lines below, explain what those SHOW not tell about the character." The worksheet drew students' attention to specific techniques which authors use for indirect character development, such as showing the character's thoughts, speech, appearance, feelings, actions, and the reactions of other characters. Students filled out these characterization worksheets before beginning to write their essays.

These assignments demonstrate a way that eighth-grade teachers prepared students to write about disciplinary content in English (i.e., characterization in a novel) and to respond to on-demand writing tasks with substantive content and appropriate form. Taken together, the worksheets asked the students to first use writing to help them interpret the writing task (unpack the prompt), then analyze their focal character (by identifying and interpreting quotes about characters on the indirect characterization worksheet), and then to plan their essay (using the space for creating a list, outline, or bubble cluster). While all of these stages were presumably intended to prepare the student to write the essay, it is worth noting that they were nonetheless *writing* activities and strategies, through which students made sense of and organized their thinking about the text and the task. Only then did students write the on-demand, timed essay, knowing that they would be assessed using the district assessment rubric, with which they were also familiar.

This example also shows a way that the eighth-grade teachers focused curricular decisions and some writing assignments around the high-stakes tests their students would take. Each month students wrote one of these timed essays on their independent reading books, each time with a focus on characterization. The prompts changed, however: One might ask students to explain how life events shaped a person's life in a biography; another, to compare the personalities of two characters from a historical fiction play. It is also important to note that these were not the only things students wrote that year. Among other things, students also wrote poetry, how-to articles, and end-of-year reflections on their personal growth at John Adams Middle School.

Using Models to Revise. We also had an opportunity to observe eighth-grade English teacher Ms. Rudolph as she led her class at John Adams Middle School through a discussion of students' responses on the district writing assessment. We observed the class after students had taken the Santa Monica–Malibu Unified School District Writing Assessment, in which they had read a brief excerpt from Tobias Wolff's *This Boy's Life: A Memoir* (1989) and then had written responses to the question, "What kind of person is Toby's mother? How do details of the passage support your judgment?" Note that the test question followed the consistent focus on characterization and character analysis.

Ms. Rudolph began class by asking students to copy the following notes into their writer's notebooks:

> Effective writers review their past writing to find areas of strength
> and weaknesses to improve skills for future writing. How?
> 1. Look at a sample of a good essay.
> 2. Read your essay out loud to yourself.
> 3. Note places where it does not make sense or where meaning
>   breaks down.
> 4. Rewrite your essay to show how you would improve it—typed by
>   Tuesday.

These questions explicitly framed the lesson as a study of (and inquiry into) writing techniques, including looking at models (to understand genre conventions and audience expectations) and reading one's own essay aloud (to aid in clarifying and adding details to the writing).

After the students had copied the instructions, Ms. Rudolph handed out packets of "anchor papers" (sample student responses) from the previous year's district writing assessment, and she discussed the way teachers use anchor papers like these to calibrate their scoring. In this way, she called attention to the audience for such essays, and the criteria that the audience used to assess what they read. She then read aloud the first essay in the packet, which had earned a top score the previous year, and asked the students if they could recognize the outline or global statement of the essay. She also asked the class, "What does the writer do well?" Students provided responses, observing vivid language, good transitions, and the way the essay "made me think." When Ms. Rudolph asked if anything was not correct in the essay, students observed some grammatical mistakes, such as tense changes.

As Ms. Rudolph continued to walk her students through several other anchor papers, she facilitated a discussion on the importance of the essay responding to the prompt, the range of scores students could receive in order to be "proficient," and the various places a writer might put a thesis statement. The lesson provided an opportunity for students to explore, through class discussion, some aspects of audience expectations for their essays, as well as different ways they might approach similar tasks.

Throughout this portion of the lesson, Ms. Rudolph was teaching her students techniques for examining a model and observing strengths and weaknesses, which student writers could then apply to their own writing.

After finishing with the anchor essays, Ms. Rudolph returned the students' district assessments without the rubrics or scores on them, and she asked students to find a place in the room to read their papers aloud to themselves. She explained that reading their writing aloud is a revision strategy they could use, since it could help them "catch some mistakes" that they might have missed when they reviewed their essay silently. After they read their papers aloud, students were to write down three things they planned to revise. Only then would they receive their scores and rubric assessments.

In making these pedagogical decisions, Ms. Rudolph was disrupting the normal approach implied in high-stakes testing, where the students merely take the test and receive the grade. In this case, however, Ms. Rudolph invited the students back into their writing, asking them to use model essays to help them evaluate their texts before finding out their scores. Later, students would revise their essays and assess their own writing using a checklist derived from the rubric, again shifting ownership and purpose from the district assessment to the classroom and student writer.

Looking across both the monthly on-demand writing about independent reading and the observation of Ms. Rudolph's lesson, we can see several elements of process-oriented instruction. In both examples, there was an effort to analyze a genre (the character analysis essay) and to identify the features of an effective text (through the rubric, unpacking the prompt, and discussing anchor texts in class). Instruction on writing techniques also was woven throughout these lessons, as students practiced organizing strategies (indirect characterization worksheets to assemble evidence, list/outline/bubble clusters to organize writing) and revision strategies (reading their work aloud to help them identify areas for revision). In these examples, the characterization essay was taught as a particular genre, with particular conventions and expectations, rather than as a decontextualized formula to be remembered and duplicated.

Modeling Revision Strategies in an Inquiry-based Workshop Setting

The preceding examples reflect writing instruction designed to engage students in disciplinary conversations about character analysis and to analyze genre expectations associated with high-stakes testing. Yet these are only some of the many writing contexts for which English language arts teachers must prepare their students. As noted previously, English teachers also are called on to help students develop writing strategies they can use across writing contexts. At Amadon High School, we observed Ms. Greene, a 12th-grade English teacher, leading her students in a writing lesson during an interdisciplinary unit on privacy rights. Unlike the John Adams examples, Ms. Greene's students were not writing about content specific to English as a discipline, and they were not explicitly preparing for high-stakes assessments.

When we observed the school, Amadon High School teachers participated in interdisciplinary Small Learning Communities (SLCs), and Ms. Greene's SLC emphasized backwards design around culminating, interdisciplinary essays. There was also a strong National Writing Project presence in the English department, both through department work and through individual teachers' participation in a local Writing Project site. Ms. Greene herself was a Writing Project teacher consultant. Across the school, the majority of writing instruction that we observed was process-oriented, with a great deal of collaborative group work and class discussions. As at John Adams Middle School, even when students engaged in on-demand writing, they spent class time in relevant process-oriented practices, such as drafting, sharing, and analyzing student writing.

Ms. Greene and her colleagues had received a grant to support the development of the unit on privacy rights. Students began the unit by researching privacy rights (e.g., relating to Facebook, backpack searches, and airport travel), and then worked collaboratively to write essays or action plans. Ms. Greene took responsibility for teaching the students research skills and bibliography formatting, while a colleague from social studies focused on government issues related to privacy. The teachers collaboratively covered how to address a privacy question, and they collaboratively evaluated the projects.

In the lesson we observed, Ms. Greene focused on helping students engage in purposeful revision practices. The activity not only provided students insight into how peers read their work, but it also demonstrated how to take an authentic inquiry stance as readers and how to collaboratively revise writing. On the board at the front of the room Ms. Greene had written, "Revision Activity: Modeling the Process." She began by passing out a sample student text and asking students to write questions for the author on Post-it notes. She told students to place the notes directly on the paper in the places where their questions arose. Here is an excerpt from the beginning of that sample student text:

> Security has become a prominent issue in the United States since the turning of the century. In order to maintain the privacy of civilians protected, as given to us in the Fourth Amendment, which states: "the right of the people to be secure in their persons, houses, papers and effects against unreasonable searches and seizures shall

not be violated . . . " we must act upon the responsibility of the abuse and make that the technology such as video surveillance in businesses is free from this problem. Our group came up with a list of ideas that would help keep civilians safe without being cheated of their privacy.

"Think about clear writing," Ms. Greene advised her students as they read. "It's great that you learned something [about privacy rights]," she said, but their job was also "to learn about how to convey what you learned clearly in writing." In this way, Ms. Greene highlighted the layers of purpose from the unit: to inquire about privacy rights and to convey this learning clearly to their audience.

In facilitating this revision lesson, Ms. Greene emphasized the importance of students making their Post-it questions specific, to point out any areas that were not clear, and to observe if there were details missing. "Don't correct grammar," she advised, asking them instead to "ask questions about ideas, wording, [and whether the writer is] conveying the message clearly." In this way, she called students' attention away from merely correcting surface errors, and focused them instead on asking the writer authentic questions about content and clarity.

After students had a chance to read the text silently, recording their notes and questions on Post-its, Ms. Greene led them in sharing their questions as a group. She placed a copy of the same sample text on a document reader and read through it sentence by sentence. "Stop me when you have a question [from your Post-its]," she told the class, reminding them that the point of the lesson was to "pose an honest question that the reader might have." It is noteworthy that in this lesson the students were the primary ones asking questions, rather than the teacher.

As the lesson progressed, with the class reading sentence by sentence together, they accumulated questions: The "turn of the century" refers to which century? Is there any way to make this sentence shorter, or to get rid of that run-on? Is sentence #3 the thesis? Is this sentence too informal? While these questions may be seen as relatively at surface level (not yet getting at the deeper issue of the organization or argument of the text), they do demonstrate students learning to ask authentic questions about focus, sentence construction, and appropriateness of language for an audience. After one student asked a question, Ms. Greene interjected, "I had that same question, only the way you phrased it is actually better than the way I did. The better the questions you have for people, the better revisions will be." Here again, she focused the students' attention on the relationship between a reader's specific questions and the usefulness for the writer in making revisions later. She also purposefully positioned herself as a fellow reader with questions of her own.

This first part of the lesson served as an in-depth model of a new peer-revision strategy. As a next step, students worked together in groups to practice this strategy, reading silently and using Post-its to annotate another group's collaboratively written paper. They then discussed their Post-it questions and combined them onto one document, which they returned to the authoring group. When a group received its own paper back, Ms. Greene asked them to number the Post-its in the order they believed they needed to be addressed in the text, and then to work together to respond to the questions.

Once again, this approach highlighted a sense of student agency and authority in using what they had learned as writers, expecting them to collaborate to determine to what extent and in what order they would respond to peer questions. As the class ended, Ms. Greene asked the students, "Do you think the groups will get duplicate questions?" When students responded affirmatively, she observed, "That will be really good evidence that this is a part of the writing that needs to be addressed."

Throughout this lesson, Ms. Greene discussed writing in multiple ways: as a means to learn about the topic (privacy rights), to communicate that learning to an audience (in an essay or action plan), to pose questions about clarity and content as readers/reviewers (through Post-it notes), to make a plan for revision (by organizing and numbering the Post-it notes), and to revise the draft text in response to reader feedback. She also used student work to model a revision strategy that students could use beyond this particular writing situation. Ms. Greene's instruction emphasized the need to consider the author's purpose, to take an inquiry stance when reading a peer's paper, to pose authentic questions to the paper's author, and to collaborate as a group around complex tasks of drafting, writing, responding, and revising. Each of these strategies is supported by the research on effective writing instruction.

Connecting Multiple Writing Strategies in a Literacy Curriculum

Like the students at Amadon High School, students at College View Middle School in Kentucky were immersed in learning writing strategies that they could use across writing contexts. The language arts department chair described the school as having a strong emphasis on writing. Language arts teachers had double blocks for instruction, they shared planning periods, many had been involved in professional development for writing (several through the National Writing Project), and the department chair had attended workshops with literacy leaders such as Harvey Daniels and Nancie Atwell. Additionally, at the time of our study students in College View Middle School kept cross-subject writing portfolios as part of the state writing assessment, and they used these portfolios to reflect on their writing growth.

Some of the sixth-grade assignments from College View stand out in the way that they demonstrate teachers' commitment to integrating literacy practices. The assignments guided students in exploring both how writing choices affect readers' experiences and how to apply those writing strategies in their own compositions. For example, one set of sixth-grade assignments focused on *revealing dialogue*. Students began by reading an excerpt from a story, using colored pencils to underline the dialogue in the story, with a different color for each speaker. "Notice how the author changed paragraphs each time she changed speakers," the directions advised. Following the excerpt, students were asked to write about what they learned about each speaker "just from reading the way they talk." This exercise invited students to attend to a writing strategy (the use of dialogue) as well as the effect that strategy had on them as readers (revealing information about the characters).

Students then read another narrative and marked "three spots where the author could add revealing dialogue." Then, "mak[ing] sure to punctuate correctly," students picked one of these spots and wrote a piece of revealing dialogue, reflecting afterwards on what it told a reader about the characters. In this exercise, students moved between roles of reader and writer, noticing the effect of a writing strategy on their experience as a reader, and then observing opportunities to use this technique in revising a different narrative. As a final stage in this set of activities, students returned to their own drafts of a story begun earlier, to find three opportunities to add revealing dialogue to their own work.

Through this set of writing activities sixth graders were learning writing and revision strategies in the context of a process-oriented pedagogy. As in the previous examples from John Adams Middle School and Amadon High School, students were learning to read closely in order to discern and apply effective strategies in their own writing.

Other assignments at College View engaged students in trying out a wide variety of writing strategies. These included *show-me paragraphs* (where students focused on using sensory detail to "show" rather than "tell about" a scene), *snapshots* (where they used specific details to describe a particular moment in time), *thoughtshots* (where they presented someone's thoughts in a scene), and *exploded moments* (where they used details to slow down the pace of a scene). (See Lane, 1993, for further descriptions of these strategies.) For example, in a notebook entry, sixth grader Elise (an English language learner) practiced writing a snapshot of a scene:

As I open my eyes and feel the afternoon moist cloudy sky, I feel like a storm is waiting around the corner. The mountains surround me like a blanket feeling rough and dry. The sun makes the water seem like an endless desert of death. The mountains shining bold and almost touching the sky. What a beautiful scene.

In this example, we see Elise practicing the snapshot strategy to weave together sensory language to show the moment in time to her readers.

Clearly Elise's teacher was helping her students develop specific written texts (e.g., narratives), while also purposefully teaching them strategies that extended beyond and across writing tasks. The students were learning the importance of word choice and phrasing in effectively communicating what they wanted their readers to see and feel. There was attention to reading model texts and identifying writing techniques, and the instructional materials provided scaffolding to help students observe writing techniques and emulate them in their own writing. There was also attention to helping students name writing and revision strategies, as they attended to specific effects (e.g., revealing dialogue, thoughtshots, snapshots, exploded moments, and show-me paragraphs). As with the previous examples, Elise and her classmates used writing in multiple ways: To identify writing strategies and their effects in texts, to suggest changes and writing techniques for another author's work, and ultimately to use new techniques in their own writing. Across these examples, the focus remained on the development of effective strategies that could be used purposefully across multiple writing texts and contexts.

These writing and instructional strategies also imply teachers' use of professional development resources to inform instruction. Just as Barry Lane (1993) suggests in *After the End: Teaching and Learning Creative Revision*, in which he discusses techniques like snapshots and thoughtshots, Elise's teacher emphasized not only the understanding of specific revision strategies, but also the purposeful selection and use of strategies to create desired effects through writing.

Schoolwide Curricular Cohesion for Writing

Like John Adams Middle School in Santa Monica, College View Middle School offered an excellent example of a school with a shared commitment to writing instruction. Even beyond this, at College View Middle School we saw evidence of a common curricular story that extended across students' experiences in that building. Every year, College View's seventh-grade teachers compiled a writing handbook called *The College View Compass*, which followed up on the writing instruction from sixth grade (Elise's grade) and brought together writing strategies, activities, and sample student writing. *The Compass* was printed each year, and every seventh grader received a copy. The intention was that *The Compass* would reinforce the writing strategies students had learned in sixth grade and serve as a support for new writing strategies they would learn throughout seventh grade. The handbook became a tool that students could consult about their writing in each of their subjects.

The year we visited the school, *The Compass* was divided into sections that corresponded to the types of writing required for the Kentucky seventh-grade portfolio assessment, including personal writing, literary writing, transactive writing, and reflective writing. In this way the handbook supported student writing that was specifically related to English as a discipline as well as writing that extended beyond disciplinary boundaries. Each handbook section contained strategies students could use, questions they could ask themselves as they wrote, activities they could do to support their writing, and examples of student work. The handbook also had reference materials for help with literature circle roles, technology, spelling or grammar, writing strategies, and a number of other topics. In fact, the reference section contained pages on thoughtshots, snapshots, and exploded moments in writing, as well as the assignment sequence on revealing dialogue which Elise and her sixth-grade classmates had completed. Students were encouraged to insert their own pages into their handbooks, allowing them to personalize their handbooks and positioning them as contributors of knowledge and writing strategies.

Although structured around the requirements of a state assessment, the handbook was aligned with a vision of students growing as writers who compose with purpose and intent and who mobilize particular writing strategies for desired effects. The handbook also communicated values and beliefs about writing, about what makes writing powerful or meaningful, about a writer's relationship with a text, and about what it means to be an author. The language of the handbook itself reinforced these messages and added to the sense of curricular cohesion. For example, the handbook opened with an invitation for students to write a letter to their seventh-grade teacher (Figure 3.1), introducing themselves as writers. Notably, this invitation began with a quote about the power of writing, written by a former College View Middle School student. Directly below the quote is a "Writing Situation" that says, "To help me understand who you are as a reader and a writer, I want you to reflect over your reading and writing experiences in sixth grade and elementary school." By framing the invitation with a quote from a student and creating a writing situation that is written by an interested teacher audience, teachers gave students a clear reason for writing and encouraged them to share a vision of who they were as readers and writers. This assignment also provided a powerful introduction for the handbook.

FIGURE 3.1. Letter to My Teacher

LETTER TO MY TEACHER

Reflect—*to think about seriously; careful thought and serious consideration of past events. "Even if the rest of the world only sees me outwardly, I will always have my pen and paper to show my 'true colors,' to allow the center of my soul to shine brighter than my eyes."*
—from a former student's letter to the reviewer

Situation: When we write, we are able to tell our audience a lot about ourselves. To help me understand who you are as a reader and a writer, I want you to reflect over your reading and writing experiences in sixth grade and elementary school. Consider some of the following: (You may add other topics, if you wish.)

- Tell about your writing and reading experiences in the sixth grade.
- You probably did a lot of writing in the fourth grade. Tell about that experience and your other writing experiences from first through fifth grade.
- Compare your reading and writing experiences from elementary to your experiences as a sixth grader.
- Tell about your strengths and weaknesses as both a reader and writer.
- Reflect over how your reading and writing abilities have grown.
- Does reading help you as a writer? Explain how.
- Do you have any goals for this year in reading and writing?
- How do you write? Strategies, special place, inspirations, special influences, etc?

Writing Task: Write a letter to your teacher reflecting over your growth as a reader and a writer.

Key Points to remember as you write:

- Start with a strong lead (list, quote, anecdote, starting fact or statistic)
- Organize your ideas (paragraphs, transitions)
- Develop and support your ideas (sensory details, vivid verbs, snapshots, thought shots, etc.)
- Use a variety of sentences
- Have a strong conclusion
- Revise and edit.

Toward the end of the handbook section for each type of writing (i.e., personal, literary, transactive, and reflective), students would find a checklist or opportunity to reflect on their final products. Figure 3.2 shows the Personal Writing Checklist, which prompted students to ask themselves if they had included "an attention-getting lead," if they "show" rather than "tell" (again referencing familiar strategies like thoughtshots, snapshots, exploded moments, and revealing dialogue), whether they organized their papers logically, and so on.

The handbook section on personal writing concluded with an opportunity for students to reflect on their writing, recording the strategies they used to gather ideas, their thought processes in deciding a focus, what they "realized" after writing their first draft, what changes these realizations led them to make, what they found easiest and most difficult as they wrote, and what they ultimately learned from writing that piece. Process-oriented instruction, understood as rhetorical and recursive in nature, was embedded throughout the writing strategies, leaving students with a record of what they did as well as a reflection on what this meant for them as writers.

Taken together, student work from sixth graders and these excerpts from *The College View Compass* provide evidence of a curricular conversation about writing that began in sixth grade and extended throughout the middle school experience. Students at College View Middle School were learning writing strategies and being called to use these in purposeful ways across their years and across all of their subjects.

ENGLISH AND THE COMMON CORE STANDARDS

We have seen that good writing instruction goes far beyond the confines of any one lesson. It involves activities that occur over time to support the range of writing in which we want students to excel. All of the examples in this chapter address important elements of the *Common Core State Standards* (CCSSO & NGA, 2010). Indeed, virtually any effective writing task addresses aspects of three of the standards:

Standard 4—Produce clear and coherent writing in which the development, organization, and style are appropriate to task, purpose and audience

Standard 5—Develop and strengthen writing as needed by planning, revising, editing, rewriting or trying a new approach, focusing on how well purpose and audience have been addressed

Standard 10—Write routinely over extended time frames (time for reflection and revision) and shorter time frames (a single sitting

FIGURE 3.2. Personal Writing Checklist

Is your personal writing a
_____ personal narrative, _____ memoir, or _____ personal essay?

Have you included why this is significant in your life?

Have you used an attention-getting lead?
- Startling statistic
- Quotation
- Anecdote
- List or series

Do you "show" rather than "tell" through the use of:
- Snapshots
- Thoughtshots
- Exploded moment
- Dialogue

Is your paper logically organized?
- Uses transitions
- Divided into paragraphs

Is your paper focused on YOU? Have you included your:
- Thoughts
- Feelings
- Reactions

Do you have a conclusion that:
- Sums up?
- Reflects?

Have you edited your paper?
- Capitalization
- Usage (run-ons, fragments, subject/verb agreement, and so on)
- Punctuation
- Spelling

---

or a day) for a range of discipline-specific tasks, purposes and audiences

Each of the examples discussed in this chapter also prepares students to meet additional standards. For instance, in addition to the three above, Ms. Greene's unit on Privacy Rights also addressed:

Standard 2—Write informative/explanatory texts, including the narration of historical events, scientific procedures/experiments, or technical processes

Standard 6—Use technology, including the Internet, to produce and publish writing and present the relationship between information and ideas clearly and efficiently

Standard 7—Conduct short research projects to answer a question . . . drawing on several sources and generating additional related, focused questions that allow for multiple avenues of exploration

Across all examples, we see not merely interesting activities, but also instruction that incorporates effective, research-based teaching strategies. In each case, the teacher or group of teachers has set particular purposes for the lessons and structured students' engagement in the activities so as to scaffold their learning. In such instruction, standards like those in the Common Core provide a way to reflect on the breadth and depth of students' literacy learning, but they do not outline a curriculum or prescribe a particular approach to teaching and learning.

THE BOTTOM LINE

Looking across these examples from schools with local reputations for excellence in writing instruction, we see teachers creating cohesive writing curricula that emphasized preparing students to write for multiple purposes and audiences. At John Adams Middle School, we observed student writing that was focused on English disciplinary conversations related to character development in literature. While engaged in this literary analysis, students also were preparing for high-stakes writing assessments by learning to unpack writing situations (and audience expectations) and to use multiple organizational and prewriting strategies. Ms. Rudolph's lesson also showed students analyzing anchor or model essays to help them understand qualities such as organization, evidence, and sentence construction. Students used these insights to target areas for revision as they reentered their own timed essay attempts.

At Amadon High School, Ms. Green's use of the Post-it revision strategy illustrated a way of engaging students in authentic inquiry-based peer review. Her lesson also emphasized students collaborating around complex tasks as they worked in groups to read peer work and to use feedback in revising their own writing. In Ms. Green's classroom, students used a variety of types of writing for a variety of purposes, including inquiry, communication, reflection, organization, and revision.

Similarly, Elise and her sixth-grade classmates at College View Middle School engaged in a variety of writing activities to help them both compose and revise their writing. Their teachers demonstrated ways to connect their experiences as readers and writers, observing the effect of techniques like revealed dialogue and snapshots in helping an author create a specific effect in a text. College View Middle School also clearly had a schoolwide vision of writing instruction, further adding to the sense of curricular cohesion observed in student writing samples. This cohesion was best observed through the student writing handbook, which teachers created each year in anticipation of a seventh-grade state portfolio exam, now abandoned. That handbook not only reinforced writing strategies, but also consistently emphasized the significance of writerly purpose and understanding of audience in one's writing processes.

Looking across all of the classrooms we studied, we find a number of practices that contribute to successful teaching of writing in English and the language arts, including addressing the demands of the Common Core:

Curriculum and Instruction

- Organize curriculum around "big ideas" appropriate to the study of literature, language, and composition, and to the grade level of the class.
- Explicitly teach strategies for generating ideas, drafting, revising, and editing.
- Emphasize authentic discussion and writing tasks based in inquiry, as writers focus on purpose, audience needs, desired effects, and strategies that might achieve these effects.
- Across the year, ensure that students will be engaged in a wide variety of writing tasks for varied audiences and purposes, including systematic attention to the argument, informative/expository, and narrative tasks of the Common Core.

Assessment

- Use writing tasks as ways for students to demonstrate their knowledge and understandings of the English content.

Schoolwide Initiatives

- Provide time for shared planning meetings and participation in professional learning communities committed to continual improvement of writing instruction. These may be school or department-based or rely on external networks such as the National Writing Project, the National Council of Teachers of English, or school-university collaboratives.

FUTURE DIRECTIONS

Across all the examples in this chapter, there is evidence of cohesive writing curricula, an emphasis on authentic and discipline-appropriate discussion practices and student inquiry around complex tasks, and a commitment to explicitly teaching writing strategies that are appropriate to the field of English. These are the very qualities of effective writing instruction supported by the research reviewed at the beginning of this chapter, and could well be embraced by all English and ELA programs in their efforts to guide student development of strong writing abilities.

Still of concern, however, is the widespread trend in English classrooms to mirror the kinds of writing asked for on high-stakes tests. This emphasis constrains the genres and purposes for which students are asked to write, narrowing the audiences and the types of writing students are learning to address. It also runs counter to the larger goals of the English curriculum, which include apprenticing students into the various disciplines of English as well as preparing them to engage in the public discourse of a democratic society. To reverse this trend, teachers will need to help students learn to consider the context, purpose, and audience for their writing and how these affect the choices they make about genre, organization, and language. In this way, teachers and students can be freed to treat test writing as one of many writing situations, with prompts that need to be analyzed and reflected on to understand what is being asked and what is expected. The instructional activities described in the "Portraits of Success" section suggest some ways this can be done by engaging students in the kinds of reflection and revision that are the mark of successful writers.

It is also worth noting that the schools featured in this chapter share a commitment to supporting teachers in developing and refining these instructional strategies through ongoing professional development and collaboration. Together, the examples are good models of ways in which teachers and schools can work together to offer students significant writing instruction that will position them to successfully undertake the complex writing tasks they will encounter in their future years in school, work, and life.

Reflect and Discuss

1. What are some of the big ideas you want students to learn from their study of literature this year? Choose one, and develop a range of writing activities around it.
   a. Use writing to draw on related knowledge, consolidate under-standing, and reformulate and extend understandings of litera-ture and life.
   b. Ask students to explore different works by the same author or works on similar themes by different authors.
   c. Read and analyze conflicting reviews of the works (or authors).
2. Look back at the section on "Portraits of Success." In these exam-ples, students are identifying and practicing strategies for composing and revising their work, which they can use across many writing contexts.
   a. With colleagues, identify your students' writing needs. Develop a chart that you can use as a reminder about particular writing strategies you can teach when your students need them.
   b. Develop writing activities that provide opportunities to teach these strategies and to monitor students' growth.
3. With your colleagues, develop rubrics for students to use as they plan and revise each of the types of writing required for success in English.
   a. Include separate sections for Content, Organization, Language, and Conventions.
   b. Collect a set of writing samples for students to analyze that high-light the features of more and less successful writing of the vari-ous types (e.g., literary analysis, imaginative story, explanation, and argumentation).

CHAPTER 4

Writing in Social Studies/History

Although the national survey (see Chapter 2) found relatively little writing taking place in any of the subjects studied, the field of social studies/history has long treated writing as an integral part of the instructional activities in which students are expected to engage. Further, over time many researchers and scholars have noted the importance of writing in the learning of the discipline. Clearly, there is a disconnect that needs to be understood.

THE BACKGROUND FOR WRITING IN SOCIAL STUDIES/HISTORY

As early as 1978 Henry Giroux argued that "a pedagogy of writing can be used as a learning vehicle to help students learn and think critically about any given social studies subject" (p. 291). This was at the beginning of an era of focused and widespread research on writing to learn as well as on writing across the curriculum in schools and universities. It also corresponded with the start of the National Writing Project. Together, these created a wave of professional activity around uses of writing to support students' subject-area learning. Since then, social studies/history teachers in many schools across the country have incorporated various kinds of writing into their class activities, such as journal writing to reflect on and raise questions about new learnings, as well as carefully structured assignments for completing longer research, analytic, and argumentative papers. While these practices did not necessarily represent the national norm, collaborative work through peer project planning, reflection, discussion, and writing became more popular. Steffens, Dickerson, Fulweiler, and Biddle (1986) marked historical writing as an intellectual activity. They argued that writing goes beyond merely communicating what has been learned, but also inherently affects the learning of history by engaging students in discovery, problem solving, and organization. They went on to explain that the act of composing helps the writer learn history as well as clarify understanding of the subject. As a result, they called for daily writing in social studies/history classrooms. (See Langer, 2011a, Chapter 5, for examples of such classroom activity in social studies/history.)

During the 1980s some states began to include prompts requiring extended analytic or persuasive writing (and sometimes writing for other purposes) in their social studies/history assessments. By and large, this reflected a growing attempt on the part of educators, researchers, and test developers to treat writing as a cognitively engaging process not only for thoughtful learning activities, but also as a way to evaluate students' abilities to think through, analyze, or in other ways manipulate content-specific material in order to arrive at defensible interpretations or points of view. The move differed considerably from using writing merely as a vehicle to prompt students' recall of material they had already studied.

By the 2000s the forefront of pedagogical scholarship in social studies/history focused on the learning of history as developing interpretations rather than finding truths about events. From this perspective, it became important that historical sources—whether primary or secondary—be questioned, examined in terms of the time, situation, author, and audience in which they were written, and verified as students built connections and searched for patterns that would support their developing interpretations (e.g., see Wineburg, 2007). This approach is developed most fully in Wineburg, Martin, and Monte-Sano (2011), which includes guidance for teachers as well as source materials for students. It is anchored in the practice of teaching history through contextualization and is laced with writing activities that are fully integrated into the processes of historical interpretation. In such an approach historical knowledge must be seen as provisional, and students must become active participants in developing reasoned interpretations.

The ongoing emphases on writing to learn and on writing in the disciplines of social studies would seem to offer a wealth of opportunities for activities in which students could explore the historic past from a variety of vantage points. And supporting this emphasis, the social studies community has continued to affirm its belief in the benefit of writing as an integral part of learning the content. In a position paper written in May 2008, the National Council for the Social Studies stated simply that a challenging social studies curriculum "makes use of regular writing and the analyses of various types of documents, such as primary and secondary sources, graphs, charts and data banks."

THE WRITING STUDENTS ARE ASKED TO DO IN SOCIAL STUDIES/HISTORY

We explained in Chapter 2 how the pressures of high-stakes assessment have often worked against attention to writing. This played out in a particularly vivid way for us in social studies/history. Early in the project, when selecting the states to include in our five-state study, we examined the formats used for testing student performance in each of the four core subject areas. In the five states we chose, social studies achievement was assessed solely with multiple-choice items in California and Texas. Multiple-choice questions were supplemented with essays in New York and Michigan, and portfolios of student writing (including work written for social studies) in Kentucky. By the time our study ended, Michigan had switched to multiple-choice and Kentucky to short-response formats. Thus New York was the only one of the five states that continued to test social studies/history knowledge by having students write essays.

New York is also unusual in requiring document-based essays as part of state social studies exams, which in turn influenced the kinds of writing students were asked to do. (Such questions are also part of Advanced Placement history exams.) In the national survey, teachers from New York were significantly more likely than their peers in other states to emphasize the kinds of analysis and synthesis of material across texts that are required by document-based questions. Such writing was rated as very important by 62% of New York middle and high school teachers, compared with only 40% of teachers in schools in all other states.

In the national survey, teachers were asked directly about the importance of high-stakes state exams in shaping their curriculum. Eighty-two percent of high school social studies/history teachers and 38% of middle school teachers reported they considered them important. To prepare students for these exams, 67% of social studies/history teachers reported using rubrics in their teaching of writing, 57% practiced on similar tasks, 56% practiced on old exams, and 54% ensured that the skills necessary for the high-stakes tests were incorporated into their curriculum, rather than focusing directly on "test prep."

We also asked teachers to estimate the percentage of the high-stakes grade that was based on open-ended responses. The high school teachers reported 27% and the middle school teachers reported 4%. Thus, although the high-stakes tests clearly affected what teachers from Grades 6–12 did in their classes, only a small percentage of longer, open-ended writing was included on the high-stakes tests. One social studies/history teacher described the result:

> I've tried to push my department to have some form of written assessment on their major unit tests. . . . at one point I tried to go toward almost completely essay, and because of the TAKS test [Texas Assessment of Knowledge and Skills, which is all multiple-choice], because of the state tests and having to prepare the kids for a mul-

tiple-choice test, it wasn't necessarily [a good thing]. . . . I think writing is just as good a preparation as multiple-choice, but it was stressed the district wanted us to have some multiple-choice. (Middle school social studies chair)

The Amount of Writing Students Do

Asked how many writing assignments of differing lengths they had assigned over a 9-week grading period, teachers reported an average of 4.3 papers of a page or less, 1.9 papers of one or two pages, and 0.5 papers of three pages or more. In our five-state study such extended writing represented 19% of the social studies/history assignments collected from high school and 22% from middle school. Clearly some, though not much, longer writing was taking place beyond exercises and short answers, copying, and taking notes, whether these formats were used in the high-stakes tests or not.

The Writing Instruction Students Receive

Regarding the frequency with which they had students engage in various process-related instructional activities to support writing in their discipline, 59% of the social studies/history teachers reported they frequently had their students spend class time generating ideas and 39% reported they had their students engage in inquiry tasks. Other instructional strategies the teachers reported using frequently included providing rubrics (63%), studying models (57%), and teaching specific writing strategies (42%). Teachers were also asked about the uses of writing they considered very important for learning social studies/history. In order of importance, they valued:

1. Explanation of subject-area concepts (68%)
2. Critical analysis of an issue or text (60%)
3. Applying concepts to new situations (51%)
4. Analysis and synthesis across multiple texts (41%)
5. Student response and interpretation (35%)
6. Précis or summary writing (32%)
7. Definitions of concepts or terms (27%)

Taken together, these results indicate that social studies teachers consider a wide range of writing activities as very important in supporting subject learning, and that these serve a variety of purposes.

The Big Picture

In all, these results leave us with a mixed picture of the uses of writing in social studies/history classes. Clearly writing is being assigned in many classes and has become integrated into social studies/history teaching and learning. When we examined all of the writing that students had completed in their social studies/history classes across a semester, we found evidence of close adherence to the activities presented in textbooks and other instructional materials, with fewer teacher-generated activities and prompts. However, many of the assignments called not only for multiple choice and fill-ins, but also for short constructed responses. Some offered models of, and required students to complete, longer writing assignments, often echoing formats called for by statewide tests or Advanced Placement exams. Whether shorter or longer, such assignments provided strong scaffolds to guide students in understanding the material presented, with frequent interspersed requests for students to explain their understandings and to provide evidence in short written responses.

Longer writing assignments most often asked students to write about a big idea or theme and sometimes to provide supporting evidence. Less often, we saw student writing that involved the reading of multiple texts, or assignments requiring students to use the Internet as a source of data for their papers. (Document-based questions are one set of tasks that require the use of multiple source documents that are supplied with the test question; for an example, see Chapter 2, Figure 2.2.) Much of the student writing we saw involved connecting, synthesizing, or summarizing ideas from readings and class discussions. Occasionally, we saw analyses leading to student-constructed interpretations. Sometimes these included defense of the position taken; many did not.

The types of writing assigned tended to differ from school to school. We saw more writing in schools where recent professional development initiatives had focused strongly on writing (e.g., National Writing Project [http://www.nwp.org], AVID [http://www.avid.org], CRISS [http://www.projectcriss.com]). In other schools, particularly in states whose high-stakes tests in social studies/history required no writing, teachers told us they had no time for writing because they had to prepare their students for multiple-choice exams.

Across schools and states, we did not see the depth or breadth of "contextualizing" that Wineburg and colleagues (2011) call for. That is, students were not asked to develop interpretations of historical material by systematic and in-depth questioning of sources, establishing their context, seeking corroboration, and making generalizations. However, we did see activities where students read documents with divergent points of view, after which they had to present and explain and defend their own stance. The majority of the longer writing we saw presented textbook interpretations or summarized the student's own or others' points of view. At times we saw helpful written feedback from teachers; only occasionally were students asked to write second drafts in response.

Overall, we can see that the tradition of writing as a valued aid to learning has by and large been set aside, with goals having shifted from teaching to ensure disciplinary competence to teaching to ensure test competence. Not a lot of writing was taking place in social studies/history classes, and where it was, much of it was not engaging students in thoughtful learning of the material through writing.

PORTRAITS OF SUCCESS

Yet against this somewhat discouraging backdrop, we did see examples of effective uses of writing. In our close-up studies of classes in action, some individual schools, departments, and teachers maintained the belief that highly engaging activities around challenging and interesting curricular materials could both ensure high-level disciplinary learning and also prepare students to do well on the high-stakes tests that were in place. The sections that follow present examples of ways in which writing in social studies/history was put to good use as an aid to thinking and learning within the disciplines of social studies/history.

Using Writing to Develop and Share Understandings

In Skansen Middle School, one of the schools we studied for a year, Mr. Garcia, an eighth-grade social studies teacher, used a textbook to structure the content of his course. He also had his students keep journals in which they took notes of what they read; defined new vocabulary; created timelines, concept maps, T-charts, and other graphics; and wrote shorter and longer responses to a variety of assignments. Each section of the journal was aligned to a particular section of the textbook, with the writing serving as an aid in the development of understanding. For their unit on the Industrial Revolution, for example, the students took notes, developed concept maps, and completed a longer writing task for four separate sections of the chapter.

Mannie, an eighth-grade higher achieving student, kept a journal that illustrates the typical pattern: His entries for Section 2 began with notes highlighting vocabulary and organizing important information,

FIGURE 4.1. Mannie's Concept Map on Inventions and Industry

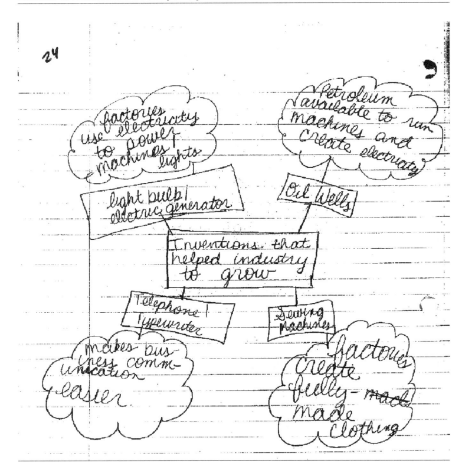

then moved on to a longer writing task. He began by identifying two new vocabulary words and defining them (and added others later):

> *Transcontinental Railroad—completed in 1869. It linked the East + West coasts by rail.*
> *Standard Time—System developed by rail companies + adopted by the U.S. govt in 1918 that divided the United States into 4 different time zones.*

He also listed six factors that led to growth of industry in the United States: "Investment capital," "Resources (Plentiful Natural Resources)," "Im-

FIGURE 4.2. Mannie's Concept Map on Railroads

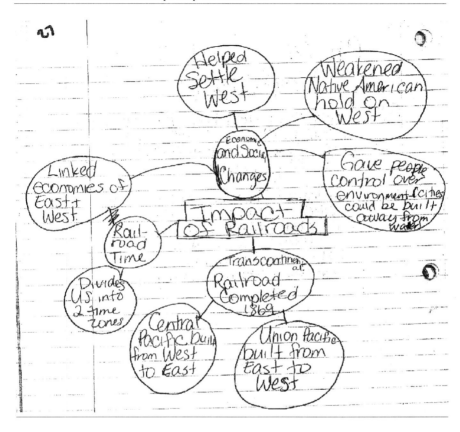

migration (High Immigration)," "Population (growing)," "Inventions," "Transportation (improved) (trains)." At different points in his notes on Section 2, Mannie also created two concept maps: One focused on inventions that helped industry to grow (Figure 4.1), and another, added sometime later, on the impact of railroads (Figure 4.2).

These shorter notes and concept maps were followed by an assignment requiring the class to write a letter in response to an editorial about the actions of John D. Rockefeller and Andrew Carnegie, drawing on their previous reading, writing, and class discussion. Mannie wrote a first draft in his journal, replete with cross-outs and later additions. The beginning of his draft is displayed in Figure 4.3. His final draft, produced on a word processor, read:

FIGURE 4.3. Draft of Mannie's Letter to the Editor (Paragraph 1)

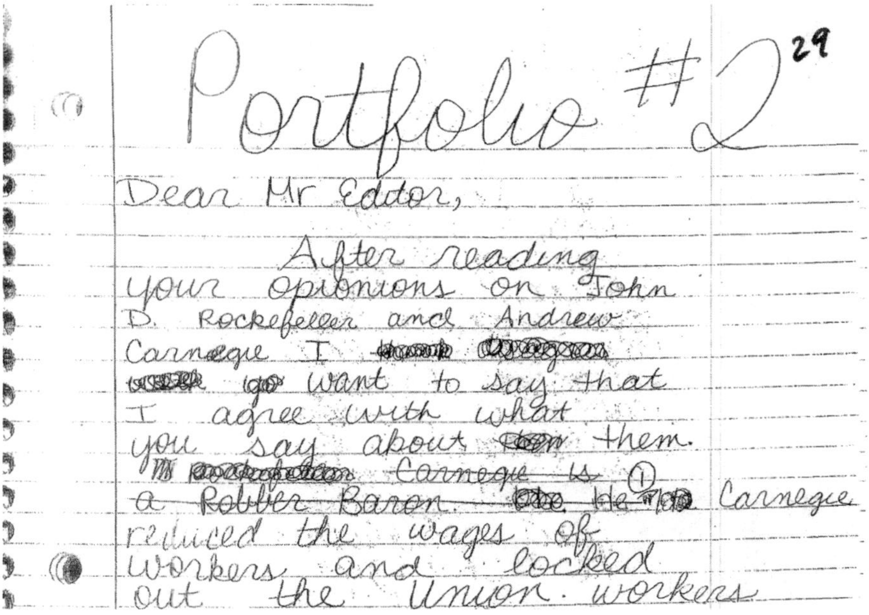
Portfolio #2 29

Dear Mr Editor,

After reading your opinions on John D. Rockefeller and Andrew Carnegie I want to say that I agree with what you say about them. ~~Carnegie is a Robber Baron.~~ ① Carnegie reduced the wages of workers and locked out the Union workers

Dear Mr. Editor,

After reading your opinions of John D. Rockefeller and Andrew Carnegie, I want to say that I agree with what you say about them. I feel that both men are robber barons. Although they were both men were philanthropists, giving millions of dollars to libraries, universities, and other charities, they both have done much to hurt society.

Carnegie reduced the wages of workers and locked out the Union workers. He hired new workers that weren't in the Union and hired armed guards. The armed guards had a gunfight with the Union workers. There were ten deaths and the Union was broken when the state militia was called in. He then kept prices high through monopoly. People had to pay for whatever he asked for.

Rockefeller had also done many things to hurt society. He eliminated his competition by taking over small businesses. He also had secret deals with the railroads. He used trusts to create a monopoly. Like Carnegie, he kept prices high which forced people to pay whatever he charged.

As you can see, I feel very strongly that these men have scammed society into a monopoly and have used other forms of dishonest business to get money. They are robber barons in my opinion. Carnegie and Rockefeller didn't earn their money. I feel they stole it.

Sincerely,

These examples from Mannie's work show how writing was integrated into the fabric of learning in his class: Reading, writing, and discussion were each used to support students' inquiry and idea development. Mr. Garcia gave them support and time to understand the troubling as well as positive aspects of the industrial era and the roles Carnegie and Rockefeller played in it. The final draft shows that the student understood the genre of a letter to the editor (including the need to begin agreeing or disagreeing with the newspaper's position, giving specific details to support a position, and closing with a strong personal statement). He also showed a good understanding of the historical material that made up the content of the unit.

Other longer writings that were part of the same unit included a "stump speech" as a Populist Party candidate for the U.S. Senate, in which Mannie appealed to the farmers of Nebraska, and a project exploring important events during this period (including the Haymarket riot, the founding of the American Federation of Labor, and the Homestead strike) from the conflicting points of view of prounion advocates and their antiunion adversaries. The variety of activities that engaged the students in organizing, connecting, comparing and contrasting, synthesizing, reflecting on, and writing about historical events created a supportive and cognitively engaging context for learning.

Using Writing to Explore Multiple Documents

Document-based questions (DBQs) play a significant role in Advanced Placement exams in U.S. history, European history, and world history, as well as in some state assessments (e.g., New York). They typically include a range of primary source documents, including charts and graphs, political cartoons, newspaper accounts, and other contemporary materials presenting a variety of perspectives on a historical event. As Mr. Khan, a 10th-grade social studies teacher described it, DBQs require students to "read, analyze, and make sense" of primary source documents, group related items together, and use the documents and their knowledge of history to support a thesis. In practice, however, instruction focused on document-based questions often becomes quite formulaic. Kevin, a 10th-grade lower achieving student, captured this, noting in an interview that for the DBQ he had to "learn how to write the thesis statement, and write quick, and get it simple and to the point, get the facts . . . completely opposite than in English [where] she teaches you how to write insightfully."

We can see the emphasis on responding to the examination question format playing out in a social studies class in Port Chester Middle School. This National Blue Ribbon school is in an old manufacturing town about 25 miles from New York City. It had been a manufacturing hub, but it fell on hard times and is now in the midst of a revitalization effort. Because it is in New York State, the students would take a high-stakes test requiring them to read several historical documents about a particular topic and respond to document-based questions. (See Chapter 2, Figure 2.2, for an example of a document-based question on the causes of the French Revolution, and the generic rubric recommended by New York State.) The teacher, Mr. Sanchez, shared the generic rubric for DBQs with his students, used it for his feedback and grading of papers throughout the year, and also encouraged his students to use it for self-evaluation and editing as they completed their own responses to DBQs.

In addition to using the rubric to help his students understand what was required in an effective response to a document-based question, Mr. Sanchez structured individual lesson sequences around the parts of a typical DBQ. This included helping students unpack the scaffolding question for each document and engage in the analysis and synthesis required to answer the major writing prompt. For a two-part question on the Great Depression, for example, Mr. Sanchez gave his students a preview of the document-based writing question: (1) to discuss the problems that Americans faced during the Great Depression and (2) to discuss actions taken by individuals, groups, and the government in their attempts to solve the problems.

Mr. Sanchez then presented the documents one at a time, following each one with a focusing question designed to help the students explore the document. Only after a detailed exploration of each of the documents did they return to reread the two-part question. At that point Mr. Sanchez also provided them with a paragraph outline to use for organizing their papers (Figure 4.4).

Following is Yasmine's (Grade 8, English language learner) response to the two-part DBQ:

> *The Great Depression brought many problems to the people. After the stock market crash of 1929, the United states went into a period of economic crisis known as the Great Depression. During this time, the political, economic and social institutions of the United States were in turmoil. The government, various groups and individuals sought ways to adress the problems that Americans faced.*
>
> *Americans faced many problems during the Great Depression. People tried to withdraw their life's saving which was often too late, making the banks collapse (Doc 2). Also, people didn't have jobs, they were hungry and looking for opportunities to at least pay their rent (Doc 3). Lastly, the taxes were rising (Doc 5). Those are problems that Americans faced during the Great Depression.*

FIGURE 4.4. DBQ Paragraph Organizer

Paragraph 1:

- Background: Explain what was happening at that time, including problems Americans faced
- Then write a topic sentence about what the entire paper will be about

Paragraph 2:

- Begin with a topic sentence telling what this paragraph will be about
- Discuss actions taken by the government, with details about specific actions
- Cite the documents you used for your information
- End with how these actions were received and/or worked out

Paragraph 3:

- Begin with a topic sentence telling what this paragraph will be about
- Discuss action taken by certain groups of individuals to help solve the problem, with details about specific actions
- Cite the documents you used for your information
- End with how these actions were received and/or worked out

Paragraph 4:

- Restate your introduction; use other words
- Add outside information that is relevant and adds to an understanding of the issues of and solutions to the Great Depression
- End with a closing statement about the difficult times, the problems, possible solutions, what we might learn from them or about differing points of view

---

The government and various groups take some actions in an attempt to save the problems brought by the Great Depression. Various individuals or groups opened many "kitchens" that gave the unemployed free coffee or free soup (Doc 4). Also the president Franklin Roosevelt created the New Deal remedies (Doc 6).

Lastly, Dr. Francis Townsend proposed a pension plan that will benefit a [older] woman and a man with $200 dolars per month, but they don't have to do any labor or profession. By doing that, other people will take the jobs that the elderly people had, which was a little success in those tuff times (Doc 7). Those are some of the actions taken by the government and various groups in an attempt to solve the problems brought on by the Great Depression.

In conclusion, the Great Depression was a period in time where the political, economic and social institutions of the United states were in turmoil, luckily the government and various groups sought ways to address

*the problems that Americans faced. Hopefully we will learn from our
mistakes and not get into another depression.*

When evaluating her written work the teacher wrote, "Could have
added more details; include outside information wherever possible." Her
teacher gave her a DBQ score of 3 out of a possible 5. While 3 out of 5
may not seem like a high score, for Yasmine it represented a substantial
achievement. As an English language learner, the use of the paragraph
organizer allowed her to touch on all the required parts of the task, although she did so with little depth or complexity. It is important to note
that Yasmine had spent the semester gaining fluency in the English language, mastering the special register and vocabulary of history, and also
learning to express herself clearly in writing while responding to the high
expectations of DBQ prompts.

Using Writing to Step Back in Time

Another kind of writing task that is used regularly in social studies/
history asks students to write from the point of view of a historical figure
(famous or not), using knowledge of history to explore life and opinions
in the period under study. Let us look at a 10th-grade Global History class
in Batavia High School, a small school where writing and literacy were of
paramount importance. Located in the far western section of New York
State, Batavia is a small city of 16,000 people.

The teacher of this class, Ms. Young, used another kind of rubric and
written feedback on students' writing to support their developing understandings of history and of historical writing. Ms. Young's assignment
asked students to imagine they were a newspaper editor during the reign
of Louis XIV, and write an editorial about some important aspect of the
period. To guide the writing, Ms. Young provided a simple rubric that
highlighted the components that would be important, ranging from spelling to creativity, as well as knowledge of the history (Figure 4.5).

Ms. Young discussed each of these features with the students and
they were expected to use the rubric as a guide to consider before and
after writing their historical editorials. Davie (Grade 10, lower achieving)
decided to write his editorial about Louis XIV himself. On the first page of
his draft (Figure 4.6), we can see Ms. Young's comments drawing Davie's
attention to the need for elaboration of the points he had made (what and
why questions), the need for greater specificity, and the need to be sure
the comments were well connected to the entire essay.

On the second page of the essay (not included here), Ms. Young
pointed out the need for clarifying some statements to make them more
easily understood, and the need to make a stronger comparison between

FIGURE 4.5. Rubric for Historical Editorial Assignment

FEATURES	SCORE
Grammar, Spelling, Punctuation	/5
Opinion	/5
Facts from era	/5
Facts before era, reflection	/5
Persuasion/Creativity	/5

FIGURE 4.6. Davie's Essay on Louis XIV

Global 10E

Block 4 BD

Louis XIV Takes Over Completely!

The "Sun King" Louis XIV has been in power for awhile and has changed the
way France is viewed in the European world. As King Louis XIV lives a lavish life style
we the people have been taxed and fined. We are paying for King Louis's mistakes.

As the start of the king's reign Louis started out with doing what he had promised
to do. He helped by taking the noble's power down and increased the power of the
government intendants. From then he was doing what he had promised, but things
occurred. Then King Louis made a move that will be remembered. He hired Jean Baptiste
Colbert as his financial advisor that wanted to do a lot to help France. Colbert tried to
start Mercantilism and make France self-sufficient. King Louis did support this until
Colbert's death awhile back. Then something terrible happened that the king did and the
people did not approve of it. King Louis did cancel the Edict of Nantes. Then friends and
family fled from the country to escape. Many jobs were left open and the economy fell
drastically.

King Louis XIV has been a leader to remember such as a leader a long time ago
by the name of Shi Huangdi, a ruler of ancient China. Just like King Louis, Shi Huangdi
was liked at the beginning of his rule but as the time went on Shi Huangdi lost his respect
from his people and was not liked. Just as China was the most powerful country during
its Qin Dynasty, France is most powerful so far under King Louis. King Louis has

[Handwritten annotations:]
(B) What are intendants? Why would he do it "so"? Why did he want to reduce the power of the nobles?
(A) be careful of speaking such in general
You need to provide some specific information — What you have written in the ¶ above — could have been done much more succinct
perhaps develop this to Louis XIV & Shi Hu
Good
develop —
How Does this relate to the rest of your essay — or to China & the Qin Dynasty

FIGURE 4.7. Completed Rubric for Davie's Essay

FEATURES	SCORE
Grammar, Spelling, Punctuation.	4/5
Opinion: You need more info pertinent to your topic.	3/4
Facts from era: Must be relevant to your editorial perspective.	3.5/5
Facts from before era, reflection: See above. Also you need to do more to relate Shi Huangdi's accomplishments to Louis XIV.	3.5/5
Persuasion/Creativity: See comment above.	2/5

Louis XIV and Shi Huangdi. The rubric in Figure 4.7 shows Ms. Young's grades and comments for Davie's essay.

In this as in the previous examples, we see that writing was an integral part of the fabric of learning and thinking about history. Across the semester, Ms. Young used her writing assignments to focus students' attention on what was important in the content, on ways to contextualize and extend learning, and on ways to express their developing ideas in writing.

Summarizing and Responding to Current Events

Another common writing activity in social studies/history requires students across grade levels to summarize information from contemporary sources (newspapers, magazines, Internet news sources), and then to explain their reaction in writing. Such assignments help students learn to summarize by pulling out the main idea and key points, and to do so using their own words. In formulating responses or reactions, such assignments ask students to comment on specific items in their summary, drawing from their knowledge of social studies/history to explain their point of view.

For our first example, let us look at Highland Middle School in Louisville, Kentucky. Highland has a challenging curriculum, with a Fine Arts Program, an International Studies Program, and an International Baccalaureate Program.

Mr. Sintry, a sixth-grade teacher, had his students read about current events on a weekly basis and, for extra credit, summarize each article and react to it. Missy (Grade 6, higher achieving) completed the Cur-

FIGURE 4.8. Missy's Completed Current Events Log

News Story Title: City Seeks Money for Downtown Bicycle Station

Source (circle one): Newspaper, Television News, (Magazine)

Scale (circle one): International, National, (Local)

Article Summary (One Paragraph):

The city is seeking federal money to pay for most of the cost of developing a large bike station intended to encourage more bicycle commuting into the central business district. The request isn't approved, the city is trying to find other sources. They have been discussing this project for a while now. The project will be discussed Friday at Bike Summit II which involves discussions. The intent is to have a secure parking for bikes, as well as lockers and showers, a bike shop with repair services close to the bus lines.

Your Response to the Article (One Paragraph):

I think this is a good idea that they are trying to open a bike shop. It is good because it will be very convenient to have, especially right next to the bus route. And it could get Louisvillians to be more active to exercise on bikes because everyone always says that humans are soo lazy. And it will be helpful also because it is like an everything bike store so its somewhere you could easily get to for everything, not travel around everywhere to find certain parts.

---

rent Events Log shown in Figure 4.8, one of a variety of logs that she completed during the semester in response to international, national, and local news.

Clearly one purpose of this exercise was to encourage students to keep up with the daily news—to build a growing bank of knowledge about current events and also to get hooked as a news-follower. Missy was well on her way, as was evident in the variety of logs that she had completed. These logs also provided an ongoing opportunity for Mr. Sintry to help Missy and her classmates refine their ability to write concise and accurate summaries, as well as to select arguments and evidence in sharing their own opinions.

Now, let us look at an example of a somewhat similar task from an Advanced Placement U.S. Government and Politics class at New Paltz High School. New Paltz is in the Hudson Valley, 80 miles north of New York City, and is the home of the State University of New York at New Palz that was founded in the 1800s and continues to have a strong effect on the community. For this particular assignment, Ms. Cordell, the teacher, had the students read five articles taken from various magazines and newspapers, including *The Economist*, *Time*, and *The Washington Post*.

They were expected to write an "integrated summary," by synthesizing the critical ideas expressed in the articles and also to respond to them, using information from within the particular articles as well as outside information to explain and defend their views. Here are excerpts from what Clara (Grade 12, English language learner) wrote:

> *There is one universal factor to all of the political articles these days, and that's Barak Obama. It has been like that for months now, but since his inauguration and his actions following his less than smooth swearing in, the substance of these articles has changed. Now he invades articles on all aspects of national government. He is a crucial part of any discussion of current legislative debates and votes, and the only news on the judicial front is relative to the new president. He is the man. It is obvious from the articles that he is carrying into office a different sort of focus, a new era. He is attempting to usher in a new age of governmental competency and responsibility, and he's trying to forge bipartisan relationships in order to unify all three branches of government so they can work on this new agenda too. However, as almost all of the articles pointed out, there are bumps in the road.*
>
> *One trend that is apparent is that the tone of these articles is sounding increasingly more anxious and more negative. A couple of months ago almost all of the papers, with the exception of the conservative ones, talked reverentially about Obama, when he was a candidate and then when he was President Elect. That tone has changed. People are still reluctant to criticize Obama too heavily, but there is a note of worry that has come up. The recent tax-evasion scandals involving Tom Daschle and Timothy Geithner were embarrassing to the Obama campaign. . . . But now that Obama is actually president, all of his mistakes serve only to invalidate the nation's hopes. The nation doesn't want to let him down, which is the cause of the tone. . . .*
>
> *Another trend has been articles detailing partisan struggles. . . . The Citizens wish to see a change and it is frustrating to see the economic package hoied up in the House or Senate. . . . The press is so worried about partisan struggles that they are predicting. . . . Also a worry is the intra-party disagreements between Nancy Pelosi, speaker of the House, and Barak Obama, which is unfortunate. . . .*
>
> *All of this is well, worrisome. I fear that Obama, with his amazing rhetoric about hope and change, might have raised our hopes up too high. I fear we may have put all of our hope too much into one man. . . . More and more it seems that the fate of the nation rests on his skinny shoulders. He needs to keep his campaign promises, or else the nation might stop believing in hope.*

Clara's essay is a much more sophisticated extension of Missy's sixth-grade current events summary and response. To complete it, Clara needed not only to read the five articles and understand them, but also to find critical issues that were raised by (if not directly in) the articles, calling on a wealth of other information to explain why these issues were important. In a way, we can see that the summary task discussed above, as well as the various across-text tasks discussed earlier, provided scaffolds that helped students develop the disciplinary knowledge and writing skills to write the kind of essay we have just read. It is not only cognitively more challenging, but also presents the kind of pieces that historians, political commentators, and others write, reacting to ideas and interpretations and explaining their own. Together the examples offer a way to think about how we can offer developmental support for students' learning—writing to learn and learning to write social studies/history, across the school years.

SOCIAL STUDIES/HISTORY AND THE COMMON CORE STANDARDS

We have seen that the Common Core State Standards, introduced in Chapter 1, highlight the importance of writing in social studies/history as well as in other subjects. The National Council for the Social Studies has joined other education associations in a jointly issued position paper, *Principles for Learning: A Foundation for Transforming K–12 Education* (2010b), which also emphasizes the importance of disciplinary literacy. The first bullet states, "Being literate is at the heart of every subject area" and goes on to argue that, as students progress through school, they need to learn to use increasingly sophisticated and more complex evidence and reasoning pertinent to the subject area in their reading and writing.

From our perspective, both this position paper and the Common Core strongly support the kinds of social studies/history teaching described in the examples presented in this chapter, in which students have integrated practice in the uses of writing to learn and the learning of disciplinary literacy with increasingly complex material, formats, and expectations across the grades. The letter to the editor, for example, addressed Standards 1 (argument), 4 (coherent writing appropriate to audience and purpose, 5 (appropriate writing processes to develop and strengthen writing), 8 (multiple sources), and 10 (write routinely). The Document-Based Question activity addressed the same set of standards, except focusing on informational/explanatory writing (Standard 2) and drawing evidence from texts (Standard 9).

If we were to look across all the writing described in this chapter, we would see that, to some extent, each of the anchor standards was addressed in one way or another. At the same time, each of the activities helped students develop their interpretations around appropriate issues in social studies/history. The standards become helpful when used by teachers to plan as well as reflect on their own teaching to decide which standards are appropriate for a given social studies learning activity, and to cluster them in ways that lead to the most effective and engaging learning experience for the students. In a similar way, the National Council for the Social Studies' *National Curriculum Standards for Social Studies* (2010a) may provide helpful suggestions. Although there is no section devoted directly to writing or literacy in the social studies standards, the Snapshots of Practice generally include uses of writing as an integral part of the social studies/history learning experience.

THE BOTTOM LINE

Overall, we have seen that writing has a long history of being used to support students' social studies/history learning. Although the pressures of No Child Left Behind and related reforms moved the focus away from writing in social studies/history as well as from writing in other subjects, we have evidence that writing has continued to be used by effective teachers, in supportive schools, as a way to assist student learning.

However, the examples in this chapter do not represent the majority of work we observed; in fact, activities like them were rare. As a profession, we need to help other teachers find ways to incorporate similar integrated activities into their instructional routines. The examples in this chapter can be seen as a beginning, a way to start addressing the goals of the Common Core.

Looking across all of the classrooms we studied, we find a number of practices that contribute to successful teaching of writing in social studies/history:

Curriculum and Instruction

- Invite students to develop discipline-based interpretations of issues or events by investigating the original contexts that surrounded an issue or event, and the contexts in which it was written about over time.
- Engage students in "minds on" writing tasks that require analysis and synthesis of available information, including the evaluation of the trustworthiness of sources, the contexts in which

they originate, and the relationships they have to one another and to other available information.

- Across the year, ensure that students will be engaged in a wide variety of writing tasks for varied audiences and purposes, including systematic attention to the argument, informative/expository, and narrative tasks of the Common Core.

Assessment

- Provide students with rubrics that clarify expectations about the different kinds of writing required in social studies/history. For example, different rubrics may be required for document-based questions and for thematic essays.

Schoolwide Initiatives

- Provide time for shared planning meetings and participation in professional learning communities committed to continual improvement of writing in social studies/history. These may be school- or department-based or rely on external networks such as the National Writing Project, the National Council for the Social Studies, or school-university collaboratives such as the Stanford Reading Like a Historian project.

FUTURE DIRECTIONS

More input from the field will be needed to create even more challenging, engaging, and discipline-appropriate activities. None of the classrooms in our studies, for example, were based around the in-depth examination of primary sources advocated by Wineberg and colleagues (2011) and their Stanford Reading Like a Historian project. That project shifts the focus from historical information to historical interpretation, in which students "evaluate the trustworthiness of multiple perspectives on issues from King Philip's War to the Montgomery Boycott, and make historical claims backed by documentary evidence" (Stanford History Education Group, 2012, para. 2). Writing is deeply embedded in the materials developed by the project, which challenges students to construct their own historical interpretations as they examine the trustworthiness of sources, the contexts in which they originate, and the relationships they have to one another and to other available information.

In general, the writing activities that we found to be most successful offered cognitively challenging experiences that used writing to engage students in developing and defending their own interpretations in engaging and thought-provoking ways. For them, writing is an act of contextualizing, analyzing, problem solving, clarifying and developing defensible historical interpretations that are themselves provisional in the face of new data. Such activities build up over the days of a unit in ways that invite students to develop their own understandings and interpretations. In doing so, students are helped, gradually, across the years, to gain the ability to think, know, communicate, and write in ways appropriate to history and the social sciences embedded in the social studies curriculum.

Reflect and Discuss

1. Choose key events and issues that underlie the year's curriculum. Select one, and invite students to examine the contexts that surrounded it.
    a. Ask students to write an analysis of the various contexts and perspectives that existed at the time.
    b. Ask students to write an analysis of the contexts in which this issue or event has been written about, capturing changing perspectives over time.
2. Develop sets of activities that invite students to write frequently.
    a. Ask students to write a ticket-out every day, where they jot down what they understood and what they're having trouble with.
    b. Have students reflect on their own ongoing inquiry. Ask them to explain what they have learned thus far, what else they need to inquire about, and where they might look for further information.
3. Look back at the Portraits of Success. Which activities can you incorporate into your coursework?
    a. Discuss with your colleagues how you might do this in a way that works for your students and your social studies/history curriculum.
    b. Be specific about your purpose for each writing activity, the content in which it might be embedded, the outcome you anticipate, and possible next steps.
    c. Develop rubrics and collect writing samples students can use as they plan and revise their writing, as well as provide feedback to their peers.

CHAPTER 5

◇◇◇◇◇◇◇

Writing in Mathematics

Michael P. Mastroianni

The current relationship between traditional understandings of writing and mathematics education is somewhat different from relationships between writing and the other subject areas. Unlike composition in English, science, and the social sciences where written language has been the usual medium of presentation, composition in mathematics has typically emphasized mathematical representations. Arguments have been expected to be cast, logic structured, and thinking executed using mathematical symbols unique to the discipline. And for many years this sole form of composition was widely accepted by mathematics educators. As Paul Connolly (1989) points out:

> Given that mathematics has its own symbol system through which practitioners can think and express themselves, it is not immediately apparent why a second "natural" written language is helpful to learning or how, exactly, it might serve a class in learning mathematics. (p. 9)

However, in the past few decades mathematics researchers, professional organizations such as the National Council of Teachers of Mathematics, and teachers alike have recognized the many potential benefits written composition in mathematics classrooms can have for students' disciplinary learning.

THE CALL FOR WRITING IN MATHEMATICS

For many years researchers have advocated for the inclusion of effective writing assignments in the math curriculum (Connolly & Vilardi, 1989; Morgan, 1998), based on findings that writing can improve students' understanding of mathematical concepts (Cross, 2009), make mathematics more meaningful for students (Porter & Masingila, 2000), and promote student engagement. Steele (2005) concluded that writing can help mathematics students explain and make sense of their lessons in a richer way than algorithmic procedural instructions: "This opportunity to explain their thinking in writing helped them develop conceptual knowledge. . . . This conceptual knowledge and sense making cannot be generated by procedures learned by rote" (p. 152).

The National Council of Teachers of Mathematics (NCTM) has also championed the incorporation of writing into mathematics instruction. In the *Principles and Standards for School Mathematics* (2000), NCTM advocated for increased opportunities for students to talk, write, and explain mathematical ideas: "Students who have opportunities, encouragement, and support for speaking, writing, reading, and listening in mathematics classes reap dual benefits: they communicate to learn mathematics, and they learn to communicate mathematically" (p. 60). Further, previous research has shown that mathematics teachers at the middle and high school levels have very positive views toward writing and toward the inclusion of effective writing assignments into math instruction (Quinn & Wilson, 1997).

Despite this momentum for writing in mathematics, the positive arguments for writing from mathematics education researchers, the curricular standards calling for writing from the National Council of Teachers of Mathematics, and the positive views of writing held by mathematics teachers, little writing is, in fact, being incorporated into most secondary school mathematics instruction. The calls for writing in mathematics have yet to sizably impact instruction or student learning. As we will see from the results of our national survey and our examination of students' work in math, writing as an act of composition in mathematics is rare.

THE WRITING STUDENTS ARE ASKED TO DO IN MATHEMATICS

Teachers' responses in our national survey provide a clear picture of typical mathematics practice. When asked about activities during the last 5 days in a focal class, 100% of mathematics teachers reported having students complete numerical calculations, 95% reported having students copy in-class notes, and 81% reported having students complete multiple-choice, fill-in-the-blank, or short-answer questions. Overwhelmingly, mathematics teachers across the country reported that they engaged their students in activities requiring memorization or replication, and not more conceptually engaging activities such as explaining processes that led students to solutions or discussing real-life uses for the mathematical concepts under investigation. And as noted by the Mathematical Sciences Education Board (1990), this is problematic: "Few [students] have the stamina to survive the curriculum of mathematics—at least not the way it is now delivered. Of 4 million [kindergartners] who begin, only 500,000 are still studying mathematics 12 years later" (p. 5). This attrition may be linked to the fact that NCTM's call for writing as a way to help students think about and learn the underlying concepts they are studying—to think through and write about what, how, and why—has gone largely unheeded.

In our survey, we also explored mathematics teachers' attitudes toward writing and writing instruction. Consistent with Quinn and Wilson's (1997) survey, we found mathematics teachers to have very positive views. Some 94% of surveyed mathematics teachers agreed with the statement "All teachers should be responsible for teaching disciplinary writing within their own subject." Ninety-seven percent agreed "All teachers should be responsible for improving students' writing skills." And 91% of math teachers rejected the statement "Asking students at this grade level to write is not necessary in this subject."

Nevertheless, while mathematics teachers' positive attitudes toward writing and writing instruction in mathematics were close to unanimous, from our analyses of student work, we saw that these views have not translated into practice. In total, we collected 2,026 examples of middle and high school student work in response to mathematics assignments. Of those assignments, 74% provided students the opportunity to compose mathematically in a variety of formats (e.g., computations, graphical representations, responses to short-answer or fill-in-the-blank exercises), and 25% were in-class notes, provided by teachers and copied by students. Only 1% of our sample consisted of assignments asking students to write a paragraph or more.

Within the 1%, however, we saw thought-provoking uses of writing that successfully demonstrated how it can be incorporated into mathematics instruction to support student learning of mathematical concepts. These assignments ranged widely, from essays on fractions, to writing in response to prompts about perimeter and area scenarios, to assignments asking students to imagine worlds devoid of certain mathematical entities (e.g., a world without parallel lines). All of these were writing assignments that engaged the students in high levels of conceptual thought about mathematics.

In the next section, we'll investigate examples of these writing assignments, as exemplars of "what-can-be" in mathematics and writing.

PORTRAITS OF SUCCESS

Writing About Fractions

Our first example takes us to Ms. Decker's sixth-grade classroom in Montebello Intermediate School in central California, where she asked her students to explore the connection between fraction operations and the common experience of baking. Montebello is situated in a semiurban community 11 miles southeast of Los Angeles proper.

Although Montebello sixth graders had to take a statewide math exam that was all multiple choice, the mathematics department still recognized the importance of writing. "Whatever you do in your life, you need to present it in oral and written form," Ms. Abraham, the chair of the mathematics department, told us. "We try to integrate as much writing as we can."

For her unit on fractions Ms. Decker used a multidraft, peer-edited, expository essay assignment to aid her students' learning of operations (addition, subtraction, multiplication, and division) with fractions. Her assignment asked students to create a procedural "recipe" for solving various problems. She outlined the expected six paragraphs on the board:

1. Introduction
2. Body
   - Addition of fractions
   - Subtraction of fractions
   - Multiplication of fractions
   - Division of fractions
3. Conclusion

This was only the beginning of the scaffolding that Ms. Decker provided to support her students' learning of the operations called for, and their writing about them. She presented a series of graphic organizers that displayed the procedural steps involved in each mathematical operation. These graphic organizers formed the basis for the content included in the essays, and provided a summary of the steps involved in adding, subtracting, multiplying, and dividing fractions. Julio, one of our lower achieving case study students, copied the teacher's graphics into his notebook. His version of multiplication and division of fractions is reproduced in Figure 5.1.

Each student completed three drafts of the fractions essay: two rough drafts and a final draft. Between their second and final drafts, Ms. Decker

FIGURE 5.1. Julio's Notebook Page of Graphic Organizers

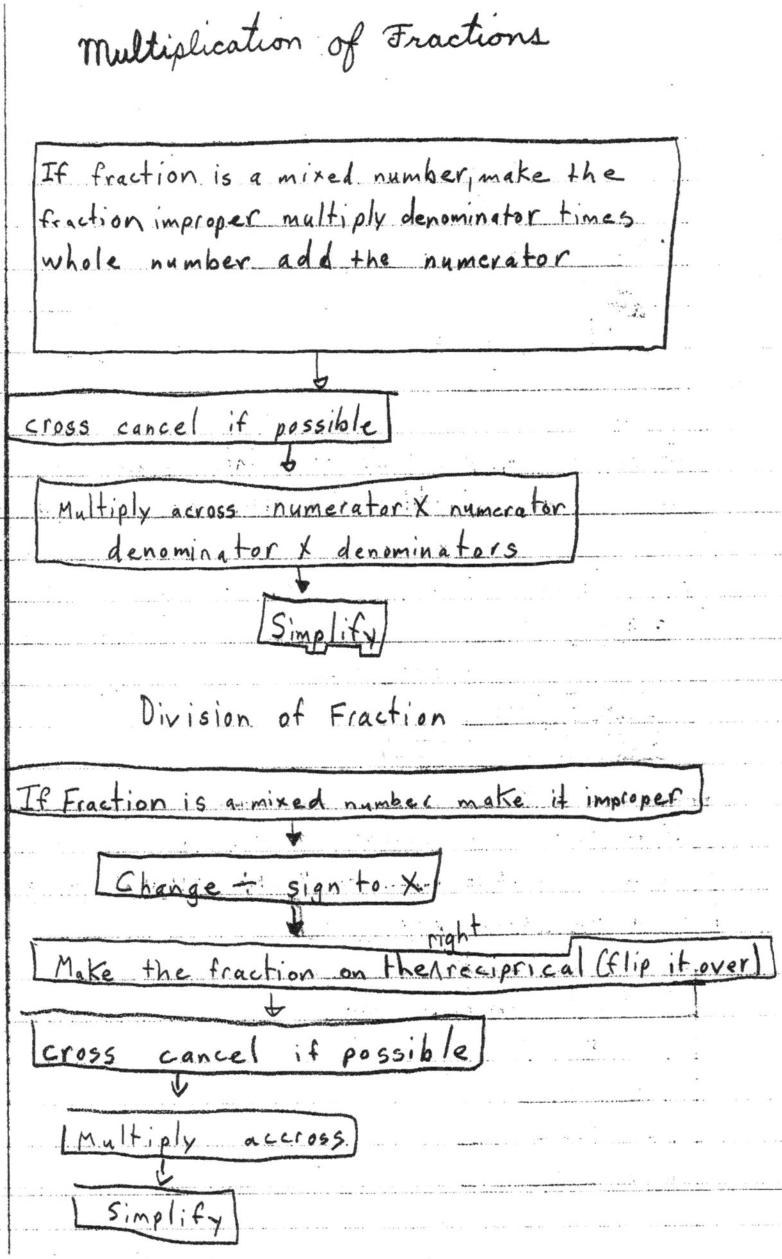

Multiplication of Fractions

If fraction is a mixed number, make the fraction improper multiply denominator times whole number add the numerator

cross cancel if possible

Multiply across numerator X numerator denominator X denominators

Simplify

Division of Fraction

If Fraction is a mixed number make it improper

Change ÷ sign to X

Make the fraction on the right reciprical (flip it over)

cross cancel if possible

Multiply across

Simplify

allotted class time for peer editing and peer feedback; she also used the time to provide feedback of her own. This was particularly important because it allowed students to assess their mathematical understanding of fraction operations against the understanding of their peers. It also allowed them to get guidance and explanation from Ms. Decker when needed. Before the peer review, she listed on the blackboard the common writing problems already discussed in class that she wanted them to focus on in their feedback:

- Indent paragraphs
- Capitalization
- End punctuation
- Spelling
- Check for meaning
- Are parts 1, 2, and 3 [from the outline] there?

With peer edits and peer feedback in mind, students made the necessary changes and began writing their final drafts. Figure 5.2 displays the first of two pages of Julio's final draft as an example of the work that resulted. He earned an A.

Ms. Decker's essay assignment began engaging students in the discourses of mathematics, as researchers Leone Burton and Candia Morgan (2000) would argue:

> We see teaching and learning mathematics not as just filling students' heads with facts and skills but as inducting them into mathematical communities. An important part of learning to be mathematical, whether in the primary school or in the university, is learning to take part in the discourses of mathematics, becoming both a consumer and a producer of texts that are recognized as legitimately mathematical within one's community. (p. 450)

Giving students opportunities to be consumers and producers of mathematics is extremely important. Sixth graders do not readily connect their everyday experiences with mathematics. Ms. Decker's essay helped them accomplish just that. Through her writing assignment, she was able to successfully scaffold students' learning both of operations and of ways to express them in extended text.

Gone to the Dogs: Writing About Triangle Theorems

Our second example comes from Grisham Middle School, an International Baccalaureate (IB) World School in the Anderson Mills com-

FIGURE 5.2. Julio's Recipe Essay on Fractions

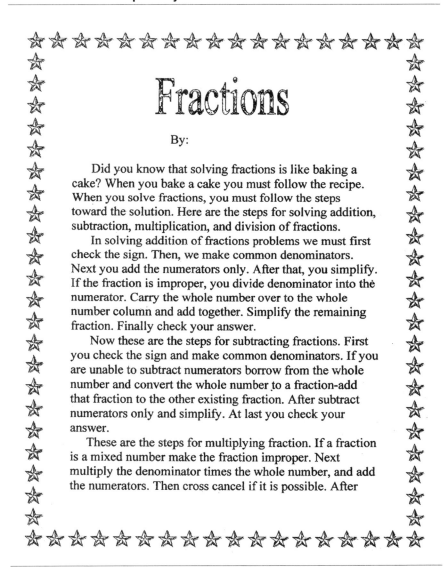

Fractions

By:

Did you know that solving fractions is like baking a cake? When you bake a cake you must follow the recipe. When you solve fractions, you must follow the steps toward the solution. Here are the steps for solving addition, subtraction, multiplication, and division of fractions.

In solving addition of fractions problems we must first check the sign. Then, we make common denominators. Next you add the numerators only. After that, you simplify. If the fraction is improper, you divide denominator into the numerator. Carry the whole number over to the whole number column and add together. Simplify the remaining fraction. Finally check your answer.

Now these are the steps for subtracting fractions. First you check the sign and make common denominators. If you are unable to subtract numerators borrow from the whole number and convert the whole number to a fraction-add that fraction to the other existing fraction. After subtract numerators only and simplify. At last you check your answer.

These are the steps for multiplying fraction. If a fraction is a mixed number make the fraction improper. Next multiply the denominator times the whole number, and add the numerators. Then cross cancel if it is possible. After

munity of Austin, Texas. As an IB World School, teachers at Grisham stressed critical thinking and making connections across disciplines. They also placed a large emphasis on student writing. Students "are expected to write in all subjects, no matter what," Ms. Quince, the English language arts chair, told us. To encourage student writing, collaboration among teachers at Grisham Middle School was high, especially within subject areas. Ms. Quince continued: "Our teams are our four core subject areas. We bring work samples and we analyze the work samples as a team to see 'How is this assignment working?', 'Are the kids learning?', 'Is the rigor high enough?' . . . And that includes writing."

Teachers in the mathematics department considered their school's emphasis on writing to be important for students' learning. "I think the emphasis takes writing to another level," the chair of the math department told us. "Besides just doing the computation, by explaining a problem or in some cases by comparing/contrasting a topic, [students are] taking it to a higher level of knowledge."

Grisham's schoolwide emphasis on writing was very evident in the student work we collected. Eighth-grade teacher Joanne Burke's "Gone to the Dogs" project was one such example. During a unit on triangle theorems, Ms. Burke asked her students to construct a short story about building a doghouse for a cold dog. The project required students to diagram a roof for the doghouse (drawing triangles on a coordinate plane), determine how to make four congruent trusses of the doghouse roof (proving congruence by using various triangle theorems), and hypothetically purchase wood from a hardware store (calculating and rationalizing material costs), with a now appreciative, warm dog living happily ever after.

This assignment was mathematically rich, requiring students to complete multiple steps and invoke several theorems throughout the development of their stories. Rosie, a higher achieving eighth-grade case study student, began her story: "There once was a girl named Rosie. She had a dog named Eley. One day, Rosie decided to build a doghouse for Eley. Rosie worked all day and by night she had a plan for Eley's doghouse." Rosie's first task was to plan four trusses to support the roof, using the side-side-side postulate to be sure the four trusses were congruent; the postulate states that if three sides of a triangle (e.g., a truss) are congruent to three sides of a different triangle, the triangles themselves are congruent.

Rosie continued by wondering aloud in her story, "Can we prove that the two sides of the triangle [adjoining triangles of a truss] are congruent?" To answer her question, she added the character of a friend (Jamie) to her story, and together they used the hypotenuse-leg theorem in a two-column proof to demonstrate congruency (Figure 5.3). Rosie added another friend to her story (Kaylin) to help her use the CPCTC theorem (corresponding parts of congruent triangles are congruent) to ensure that two adjoining legs at the base of each truss were congruent (Figure 5.4). After this, she used the Pythagorean Theorem to calculate how much wood would be needed to build the roof (not shown). Finally, Rosie determined the interior angles of the four trusses by using the converse of

FIGURE 5.3. Rosie's Doghouse: Using the Hypotenuse-Leg Theorem

"Hi Jamie!" Rosie exclaimed. "I was wondering if you could show me if the two halves of this truss are congruent."

"You will need to use HL theorem to prove this. Here, let me show you using this two column proof," said Jamie.

Statements	Reasons
$AC \cong CB$	given
ADC is a rt $\angle$	given
$ADC + BDC = 180°$	def of supplementry $\angle$'s
$ADC = 90°$	def of a rt $\angle$
$90° + BDC = 180$	substitution
$BDC = 90$	subtraction POE
BDC is a rt $\angle$	def of rt $\angle$
ADC and BDC are right $\triangle$'s	def of rt $\triangle$
$CD \cong CD$	reflexive POC
$ADC \cong BDC$	HL

the isosceles triangle theorem, which states that the base angles of an isosceles triangle are congruent. Three pages later, with costs calculated (Figure 5.5), Rosie purchased the necessary materials, and as she wrote in her concluding sentence, "built her dog, Eley a doghouse where Eley lived happily ever after." In all, Rosie's narrative was a full 14 pages long, with each page containing both narrative and supporting mathematical diagrams and explanations. On the one hand, we can see that the mathematics was a driving force behind the narrative story line. On the other hand, the narrative story line was also a driving force behind the mathematics. They supported each other.

FIGURE 5.4. Rosie's Doghouse: Using the CPCTC Theorem

"Hi Kaylin," Rosie said. "Can you help
me prove that AD and BD are congruent?"

"Well," said Kaylin, "Since you already
know that triangle ACD is congruent to triangle
BCD you can use CPCTC or congruent parts of
congruent triangles are congruent to prove that
AD is congruent to BD."

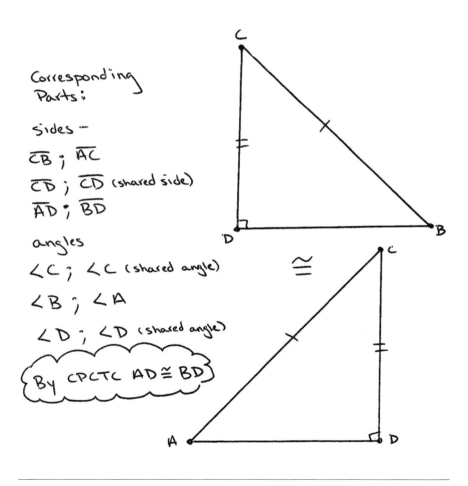

FIGURE 5.5. Rosie's Doghouse: Cost Calculation

At Sally's Tacky Hardware they sell
wood in 6-foot lengths only and it costs $0.80
per foot. So total it would cost Rosie $19.20 to
buy enough wood from Sally's. To see how
Rosie figured this out, look below.

- wood for 1 truss
  - add side lengths

24 + 15 + 15 + 9 = 63 (including supporting piece)

- wood for all 4 trusses

63
× 4
252 inches or 21ft

252 / 12 = 21ft

- How many 6 foot pieces?

4 pieces even though 3ft
will be left over because 3
6-foot pieces will only be
18 feet.

- Cost for wood needed

6 · 4 = 24ft

24 × .80 = 19.20

$19.20

While "happily ever after" typically signifies the end of a fairy tale, or in the case of a school project, the assignment's conclusion, Ms. Burke had her students complete a follow-up reflection on the activity. The task consisted of a series of prompts asking students to "List below all of the skills you practiced over the course of your project" and "Write a sentence about how you will continue to practice each of these skills in the near future." This type of follow-up encouraged students to be reflective and explicit about their personal learning and helped them solidify the real-world connections they constructed during the project. As Rosie wrote, the "Gone to the Dogs" activity helped her learn "how to explain math in a interesting way."

Ms. Burke also used an International Baccalaureate Middle Years Programme rubric to assess students' projects through three lenses: a formal lens assessing students' knowledge and understanding; a project lens assessing students' application and reasoning; and a presentation lens assessing students' communication and reflection/evaluation. Figure 5.6 presents the third section of the rubric, including the teacher's rating of Rosie's project on this section of the rubric. Overall, Rosie received an A and bonus points for her work. The rubric sets high expectations for Rosie and her classmates, both in the level of mathematical reasoning expected and in the specific features considered to be components of effective writing.

Open-Response Questions

Both examples discussed so far resulted in extended student writing similar in length to writing assigned in English or social studies. These assignments provided students ample room to explore and engage with complex mathematical content for an extended period of time. However, mathematical assignments do not need to result in such lengthy writing for students to be challenged cognitively. As a teacher in another school explained to us, "Writing is different in math. We do computations, but students need to talk about the subject. The why and how of doing problems is important." Often, teachers asked students "how" and "why" through a variety of short-response writing prompts. These prompts may have resulted in only a few sentences or a paragraph, yet they often promoted student reasoning and understanding of math phenomena. Let us look at examples from the mathematics department in College View Middle School.

College View Middle School is located in Owensboro, Kentucky, a city located on the bank of the Ohio River on the Indiana-Kentucky border. College View has placed a strong emphasis on student writing in all subject areas for a number of years. Mr. Petroff, a mathematics

FIGURE 5.6. Criteria for Assessing Communication and Reflection

MYP Assessment Criteria

Criteria C and D: Communication and Reflection/Evaluation (Presentation and Projects)

Assignment: _Gone to Dogs_   Semester: _1st_

Date of Assignment: _11/14_   Grade: _5_

Level	Descriptor
0	• S. does not achieve Level 1
1-2	• S. shows little working out but may offer oral explanations. • Presentation is poor with little use of correct mathematical symbols or diagrams. • No reflection shown. • Lines of reasoning are difficult to follow. • Presentation is mediocre with features such as titles, subtitles, date, name, some use of correct mathematical symbols, but little structure. • S. writes about the methods used but does not reflect on them.
3-4	• S. shows working out and gives explanations with some interpretation of the results. • Presentation is good with main features such as titles, date, name, and some structure to the work. • Good use of mathematical symbols and diagrams. • S. offers a simple reflection on the methods used. • Lines or reasoning are clear though not always logical or complete. • S. makes some attempt to interpret the significance of their results and make predictions.
5-6	• S. can communicate and interpret the significance of their results in words, symbols or diagrams in a clear, concise form. • The work is well structured and shows clear progression. • S. gives a good interpretation of the results and makes predictions on future events. • S. gives clear reasons for the methods used. • Lines of reasoning are concise, logical, and complete. • S. justifies the degree of accuracy of his or her results when appropriate.

**Pattern: underlining order, regularity, or predictability between the elements of a mathematical system. The repetitive features of patterns can be identified and described as relationships or generalized rules.

teacher, told us, "Writing is a priority in our school and it is shown by the [professional development] workshops made available to us." The head of the science department agreed: "There is great emphasis put on writing across the building." College View's emphasis on writing extended beyond the core subject areas into art, music, physical education, and computer classes as well.

While this emphasis on writing spanned the entire school, College View made a special effort to prepare students for writing tasks on Kentucky's high-stakes assessments. One Kentucky writing task at the time of our study was the open-response question (ORQ). In math, open-response questions typically resemble multiple-part mathematical word

FIGURE 5.7. A Typical Grade 8 Open-Response Question

Susan is going to the post office to mail six items. For each item, the post office charges 33¢ for the first ounce of mail and 23¢ for each additional ounce.

a. Copy and complete the table below in your Student Response Booklet showing how much it would cost Susan to mail each of her six items if the first item weighs one ounce, the second item weighs two ounces, the third item weighs three ounces, and so on up to the sixth item which weighs six ounces.

Ounces	Cost
1	
2	
3	
4	
5	
6	

b. How much would it cost Susan to mail an item that weighs 25 ounces?
c. Write an expression that shows the cost of mailing an item that weighs n ounces, and explain your reasoning.

Note: From Kentucky Department of Education (1999).

problems. And often these questions require students to explain, describe, or justify mathematical calculations. Figure 5.7 shows a typical Grade 8 open-response question released for school use by Kentucky Department of Education (1999).

The commentary that accompanied the release of this item noted that "The ability to identify a numeric pattern, extend that pattern, and express a rule for that pattern in algebraic form is useful in many real-world contexts such as determining pricing for a business, making investment decisions, and predicting population trends" (p. 2).

Teachers at College View Middle School often wrote their own open-response questions. As one teacher told us, "Open-response [questions] . . . are given to students frequently. This is a districtwide policy." To support teachers, College View had provided many resources, including a writing consultant who had helped teachers develop effective ORQ activities. Teachers also shared writing prompts and collaborated with one another, meeting regularly in both grade-level and subject-area teams.

An eighth-grade teacher explained that the schoolwide emphasis on ORQs included "a weekly drawing of students who have scored a four [out of four] on their open-response. They win awards as a result." Rewarding students for writing trickled down to individual classrooms, where math teacher Mr. Petroff told us they rewarded "students with candy for doing well on open-response writing."

FIGURE 5.8. Lorna's Prewriting Scaffold

Score a 4!

Know Topic of question	Do List of power verbs	Plan/Support (Math: Work/Explain) Use supporting details for each part of your answer, explain, give evidence, use examples, give reasons, use quotes from reading, provide extra information
Easton was right, it is $1\frac{1}{4}$	A. Solve, compute, explain B. Answer, explain C. (if needed)	• Topic Sentence • First, you add the 2 top numbers of the fractions which are called numerators. So, I added seven to three to get the sum of ten. The bottom #, the denominator stays the same. So the answer is $\frac{10}{8}$. This fraction is what you call an improper fraction. This fraction is improper because the numerator is larger than the denominator. Next, I the problem by seeing how many times 8 will go into 10. 8 divides into 10 once, so 1 becomes my whole number. Now, I am left with $\frac{2}{8}$. So my current answer is $1\frac{2}{8}$. But now I have to simplify because $\frac{2}{8}$ is not in simplest form. So to simplify, I find the greatest common factor of 2 and 8 which is 2, and see how many times it goes into the num. and the den. 2 goes into 2 once, and 2 goes into 8 four times. So now, my answer is $1\frac{1}{4}$.

Vocabulary		
Numerator Denominator Fraction (Bar) Simplest Form Sum Add Improper Mixed Number	GCF Like Fractions	

IF I add the denominator then I change the portion size, therefore I don't change the denominator.

This schoolwide emphasis on open-response questions insured that students knew how to approach such tasks, whether in the classroom or on their high-stakes tests. For example, Lorna, a higher achieving sixth grader, was given the following scenario and accompanying tasks:

Kailyn and Easton were given the following math problem: 7/8 + 3/8. Kailyn's response was 10/16 and Easton's response was 1 and 1/4. A) Solve the problem with all computation and explanations. B) Whose response was correct? Explain your reasoning.

Lorna began her response to this open-response question by using a generic framework designed to scaffold such tasks (see Figure 5.8 for Lorna's first draft/prewriting scaffold). This four-part template (Know, Do, Plan/Support, and Vocabulary) provided a way to organize and collect ideas. It worked as a scaffold to structure her mathematical thinking and problem solving.

After this first draft, Lorna went on to complete her writing assignment. As shown in Figure 5.9, she answered Part A by describing the steps in her calculations and the reasons behind them, concluding with "now my answer is 1 1/4." In developing her explanation, she used "power verbs" in her topic sentence as suggested in the "Do" section of the framework (as seen in Figure 5.8), and 9 of the 10 vocabulary words in her response. We can see that much of what Lorna wrote in her first draft found its way into the second. After composing her own answer to Part A of the prompt, Lorna identified Easton's response as correct since she had gotten the same answer, and found two problems with Kailyn's alternative: "evidently, she added the denominators, which you can't do . . . and even if 10/16 was the correct answer, she still didn't simplify."

Lorna and her classmates were not asked to answer their open-response questions by immediately putting words on paper. Rather, they used the prewriting activity to better understand the problem, brainstormed mathematical concepts related to the questions, and then proceeded to draft their responses. In Lorna's work, we can see how the prewriting activity supported her problem solving, including the use of mathematically appropriate vocabulary in her explanations of what she had done correctly and where Kailyn had gone wrong. For many students, this prethinking of the problem, and of the mathematical vocabulary and the concepts that go with it, can be useful in shaping the ideas as well as the language with which to express themselves mathematically.

Writing About Statistics

Our last example comes from Terry Hugo's Advanced Placement (AP) Statistics course in Bowling Green High School, located in western Kentucky, 25 miles north of the Kentucky-Tennessee border. Ms. Hugo's AP Statistics course was one of many AP courses offered at the high school.

With their heavy emphasis on Advanced Placement, it should be no surprise that Bowling Green High School's administration and faculty considered writing to be a crucially important component of the school's success. As one administrator told us, "writing is an everyday activity in our school. It is used in classes all the time." A social studies teacher similarly observed, "Schoolwide writing is emphasized at BGHS [Bowling Green High School]; it is emphasized in every classroom. . . . It's really not the mandate from the state that motivates writing, [teachers] know it's a way of measuring learning. . . ." He concluded by telling us that at Bowling Green High School "writing is used to promote learning, not as a test-driven tool."

This schoolwide emphasis on writing was quite evident in Ms. Hugo's statistics classroom. Her emphasis on writing helped support students' learning of advanced statistics and allowed her to better gauge and grasp students' understandings. She encouraged them to move beyond technical explanations and "convey data in layman's terms." As she told us, "In

FIGURE 5.9. Lorna's Final Draft About Adding Fractions

MATHEMATICS

Ⓐ I will solve the problem 7/8 + 3/8 with all computation and explanations. First, you add the 2 top numbers of the fractions which are called numerators. So, I added 7 to 3 to get the sum of 10. The bottom number, the denominator, stays the same. So, the answer is 10/8. This fraction is what you call an improper fraction. This is an improper fraction because the numerator is larger than the denominator. Next, I changed the improper fraction to a mixed number by seeing how many times 8 will divide into 10. 8 divides into 10 once, so 1 becomes my whole number. Now, I am left with 2/8. So my current answer is 1 2/8. But now I have to simplify because 2/8 is not in simplest form. So to simplify, I find the greatest common factor of 2 and 8, which is 2, and see how many times it goes into the numerator and denominator. 2 goes into 2 once, and 2 goes into 8 four times. So my answer is 1 1/4.

7/8 + 3/8 = 10/8   10 ÷ 8 = 1 2/8   2 1/2   2 4/8

(1 1/4)

Ⓑ I will now tell whose response was correct and explain my reasoning. Easton's response was correct. I know Kaitlyn isn't correct because evidently, she added the denominators, which you can't do because then that changes the portion size, and even if 10/16 was the correct answer, she still didn't simplify.

7/8 + 3/8 ≠ 10/16

You did a great job (4)

STOP! ●

AP Statistics we write a lot. . . . I want to see what my kids are seeing." She continued, "There is a gray area in math. Explanations can help me understand their answers."

Ms. Hugo's emphasis on uses of writing to help students present well-defended explanations and further their understanding was evident in her students' work. As an example, Figure 5.10 displays an AP Statistics quiz completed by Grace, a higher achieving 12th-grade student in Ms.

Hugo's course. This particular quiz asked students to critically examine a study describing an unanticipated side effect of an antidepression pill: its ability to help participants quit smoking.

For this activity, students answered a series of questions regarding the study's findings, conclusions, and generalizations. These questions acted to help the students to think more deeply about what was included in the study, as well as the conclusions that were being drawn from it.

Grace's answers were brief, as called for by the short-constructed-response questions, yet sufficiently detailed and thorough. For example, in response to the question, "Can we conclude that taking Zyban causes people to quit smoking? Justify your answer," Grace responded: "No, we have not isolated factors. Perhaps one person's will is stronger than another. . . . We cannot establish causation." Grace responded to the prompt, justified her answer, provided a reasonable explanation in support of her justification, and concluded that causation could not be established. In response to the prompt, "To what population can the results of this study be generalized? Explain." Grace wrote: "It can be generalized to smokers who want to quit smoking and are not outwardly depressed. B/c this was the makeup of the sample, this is all it can be generalized to." Again, Grace responded to the prompt, and justified her answer from her knowledge of statistical theory.

Based on her comments on the student work we collected, Grace's written responses seem to be the types of explanations Ms. Hugo expected from her students during class lessons as well as on quizzes. In addition to writing about what they were learning, she asked her students to use writing to explore applications of statistics in daily life. Toward this end, she used writing to help students use the statistical principles they had studied at school to understand and make good consumer judgments about what they read. The questions in this sequence offered students models of questions to ask themselves. In this way Ms. Hugo helped students learn to use their statistical knowledge to better understand real-life situations. Such writing tasks also call for the types of mathematical explanation that help teachers better understand students' thinking and reasoning.

NCTM has long called for students to write explanations of the steps that led to their solutions of problems and their understanding of concepts. Of the explanations in the student writing we collected, those from Ms. Hugo's AP Statistics students were particularly rich. We attribute this to Ms. Hugo's expectations for students to be able to use their thorough understanding of statistics as the basis for what they wrote, and to express it in situation-specific "layman's terms."

FIGURE 5.10. Grace's Writing About Statistics

Quiz 11.3A   AP Statistics   Name

Read the brief newspaper article on using a depression pill to help smokers quit.

> **Depression Pill Seems to Help Smokers Quit**
> BOSTON — Taking an antidepression medicine appears to double smokers' chances of kicking the habit, a study found. The Food and Drug Administration approved the marketing of this medicine, called Zyban or bupropion, to help smokers in May. The results of several studies with the drug, including one published in today's issue of the *New England Journal of Medicine*, were made public then.
> The newly published study was conducted on 615 volunteers who wanted to give up smoking and were not outwardly depressed. They took either Zyban or dummy pills for 6 weeks. A year later, 23 percent of those getting Zyban were still off cigarettes, compared with 12 percent in the comparison group.

n = 615   .23   .13

1. The results of this experiment were significant at the $\alpha = 0.05$ significance level. In your opinion, are the results practically significant? Justify your position.

Np; less than 50% stuck w/ not smoking, whether they used Zyban or not.

2. To what population can the results of this study be generalized? Explain.

It can be generalized to smokers who want to quit smoking and are not outwardly depressed. B/c this was the makeup of the sample, this is all it can be generalized to.

3. Can we conclude that taking Zyban *causes* people to quit smoking? Justify your answer.

No, we have not isolated factors. Perhaps one person will is stronger than another and so on. We cannot establish causation.

4. In performing a test of significance, the researcher can choose between adopting a fixed significance level or calculating a *P*-value. Does it matter which approach is taken? If so, describe the circumstances when one should use each approach.

It does matter to get ordering. A fixed significance level must be predetermined before calculations made. A P-value w/o significance is still effectual; inference can be made in relation to the size of the P-value.

MATHEMATICS AND THE COMMON CORE STANDARDS

In addition to standards for literacy, the *Common Core State Standards* (CCSSO & NGA, 2010) include a separate specification of standards for mathematics. Although focused for the most part on different realms of mathematical knowledge (e.g., Number and Quantity, Algebra, Statistics and Probability), the math standards are equally clear about the importance of argument and explanation within the disciplines of mathematics. As the introduction explains:

> One hallmark of mathematical understanding is the ability to justify, in a way appropriate to the student's mathematical maturity, why a particular mathematical statement is true or where a mathematical rule comes from. There is a world of difference between a student who can summon a mnemonic device to expand a product such as $(a + b)(x + y)$ and a student who can explain where the mnemonic comes from. The student who can explain the rule understands the mathematics, and may have a better chance to succeed at a less familiar task such as expanding $(a + b + c)(x + y)$. Mathematical understanding and procedural skill are equally important, and both are assessable using mathematical tasks of sufficient richness. (p. 4)

The mathematical tasks that we have examined in this chapter provide rich examples of ways that such an emphasis can be incorporated into the mathematics curriculum, supporting students in the process of developing their understandings of mathematical content as well as asking them to apply their understandings in new contexts. These tasks also play an important part in the "Mathematical Practices" that are also included in the standards for mathematics across all grade levels, including in particular Practice 3, Construct viable arguments and critique the reasoning of others. The examples in this chapter incorporate these practices directly, requiring both the construction of arguments and the critique of the reasoning of others.

THE BOTTOM LINE

The four examples we have explored represent the kinds of assignments that can be used in secondary mathematics classes to challenge students cognitively, to promote their reasoning, and to help them better understand and learn mathematics content. All four assignments provided students with opportunities to be consumers and producers of mathematics (Burton & Morgan, 2000), and to make meaningful connections. Ms. Decker's fractions essay, Ms. Burke's doghouse story, and Ms. Hugo's writing about statistics helped students make connections between their mathematics classwork and the real world, while College View Middle School's approach to open-response questions helped students develop a fuller understanding of mathematical problem solving and mathematical explanation. These assignments also provided opportunities for students to move beyond the algorithmic nature of mathematical calculations and recompose mathematical knowledge in different formats for different purposes. Finally, all four assignments maintained a level of academic rigor appropriate for the grade level of the students.

It is not difficult to see how similar examples could be incorporated into all levels of math instruction. For example, a story like Ms. Burke's "Gone to the Dogs" project could be incorporated into an 11th-grade pre-calculus unit on the trigonometric functions sine, cosine, and tangent. Similarly, variations on Ms. Decker's fractions essay or open-response questions could be appropriately used at any level. Thus, while the assignments themselves are notable, far more critical is how each teacher structured and scaffolded each assignment for the students. Ms. Decker guided students through a graphically organized summary of the procedures involved in fraction operations, scaffolding both the mathematical content and the structure of their essays. The International Baccalaureate rubric used by Ms. Burke indicated to students her expectations of mathematical reasoning and the quality of writing. The scaffolds provided for College View's open-response questions helped students dissect each prompt, connect to the concepts they were studying, and see the relationships between individual content items and larger explanations. And Ms. Hugo's statistics writing provided students with the opportunity to think carefully about how statistical principles could be applied to a real-life problem at hand and used to better interpret things they read and heard in out-of-school contexts.

Looking across all of the classrooms we studied, we find a number of practices that contribute to successful teaching of mathematical writing:

Curriculum and Instruction

- Ask students to provide a written justification for why a particular mathematical statement is true or a conclusion is accurate. Prompts asking students to explain, describe, or justify can promote student reasoning and help develop students' understanding of mathematics.
- Scaffold students' learning by helping them judge relevant ideas, constructs, or procedures, organize them effectively, and rethink them in response to classmate and teacher feedback.
- Encourage regular translation across systems of representation, from mathematical formulas to graphs and diagrams, to prose explanations.

Assessment

- Include writing tasks of various types as ways for students to demonstrate their knowledge and understanding of mathematical principles and procedures. They may be asked, for example, to explain their reasoning in solving a mathematical problem or to use their understandings of mathematics to address a real-world problem.

- Provide students with rubrics that clarify expectations about the different kinds of writing required in mathematics.

Schoolwide Initiatives

- Provide support for the teaching of mathematical writing through, for example, external consultants or district leaders of curriculum and instruction. Additional resources are available from the National Council of Teachers of Mathematics and from the National Writing Project.

FUTURE DIRECTIONS

What allows these types of lessons to happen in some mathematics classes and not others? All of our examples are situated in environments where writing was explicitly emphasized. The mathematics department at Montebello Intermediate School tried to integrate writing as much as possible into math instruction. Ms. Burke's "Gone to the Dogs" project and College View Middle School's open-response questions came from school environments where students were expected to write in every subject, and Bowling Green High School, Ms. Hugo's school, was strongly in favor of writing in each of the subject classes. To support these commitments, the schools provided teachers with professional development, access to writing consultants, and opportunities for collaboration with colleagues. In turn, these initiatives had a large impact on instruction, and as we saw, they resulted in effective examples of student writing in mathematics.

Unfortunately, such writing remains rare, although writing activities that invite students to explain, describe, or justify their work in mathematics can promote student reasoning and help develop students' understanding of mathematics. By incorporating writing into everyday classroom activity as an integral part of the curriculum, teachers can engage students in thinking about substantive problems and concepts that are central to the field and relating them to situations they face in life. In doing so, the math they learn at school will be more fully understood as well as be more memorable.

Reflect and Discuss

1. Have your students write often.
    a. Ask them to do "quick writes" about what they think they know about a new concept.
    b. At the end of each class, ask for a "ticket out," telling what they have understood and what questions they still have.
    c. Develop writing activities in which the concept is used in addressing real-life problems.
2. Plan one or two activities to help students learn mathematical language and concepts as they address a particular mathematical problem.
    a. Ask students to discuss and take notes about their understanding of the problem, their efforts to solve it, and the solution they reach.
    b. At the end, ask them to explain the mathematical principles that justify the solution.
3. Look back at the section on Portraits of Success. Which activities can be incorporated into your coursework?
    a. Discuss with your colleagues how you might adapt this activity for your students and your mathematics classes.
    b. Be specific about your purpose for the writing activity, the content in which it might be embedded, the outcome you anticipate, and your possible next steps.

CHAPTER 6

◇◇◇◇◇◇◇

Writing in Science

Marc Nachowitz

The disciplines of science have long-standing traditions of making observations, experimenting, developing claims based on evidence, and communicating those findings to a larger community. Similarly, science educators have long recognized the importance of writing in their field. Traditional writing tasks such as research papers, notes, and lab reports are central to all good science teaching (Metz, 2012). However, several recent developments, both at the policy level and in pedagogical research, have affected the role of writing and writing instruction in science classrooms.

THE BACKGROUND FOR WRITING IN SCIENCE

National organizations concerned with science instruction have for many years placed an emphasis on communication skills within the disciplines of science (National Committee on Science Education Standards and Assessment & National Research Council, 1996), though the role of writing in such work remained poorly elaborated. More recently, the National Research Council published *A Framework for K–12 Science Education* (2011) calling for students to engage in building arguments from evidence, obtaining and evaluating information, and communicating "their findings clearly and persuasively" (p. 53). The report goes on to acknowledge that "reading, interpreting, and producing text are fundamental practices of science" (p. 74). And as we have seen in earlier chapters, the Common Core State Standards developed by the Council of Chief State School Officers and the National Governors Association (2010) call for substantial attention to writing within the disciplines of science in Grades 6 through 12.

Even as new standards and frameworks have emphasized the importance of writing in science, research on writing to learn science has progressed significantly. For example, Keys (2000) found that while the act of traditional laboratory report writing can stimulate science learning, the formulaic structure of such writing allowed some students to provide hypotheses and supporting evidence from memory without thinking deeply about the content while writing. Synthesizing recent research in science writing, Hand, Wallace, and Yang (2004) noted significant advances in understandings of the following three areas:

> (a) the potential cognitive mechanisms through which writing might contribute to learning; (b) the relationship between writing and conceptual understanding; and (c) the relationship between explicit writing instruction and student performance. (p. 133)

Such research investigating the use of writing as a means to prompt students to think more deeply about the content they are learning has influenced teachers' uses of writing as an instructional technique. At the same time, while there has been progress in using writing to learn science, to the extent that writing is used at all in high-stakes assessments in science, it is used to demonstrate content mastery. These uses of writing for "show-what-you-know" also have had a strong influence on the kinds of writing used in classrooms.

By examining the kinds of writing students are asked to do as well as the placement of such writing within the larger curriculum, the remainder of this chapter will help us understand how some science teachers currently conceptualize disciplinary writing in the sciences and highlight effective practices to support disciplinary thinking.

THE WRITING STUDENTS ARE ASKED TO DO IN SCIENCE

When asked about the kinds of activities students had engaged in for classwork or homework during the previous week, 90% of science teachers surveyed indicated that their students had completed multiple-choice, fill-in-the-blank, or short-answer exercises, and that their students had written at least a few sentences for some kind of writing task, formal or informal. Seventy-eight percent reported students copying notes as directed, while 81% indicated that their students had taken notes of their own from lectures, books, or discussion. However, only 53% of science teachers indicated that their students had completed at least one task requiring a page or two of writing.

These results, which suggest that the majority of the writing students do for science is limited in scope, were reinforced by our studies of classrooms. Even in the schools chosen for their reputations for excellence in the teaching of writing, there was scant evidence of extended writing in science. Of the 59 observations of science classrooms in five states, only 14% included any writing of a paragraph or more, and when this activity did occur, it was observed to happen for an average of only 14 minutes out of a typical 50-minute class.

There are, perhaps, no surprises in our observation here. Students were engaging in taking notes and completing short-answer exercises on worksheets; they were writing. However, extended-writing tasks generally require composing—that is, thoughtful reflection and manipulation of growing understandings (e.g., questioning, analyzing, synthesizing, connecting to other concepts)—and the tasks on which students spent the most time did not require much thoughtful reflection and knowledge-building.

Though the typical science classroom did not require a great deal of extended writing, science teachers in the national survey did rate certain types of writing as important for success in their classes. The tasks teachers considered most essential were:

1. Formulating hypotheses and making deductions from them (98%)
2. Explaining subject-area concepts (96%)
3. Recording observations (96%)
4. Writing laboratory reports (92%)

The majority of science teachers also rated reflective writing ("This is what I learned"; 68%) and response logs or journals (62%) as important in their classrooms. These comments suggest a primary emphasis in science on reporting the facts and explaining how problems are solved, and a secondary emphasis on using writing as a way to learn.

Data from our five-state study of schools with reputations for excellence in the teaching of writing indicate that the emphasis in classroom practice may veer toward memorization of important content. As Samuel, one of our higher achieving focal students, indicated about his advanced-level 10th-grade biology class:

> I think all we've done this trimester is note-taking. . . . He uses an overhead and we take notes from his notes. . . . Sometimes we take notes from the book. . . . We don't write much in his class.

Indeed, a clearer picture of the kinds of writing students are engaged in during science class emerges from analyses of the approximately 2,101 student responses to science assignments in the 20 schools in our five-state study. These assignments were dominated by short-answer tasks (66%), followed by fill-in-the-blank activities (24%), and multiple-choice exercises (15%); only 7% required more extended writing of even a paragraph. (Percents total more than 100 because some assignments included a mix of response types.) Thus, although science teachers reported that they value some kinds of potentially thoughtful writing about the content, these kinds of writing were quite rare.

The Lab Report

Science teachers in our national survey indicated that the most important purpose for writing was for students to summarize what had been learned (92%). By contrast, only 20% of science teachers considered providing students with opportunities to practice particular types of science writing as among the most important reasons for writing in science classrooms. That said, the lab report was a consistent feature of student work, and the focus of student activity in developing these reports changed across the grades. Most lab reports were highly structured, focusing on students' recording of observations in the middle grades and requiring more inferential thinking in the higher grades. Across the grades, however, most lab reports resembled fill-in-the-blank approaches more than true practice at scientific thinking. That is, the steps of lab reports—observing data, recording data, and extrapolating conclusions based on observable phenomena—were clearly developed from middle to high school levels, but even at the higher levels we observed little evidence of reflection, taking a critical or skeptical stance toward the data, or connecting results to other related experiments or more general scientific knowledge.

Emphasis on Form

This cookie-cutter approach to lab report writing is a reflection of the instructional approaches science teachers employed for teaching writing in general. When asked which instructional techniques they used when students were asked to write for science, 82% of the science teachers reported that they sought to clearly specify the specific parts required for an assignment such as writing a lab report. Perhaps as a result of this emphasis on form, the majority of lab reports among the samples in the five-state study involved asking students to fill in observed data in specified places and to conclude with a one or two sentence summary of findings.

The overall pattern that emerges of typical practice in science is that writing was primarily used to demonstrate students' internalization of content. Writing was used not so much to scaffold student understanding or as a way to think deeply about and reflect on the information, but rather as a means for the teacher (and student) to determine student awareness and retention of disciplinary content. As Don, a higher achieving 12th-grade student, told us about his AP Biology class, "We are always doing an essay at least once a week around ecology, the body, the cell. Mostly it is just the details. I just put in the facts."

PORTRAITS OF SUCCESS

There were, however, individual teachers and entire schools that revealed writing practices that, while in the minority, suggest productive directions for science teachers to consider. Such activities placed writing within larger curricular conversations (Applebee, 1996), such as end-of-lesson "takeaways," open-response prompts, and lab reports requiring the student to engage with content in more thoughtful, reflective ways requiring extension of student thinking or "minds-on" (Langer, 2004) thoughtful reflection and analysis of science content. In the following pages of this chapter, we provide examples not only of schoolwide or department-wide practices, but also of interesting activities from classrooms where teachers were working more or less on their own.

Writing as Daily Conversation

Teachers from a variety of schools in our study used journal writing almost daily prior to delivering new information. For example, Ms. Tyson, a Grade 7 science teacher, began a unit about the nature of matter by asking: "In the kitchen, you might find three different forms of water. What are these three different forms of water and where exactly in the kitchen would you find them? Further, how do you use water in each of these forms?"

Other teachers in our study used similar daily warm-ups or takeaways. During 1 week in Mr. Monk's chemistry class, for example, daily activities included responses to open-ended questions such as: "(1) When a candle burns, the chemical change is . . . ; (2) Which element does not conduct heat?; (3) A convection current is . . . ; (4) What I learned about chemical reactions yesterday is. . . ." Each of these examples required reflection and transformation of information if done thoughtfully and answered in the student's own words, rather than retelling or restating content.

Another promising use of daily writing in science was reflected in Ms. Carol's 10th-grade biology class, where she required responses to a "daily blog/warm-up." She posed questions such as the following:

- Polygenic traits means having many genes. List some traits you have that you think are controlled by many.
- Write about a time you wondered where you came from.
- President Obama approved the National Institutes of Health to fund research using human embryonic stem cells. These can't be made without taking apart human embryos. Do you agree or disagree?

Several things are worth noting in this example. First, the assignments did not ask students to recall information from a text, fill in data, or simply retell what they had learned. The students were asked to bring their knowledge of science, personal experience, and things that they might have wondered about or questioned related to science topics into the classroom. Second, students were being asked to engage in a larger conversation about scientific issues not just in the classroom but in the world, to reflect upon the implications of the topics under investigation, and to transform their knowledge of the topics into something personally meaningful.

Other teachers gave their students the opportunity to process, manipulate, and reflect upon science content through the use of open-response questions, sometimes as final questions on unit tests and other times as a classroom learning activity. Mr. Wright, a ninth-grade science teacher, described one such writing assignment:

Often times when you're driving down the road in a city, you can smell food cooking at a restaurant located a couple blocks away. Using the kinetic theory, explain why the smell of solid foods baking in the oven or cooking on the stove at a local restaurant can travel such a far distance.

The accompanying rubric identified important aspects of scientific thinking, giving highest marks for demonstrating "in-depth understanding of the relevant concepts and/or processes . . . [and offering] insightful interpretations or extensions (generalizations, applications, and analogies)." Rather than emphasizing restating content in written form, the emphasis here was on the student as meaning maker. Mr. Wright used writing as a learning tool to manipulate and process discipline-specific thinking and content. A rubric such as this could be used from writing prompt to writing prompt, giving students consistent practice and feedback in mastering effective science writing that demonstrated "generalizations, applications, and analogies" of the content under investigation.

Reshaping Knowledge for Audience and Purpose

Other teachers created writing tasks that asked students to recompose what they were learning in order to address specific goals with specific audiences. Mr. Sanchez, for example, used such tasks in his AP Environmental Science class, relying on the RAFT heuristic (Santa, 1988) to plan his assignments. RAFT invites students to consider their *role* as a writer, the *audience* they will address, a *form* for the writing, and a *topic*. RAFT can be used as a heuristic to guide the writing process, or as a model to follow in developing writing assignments. Teachers use this heuristic to help students understand the importance of adjusting the message to meet the requirements of the audience, topic, and form. One of Mr. Sanchez's assignments presented this problem to his students:

> You've been elected queen/king of a tropical island with a burgeoning (quickly increasing) population. APES [Advanced Placement Environmental Science] students have determined that the current percent population growth is a chilling 4.7%! Prepare a speech to your people that outlines a plan to curb population growth. It is very important that you are NOT beheaded after your speech.

This task includes all of the components of RAFT: a role (king or queen), an audience (your people), a form (a speech), and a topic (curbing population growth).

These kinds of open-response writing prompts (e.g., journal writing, warm-ups, takeaways) are examples of minds-on learning, requiring not just knowledge of content, but a deeper, more meaningful understanding of underlying processes, implications, and application of knowledge. They require deliberate and careful selection of appropriate material, transforming it into something far greater than Don's "just put in the facts" (above) when writing for his AP Biology class. Moreover, as in the RAFT assignment, students are gaining expertise at manipulating the form and message of written communication to meet the needs of a given audience—a skill usually displayed by experienced science writers.

Learning to Respond to High-Stakes Science Tests

Although the writing required on high-stakes tests can constrain the curriculum, more effective programs use the opportunity to teach students how to respond effectively to a range of science writing tasks. For example, at the time of our study, Kentucky asked open-response questions on the science portion of its high-stakes science assessments.

In a typical response, science teachers in some schools regularly assigned open-response questions (ORQs) as chapter and unit reviews, coupled with instruction on how to respond appropriately.

For example, sixth-grade teacher Ms. Michaels, at College View Middle School, prompted her students to write about metamorphosis: "*Metamorphosis* is a process in the life cycle of many animals during which a rapid change from the immature organism to the adult takes place. Describe metamorphosis in the life cycle of the butterfly." Ms. Michaels taught her students to approach such tasks by analyzing the prompt and their knowledge of the topic using the same four-column worksheet that we saw in Chapter 5 (see Figure 5.7): (1) *know*, (2) *vocabulary*, (3) *do*, and (4) *plan/support*. An accompanying rubric gave the highest score to responses that correctly listed the stages of metamorphosis and provided a specific explanation of each stage.

Such a writing task required students to organize and present appropriate scientific content while guiding them through the prewriting and drafting stages to ensure thorough responses. This particular task supported students' development of scientific vocabulary; others we observed went further, and required them to relate their understandings to broader concepts.

Ms. Pearl similarly provided regular on-demand writing practice to her students at College View Middle School, writing that helped them engage more deeply with the science they were learning. Each assignment asked students to read "the situation and writing task, determine the audience, purpose, and form," and instructed them to plan with a graphic organizer, write a rough draft, revise for content and attention-getting leads, edit, and write a final draft. An example of her assignments is as follows:

> *Situation:* For every classroom that completes the Earth Day Science Symposium on Sea Turtles, the Leatherback Trust has pledged a donation to protect nesting sea turtles, eggs, and hatchlings at Playa Grande, the last important leatherback nesting beach on the eastern Pacific Ocean.
>
> *Writing Task:* Write a letter to one of our science or math teachers here . . . to persuade them to help the sea turtles by using this symposium activity in their classes. Be sure to include supporting details for each reason.

While Ms. Pearl's students clearly needed to draw on knowledge from the unit under investigation, this task required them to select the most compelling reasons for saving the sea turtles as well as to apply their knowledge of habitat and causes for declining population. It also went further, asking students to use their developing knowledge of the science to address a real-world problem.

While these science teachers were responding to the state-mandated use of open-response questions on science content, they also seemed to embrace not just using writing-to-learn-science strategies, but learning-to-write-science strategies as well. Note that in each of these cases students were given experience and instruction in manipulating writing assignments for a specific audience and were given a purpose and form for the writing. Furthermore, students were taught to use an appropriate writing process, to plan, draft, revise for elements of effective writing (not just effective content), and write a final draft.

If on-demand writing practice exemplifies these kinds of minds-on, reflective manipulation of information requiring students to think carefully and deeply about the subject matter, then science classrooms that regularly use on-demand writing may, in fact, be using such writing to support their students' developing understandings of science. This is quite different from simply using writing to test what students already know.

A District Approach

Of the schools we studied, Grisham Middle School in the Round Rock Integrated School District in Austin, Texas, stood out in the teaching of science thanks to a clear district initiative to support science learning through the use of writing. On the Texas Assessment of Knowledge and Skills (TAKS) Grade 7 writing assessment, Grisham (see also Chapter 5) was one of the top performing schools compared with other schools serving a similar population of students. At the time of our study, Grisham was part of a local science collaborative, in partnership with the faculty at Austin Community College, which provided sustained, high-intensity professional development to pre-K–12 teachers of science and mathematics. During our site visits, Grisham was in the 2nd year of a multiyear professional development initiative in science writing, with components including science notebooks, daily writing, and nontraditional writing assignments.

Science Notebooks. Teachers at every grade level taught the following essential components of a science notebook:

1. Prediction
2. Developing a plan
3. Question, problem, purpose
4. Observations, data, charts, graphs, drawings, and illustrations
5. Claims and evidence

6. Drawing conclusions
7. Reflection—next steps and new questions (see Klentschy & Thompson, 2008)

For each of these essential components, the Teacher's Collaborative provided teachers at every grade level with clear instructional techniques for ways to scaffold students through appropriate writing tasks. There was clear evidence of vertical alignment as the sentence starters for categories such as "claims and evidence" became progressively more complex with each grade level.

Daily Writing. Science students at Grisham Middle School wrote every day. Every student in every grade at all levels maintained a daily science journal. These often featured daily warm-ups to activate prior knowledge or takeaways at the end of lessons. These warm-ups reflected the topics currently being studied, for example: "Define the rock cycle" (Grade 6); "What is Newton's law of motion?" (Grade 6); "How does caffeine affect you and why?" (Grade 8); "Name and describe the five taste sensations" (Grade 8). Responses varied from brief answers to a paragraph depending on topic and grade level, but students were expected to answer from their developing understandings without copying directly from lecture notes or textbooks.

Nontraditional Writing Assignments. The science department at Grisham Middle School also appeared to value nontraditional forms of science writing as a means to focus student learning on science content. Rather than writing a traditional report, for example, sixth-grade students completed an "Important Book of Energy" assignment, modeled after Margaret Wise Brown's children's book, *The Important Book* (Harper, 1949/1990). Teachers showed students Brown's pattern of naming items, such as daisies, and highlighting what was most important about them. The science assignment required students to describe a critical attribute of energy (what makes this type of energy different from other forms)—how it is used by consumers, its economic benefit, and how it is transformed into usable power.

The science teachers appeared to embrace creative writing assignments as well. Rather than merely keeping and maintaining a vocabulary section of important terms in their science notebook (as we saw in many other schools), students at Grisham were asked to write narratives in which they used or applied the science vocabulary in appropriate forms. One student composed "The Tale of the Gold Dust Kid" in which she applied chemical elements to descriptions of characters and setting. It is important to note in these cases that the writing assignments, while nontraditional in form for science writing, still required students to synthesize and apply their growing knowledge of content rather than mechanically repeating facts.

Summing Up. The teachers at Grisham Middle School regularly assigned writing as a means to develop and organize scientific thinking. Daily journal writing across grades and academic levels helped to ensure that writing was deeply embedded as part of the development of scientific knowledge. All of the students we studied were actively engaged in these writing activities: Higher achieving, lower achieving, and English language learner students completed the same sorts of engaging writing activities. Moreover, it bears noting that the Texas Assessment of Knowledge and Skills (TAKS) did not require extended or open-response writing in science. It appears, then, that the Grisham science teachers, whether due to their involvement in the regional science collaborative or through their own initiative, saw writing in science as a valued tool for fundamentally shaping students' disciplinary learning.

A Focus on Writing to Learn Science

Amadon High was another school where writing was deeply embedded in science teaching and learning. In their use of daily writing practices, Cornell note-taking, and explicit writing instruction, Amadon's science faculty demonstrated their recognition that writing, if used to extend students' understanding and support deep thinking about content, can improve disciplinary thinking and learning.

Daily Journals. Similar to Grisham Middle School's use of writing-to-learn assignments, the science faculty at Amadon High School used daily journal writing to stimulate thinking and reflection about content. As one of our field researchers noted, Amadon science faculty used a "what do you think question, rather than a question that demands a factual answer," to structure daily writing. During an observation of a Grade 10 biology class, for example, the teacher wrote a daily warm-up on the board: "Most people carry hundreds of mutations that have little or no effect on your evolutionary fitness. Write about the types of mutations that can have drastic effects on the fitness of your species."

Such daily use of minds-on, extended-response writing differs markedly from the directed, restricted, short-answer writing that dominated descriptions of science writing in the national survey. Furthermore, this was a practice that was not limited to Advanced Placement or honors-level classes. One of the focal students at Amadon, Daniel, a 12th-grade student identified as academically low-performing, told us that in science, "Every day [there is] a question on the board to write to. Like: Where do you think the Swine Flu virus in Mexico came from. . . . Not a right/ wrong type of question."

Reflective Note-Taking. There was more to Amadon High School's writing in science than daily extended writing. Students also were asked to make regular use of the Cornell note-taking system. This involves taking notes in a two-column format, with students using the right-hand column to record ideas and information as they are encountered (in reading or from class discussion), and the left-hand column to pull out key words or ideas when reviewing the notes later. The notetaking is followed by writing a several sentence summary of the main ideas (see also Chapter 9). Science faculty valued the reflective nature of this approach to notetaking. The science department chair noted that:

> High-quality writing to the science teacher means, minimally, it shows the teacher that a student understands and demonstrates a complete chain of thoughts. When appropriate, I expect more than a recitation of facts, but rather a clear expression of opinion based on science.

What is clear from Amadon's science faculty is that writing was not transcription of lecture or textbook notes. Writing was an opportunity for students to regularly enter into discussion, both internally and with other students, and express their thoughts about science. The science department faculty highly valued periodic assessments because they let teachers know if students were understanding the main concepts. Moreover, while there was no writing component in the state science standards, extended writing was an important part of school-based formative assessments of science learning.

Explicit Writing Instruction. Additionally, science teachers at Amadon engaged in explicit writing instruction. As one teacher indicated, "We show students good examples of writing and incomplete examples of writing." Science teachers were also observed modeling writing on the spot, demonstrating their own composing processes for the benefit of students. One of our case study students noted that his teacher modeled how to take Cornell notes using a document reader so students could understand the process of applying the note-taking system.

Revitalizing the Lab Report

The science lab report has been a part of the curriculum at least since the late 19th century. The goals for such reports have always been grounded in engaging students in the activities of science, but from the beginning they have been subject to demands for accuracy and correctness that have led to formulaic presentation of conventional understandings rather than emphasizing exploration and interpretation of scientific phenomenon (on the history of lab reports, see Russell, 1991). Certainly the majority of lab reports that we saw in our studies reflected such a reduction of the genre to a highly formulaic activity requiring recording of data and little else.

At the same time, since at least the 1980s science educators have sought to revitalize lab activities (Bybee et al., 2006). As part of that movement, the Biological Sciences Curriculum Study suggested a 5E instructional model that became popular in the sciences and mathematics, emphasizing cycles of Engage, Explore, Explain, Elaborate, and Evaluate. As a committee of the National Research Council recommended in a report on laboratory activities (Singer, Hilton, & Schweingruber, 2006), students should be "engaged in framing research questions, making observations, designing and executing experiments, gathering and analyzing data, and constructing scientific arguments and explanations" (p. 4).

We saw one version of this approach in action in a 10th-grade chemistry class. The class was using a textbook structured around a 7E instructional model, adding Elicit near the beginning and Extend near the end of the cycle (Eisenkraft, 2003). The textbook for this class used a consistent heuristic across chapters and activities, designed to reflect the 7E instructional model. The activities included:

- What do you see?
- What do you think?
- Investigate and check up.
- What does it mean?
- What do you believe?
- How do you know?
- Why should you care?
- And sometimes, What do you think now?

As the National Research Council had recommended, this particular heuristic more closely resembles the way scientists think. A chemistry teacher that we observed, Ms. Manning, began all her activities with "What do you see?" and she asked her students to observe, first, a phenomenon in the real world and then use a systematic approach to data collection to narrow potential explanations of the observed phenomenon. The process of revising predictions that she used (What do you think now? What do you believe? and What does it mean?) allowed her students to reflect on and test out their hypotheses to see if they were consistent with other established concepts. Lastly, Ms. Manning invited her students to use writing to reflect on the larger significance of this information (Why should you care?) and how this supported or contrasted with ongoing investigations in chemistry and the world at large. Each student was asked, therefore, not just to identify specific principles of chemistry, but also to explain how these principles might have significance in the world. In other words, students were asked to weigh the value of scientific knowledge.

SCIENCE AND THE COMMON CORE STANDARDS

At the beginning of this chapter, we noted that teachers of science are expected to address the Common Core State Standards for writing as part of the development of students' disciplinary literacy. That is, according to the Common Core, curriculum and instruction in science should help students learn how to develop interpretations, formulate arguments, and provide evidence that is appropriate within the context of the development and sharing of scientific knowledge.

Across the examples described in this chapter, we can see that rather than building a curriculum around each standard, most rich and engaging instructional activities address multiple standards in the course of the activity. For example, Grisham Middle School's science notebooks involved students in meeting Standard 1 (write arguments focused on discipline-specific content, . . . including clarifying claims and evidence), Standard 2 (write informative/explanatory texts), Standard 4 (produce clear and coherent writing in which the development, organization, and style are appropriate to task, purpose, and audience), and Standard 10 (write routinely over extended time frames for reflection and revision and shorter time frames for a range of discipline-specific tasks). Grisham's daily writing activities added Standard 3 (narrative elements are incorporated effectively into arguments and informative/explanatory texts), and sometimes Standard 7 (conduct short research projects to answer a question). They also incorporated Standard 4 (with some guidance from peers and adults, develop and strengthen writing as needed by planning, editing, revision . . .) in the activities that offered students opportunities for feedback and reflection on their writing and thinking about the science they were studying.

Of course none of the activities in this chapter were developed with the standards in mind, but rather in consideration of the concepts and

constructs within the discipline. The important point is that in responding to the standards, teachers of science need to keep their focus on
developing rich and engaging activities where writing is used to involve
students in the processes of science, presenting tentative understandings
for feedback from self and others as their knowledge and skill evolves.
In such contexts, the standards can be a helpful tool for reflecting on
the curriculum as a whole to be sure that the full range of appropriate
tasks is included. Without such a perspective, there is a danger that the
standards will constrain the curriculum and push instruction toward
formulaic approaches to writing in science that offer simplistic solutions
rather than enriching what ultimately students know and are able to do.

THE BOTTOM LINE

A look across the various parts of our multiyear study indicates that the
dominant trend in writing in science is the use of writing to recite information. Writing typically takes place at the end of a textbook section
or for the conclusion of a laboratory report. Moreover, the emphasis on
short responses with an expected, correct answer does not give students
room to wonder, to explore, or to create their own understandings and
interpretations of scientific phenomena. Rarely were students invited to
engage in internal conversations (what do I think?) or in socially constructed dialogue (what do I think now that I've reflected on what others
think?) in typical practice.

On the other hand, we did find helpful examples of writing in science
that allowed students to engage in internal conversations prior to or just
after engaging with content, as in the use of daily warm-up writing or
science journals. In some instances students were generating questions
or identifying phenomena in the real world that they wondered about
or establishing tentative explanations. Such practices in science writing
allowed students to engage in knowledge development and transformation. In the most productive activities, students had many opportunities
to revise and reflect on what was being learned.

Looking across all of the classrooms we studied, we find a number
of practices that contribute to successful teaching of scientific writing:

Curriculum and Instruction

- Use daily writing to help students draw on what they know or
  to reflect on what they have just learned about a particular scientific phenomenon in the physical or natural world.

- Engage students in "minds-on" writing tasks that require analysis and synthesis of new information, helping students consolidate new learnings as well as evaluate and reflect on the knowledge they are gaining.
- Use a format for laboratory investigations that reflects the processes of inquiry appropriate to the particular science discipline (e.g., the 5E or 7E instructional models), rather than treating lab reports as fill-in-the-blank exercises.
- Across the year, ensure that students will be engaged in a wide variety of writing tasks for varied audiences and purposes, including systematic attention to the argument, informative/expository, and narrative tasks of the Common Core. Such writing can explore issues within the disciplines of science as well as apply scientific understandings to problems in the world at large.

Assessment

- Use writing tasks of various types as ways for students to demonstrate their knowledge and understandings of science.

Schoolwide Initiatives

- Provide time for shared planning meetings and participation in professional learning communities committed to continual improvement of writing in the sciences. These may be school- or department-based or rely on external networks such as the National Writing Project, the National Science Teachers Association, or school–university collaboratives.

FUTURE DIRECTIONS

Rather than using writing to measure *what has been learned*, we need to move it forward, in conversations appropriate to the disciplines of science, to using writing *in order to learn*. When students are afforded the opportunity to use writing to develop understandings, sort out ideas, and engage in discussions within the community of the science classroom, students are likely to develop a deeper understanding of the underlying scientific principles.

In our studies we found numerous examples of writing being used to foster scientific thinking throughout the learning process—not just at the end. If students are given directions to use writing to activate prior knowledge, to wonder about the physical world, and to develop and re-vise explanatory models, we are more likely to see students who not only understand science facts, but also have a deeper understanding of scien-tific processes. Students will emerge from such activities able to demon-strate the abilities called for in the standards, and also with the breadth and depth of science knowledge to do well on high-stakes exams (as did the students in the schools we studied). They will also learn science more fully—in ways that will serve them well in higher education, in the work-place, and in life.

Reflect and Discuss

1. Brainstorm a list of ways in which you can use daily writing re-quiring thoughtful reflection as a way for students to activate prior knowledge or reflect on the day's activities.
   a. Begin class with students jotting down what they think they know about a new topic, or something they have seen outside of school that is a real-life example of a concept they are cur-rently studying.
   b. End class with a ticket out (jotting down what they understood from the lesson and what they're having trouble with).
2. Develop a set of explanatory and argumentative writing tasks that will get students to think more deeply about scientific principles, for example, Why is adaptation important? These may require research before writing.
   a. Develop rubrics that highlight the content, organization, and scientific language of more- and less-successful responses to the types of scientific writing you expect your students to do.
   b. Collect samples that students can analyze to understand what is expected and how the rubrics work.
3. Look back at the section on Portraits of Success. Which activities can be incorporated most easily into you coursework?
   a. Discuss with your colleagues how you might adapt these activi-ties for your students.
   b. Be specific about your purpose for the writing activity, the con-tent in which it might be embedded, the outcome you antici-pate, and possible next steps.

CHAPTER 7

◇◇◇◇◇◇◇

Technology and the
Teaching of Writing

According to a July 2011 survey by the Pew Research Center (Brenner, 2012), 95% of adolescents ages 12–17 were Internet users, up from 73% in December 2000. Of those who used the Internet, 80% used social media sites such as Facebook or MySpace; 38% shared digital content such as photographs, artwork, or stories; and 21% reported remixing online material to make their own artistic creations. Some 31% of young adults ages 18–24 reported using Twitter, dropping to 14% among 30–49 year olds (Smith & Brenner, 2012). Overall, 75% of teenagers reported texting—63% doing so every day. Texting was highest among low-income, Hispanic, and African American teenagers, and lowest among high-income and White teens (Brenner, 2012). Overall, 37% of teenagers reported participating in video chats using applications such as Skype, and 27% reported recording and uploading video to the Internet. Given such reports, there is little question that students today are indeed digital "natives" (Prensky, 2001) who take many uses of technology for granted in their out-of-school lives.

Even the digital divide between richer and poorer households seems to have decreased for many students in poverty. According to a 2012 survey of Internet access (Zickuhr & Smith, 2012), for households earning $30,000 or less there has been a substantial increase in Internet access from 2000 to 2011, from 28% to 62%. The report goes on to state that the Internet access gap "closest to disappearing is that between whites and minorities."

For at least the past 2 decades, the growing prevalence of digital media in homes and in the workplace and community has led to calls for schools to embrace the possibilities that such media can create in supporting the writing process, building community, encouraging collaboration, and providing near-instant access to information from sources around the world and across time. Yet tapping into the possibilities of digital media for instructional advantage has progressed slowly. Not only are most teachers what Prensky (2001) called digital "immigrants," navigating in an unfamiliar landscape, but the landscape itself keeps changing. The Pew surveys themselves reflect the rapid evolution of technology uses among today's adolescents. In the 2 years between 2009 and 2011, for example, the volume of texts per user rose 20% to 60 texts per day for the typical adolescent (Lenhart, 2012). In 2011 only 24% of adolescents in the Pew survey had an account on MySpace, a sharp decline from 2006, when 85% said that MySpace was the social network they used most often. (In its place, 93% reported using Facebook in 2011.) Blogging, reported by 28% of online teens in 2006, had fallen to 14% in 2011. Video chatting (using applications such as Skype), reported by 14% in 2006, rose to 37% in 2011. Only 6% in 2011 reported daily use of e-mail, down from 14% in 2006. (Brenner, 2012).

BACKGROUND ON THE IMPACT OF TECHNOLOGY ON WRITING

The rapid pace of technology change makes it difficult to study the impact of technology on writing and writing instruction—by the time the research is completed, the technology has often changed. Nonetheless there has been a variety of studies that have highlighted ways in which a variety of evolving technologies may interact with writing and learning to write. These will be discussed briefly in the following sections.

Writing on a Computer

A series of studies beginning in the 1980s indicates that using word-processing software (as opposed to writing by hand) has a positive effect on learning to write—with particularly strong effects for low-achieving students (for reviews of the research, see Bangert-Drowns, 1993; Graham & Perin, 2007). These studies found that computer-based writing tends to be longer and of higher quality, with more revisions.

When students do compose on a computer, programs that analyze what students write can provide near-instant feedback, suggesting improvements students can make before sharing their writing with teachers or peers (e.g., Criterion [Educational Testing Service, 2012], and Intelligent Essay Assessor [Pearson Education, 2010]). Although such automated scoring systems can be manipulated by savvy writers, the quality of the responses they offer has been improving rapidly (Shermis & Hamner, 2012). And they do provide a way to lighten the paper load for overburdened teachers.

Meeting Online

Another line of research has examined the impact of software that supports computer-mediated discussion forums where students present their ideas and understandings, and react to those of their peers. Such discussions can be supported on a variety of platforms, from wikis and blogs to threaded discussions (Rhodes & Robnolt, 2009), to specialized teaching platforms such as Knowledge Forum (Nachowitz, 2012; Scardamalia & Bereiter, 2006). Research in this area has been less concerned with the effects of the implementation of a particular technology intervention and more concerned with exploring how such technologies can best support the development of student interpretations and understandings.

Code-Switching

As out-of-school uses of technology have proliferated, scholars have begun to look at the relationship of these activities to the development of academic literacy. One part of this research has addressed the fear that the casual language, abbreviations, and emoticons of instant messaging and texting would negatively affect students' more formal writing. Here, the Pew surveys discussed earlier indicate that adolescents are quite aware of the differences in what is appropriate in casual personal communication versus formal school work, even if they sometimes incorporate "informal styles from their [online] communications into their writing at school" (Lenhart, Arafeh, Smith, & Macgill, 2008, p. ii). Rather than a threat to writing development, learning to use informal and formal styles in appropriate contexts may be part of a normal process of maturation. Research that has looked directly at students' language skills supports the survey results, suggesting that adolescents' texting and instant messaging is itself a systematic and complex use of language responsive to audience and purpose (Drouin & Davis, 2009; Lewis & Fabos, 2005; Tagliamonte & Denis, 2008).

Participating in Online Communities

Other studies have examined the reading and writing required in a variety of online environments, ranging from gaming to fandoms to virtual worlds (Black & Steinkuehler, 2009). At the broadest level, what such research suggests is that these platforms provide rich and complex environments for language use and language development, with layers of participation that involve mastery of the environment itself (layers of mastery within online gaming, for example), as well as mastery of ways of participating successfully in the often extensive and self-motivated on-line communities that accompany them. Such out-of-school activities can be seen as either highly supportive of the academic literacies fostered in school (Black & Steinkuehler, 2009), or as an alternative to them that may make schools as we know them obsolete (Gee & Hayes, 2011).

USES OF TECHNOLOGY FOR WRITING AT SCHOOL

Because technology has become so prominent a tool for literacy in general and for writing in particular in contemporary society, and because technology has become a critical component of college and career readiness, this chapter will examine typical uses of technology and writing across subject areas and grades. Our studies provide a detailed picture of the ways in which technology has been incorporated into school settings, providing new tools for student writing as well as new approaches to instruction.

Word Processing

As computers have become widespread, the ability to compose on the computer has become necessary for both higher education and the workplace. Results from our national survey suggest that word processing is becoming commonplace in many schools and classrooms, though it is far from universal and varies by subject and level. For example, only 3% of mathematics teachers reported frequently requiring printed work. For the other three subjects, 21% of middle school teachers said they regularly required that final drafts be typed or printed rather than handwritten, rising to 48% in high school. English teachers were more likely to ask for written work to be typed or printed (45% across grades), compared to science (32%) and social studies/history (26%).

Students seemed somewhat more interested in composing on the computer than did their teachers. Middle school teachers reported that, when they allowed it, 57% of their students on average handed in printed copies of their work, rising to 70% by high school. Again, averages were somewhat higher for English (73% across levels) than for science (63%) or social studies/history (55%).

Because so much of the writing that students do is done in class, including timed writing assignments to prepare them for high-stakes tests, these figures overestimate the proportion of student work that is actually written on a computer. Of the 1,626 samples of extended writing collected from targeted students in the 20 schools with local reputations for excellence in the teaching of writing, only 23% at middle school and 42% at high school were composed on a computer.

The figures also mask some important limitations in the ways in which students are able to use technology to support their writing for English, science, and social studies/history classes. In a pattern that also appears in the National Assessment of Educational Progress data (Applebee & Langer, 2009), students seem least likely to use the computer for their first drafts (31% in middle school, 47% in high school), somewhat more likely to use the computer for editing and revising (34% in middle school, 56% in high school), and most likely to use it for final copy (66% in both middle and high school). This reflects a pattern in which students begin their writing in class without access to a computer, copying it over later in a computer lab, the library, or at home. Not coincidentally, the first in-class draft also provides additional practice in the writing by hand required on most high-stakes tests.

Students seem to mostly use word processors as a powerful typewriter, with little embedding of video, audio, or graphics. The one exception is in science classes, where 33% of the teachers reported their students frequently embed other material, presumably as data tables, graphs, or diagrams illustrating their work. Although digital texts are easily shared, collaborative work was also rare, with only 26% in English, 12% in science, and 17% in social studies/history reporting that students frequently sent electronic versions of work in progress to peers for response or editing.

In interviews, students for the most part took word processing for granted. Patrick (Grade 6, lower achieving) was typical, noting that he was "pretty good at keyboarding" and "likes to write essays on the computer." Beth (Grade 12, lower achieving) acknowledged that she did "whatever the teacher wants" but disliked having to write something out first and then type it: "It takes forever to do it that way."

Teachers and administrators who favored word processing emphasized its importance in process-oriented instruction:

> We found that it enhances the process when you consider the focus is on writing and revising—trying to hone your craft as a writer. More kids are more willing to go through the process—not worried so much about errors—because technology allows you to clean the writing up—[it] provides the ability to move, change, cut/paste. (Middle school principal, from interview notes)

A high school principal who noted similar advantages also indicated that even the differences in conventions (language choices, including vocabulary, syntax, tone, and voice) in different forums offered an opportunity for teaching about audience:

> You have to be careful about of course if they blog and Facebook and bastardize the English language, that that doesn't transfer into their formal writing. It opens up a whole discussion about who is your audience when you write. I think our teachers are very good about doing that with kids.

In a pattern that has been observed nationally (Russell & Abrams, 2004), teachers who resisted word processing tended to do so because of the high-stakes tests their students would be taking. Classes facing hand-written state or Advanced Placement exams spent considerable time on in-class "pen-to-paper" composition, sometimes timed, in anticipation of testing.

As a 10th-grade social studies teacher described it, "In fact, when I have them do their first drafts I make it mandatory that it is handwritten. For the [New York] Regents exams they have to handwrite their essays on demand."

Technology to Support Instruction

In addition to questions about word processing, we asked teachers in the national survey whether they or their students had used any of a wide variety of other technologies to support learning and instruction during the previous 5 days of school. The specific technologies ranged from traditional presentational tools (PowerPoint, interactive whiteboards), to word-processing and related software, to technology-mediated discussions and social media.

Teachers' responses suggest that technology adoption has been relatively slow, and has primarily been used to reinforce a presentational mode of teaching. Across subject areas, for example, 60% of the teachers reported using a PowerPoint presentation in the targeted class during the last 5 days, 62% reported using an overhead projector or ELMO document camera, and 37% an interactive whiteboard. Some 52% also reported showing a film or video presentation. In fact, the Internet has become a powerful resource for teachers: 60% reported presenting audio or visual materials directly from the Internet, and 75% shared materials previously collected from the Internet.

A smaller group of teachers reported using technology to facilitate some of the routines of instruction. Across subjects, 36% reported using a website for assignments and course-related materials, and 27% used e-mail or instant messaging for class-related tasks.

Students' uses of technology during the same 5-day period were much more limited, consisting largely of accessing the Internet for course-related materials (67%) and word processing (48%). Only 17% of the teachers said that their students had created a PowerPoint presentation, 34% reported students had used an overhead projector or ELMO, and 25% reported students had worked at an interactive whiteboard. At the middle school level, some 36% of teachers reported that their students had used computer-based simulations or games, dropping to 16% by high school. These were particularly popular in science (51% at middle school, 20% at high school) and mathematics (37% at middle school, 33% at high school). Both subject areas have a rich array of such materials available to support instruction, often with free access on the Internet.

In comparison, socially mediated discussions were rare: Only 6% of the teachers reported students had participated in an online discussion board such as BlackBoard, 5% had used other social media for class-related purposes, and 2% had been asked to create webpages or blogs.

Classroom observations in the schools with reputations for excellence in the teaching of writing suggest that these teachers' reports overestimate the use of technology. With the exception of math, where calculators were common, less than a third of the classrooms observed made use of any technology. And when technology was used, it was usually used by the teacher. Paralleling teachers' responses in the national survey, the technologies we observed in use were primarily presentational. This is clear in a list of the types of technology in use in at least 5% of the 260 classes that we observed:

- Overhead projector or ELMO used by the teacher (29% of the classes)
- PowerPoint used by the teacher (12%)
- Internet used by the teacher (8%)
- Film or video shown by the teacher (6%)
- Word processing used by the students (5%)

PORTRAITS OF SUCCESS

Like those in the national survey, teachers in the schools we studied usually used technology to enliven a relatively traditional, presentational pedagogy. We also saw some interesting and sometimes innovative uses of technology for writing to learn. As in the previous chapter, the examples used in the following pages of this chapter come not only from school- or department-wide programs, but also from the classrooms of individual teachers working on their own.

Presentational Aids for Traditional Teaching

Across all subject areas, by far the most frequent uses of technology in the classrooms we studied were to support traditional, teacher-centered instruction. Mr. Gonzales, a middle school science teacher, was enthusiastic, even as he revealed the limits of his approaches. After mentioning that his room was "the first pilot for the multimedia classroom," he continued, "I scan the worksheet in and project it onto the whiteboard, then write on the whiteboard, do diagrams. I use PowerPoint all the time. Technology-wise, I use anything and everything I can."

In addition to PowerPoints and the whiteboard, Internet-based simulations of processes or experiments enhanced the presentations of many of the science teachers we interviewed. As Ms. Germino, a high school science chair, put it, their computers were used "for running simulations that are too dangerous for the classroom" or that required equipment that was not available for students to use. Ms. Jones, a sixth-grade teacher, praised the combination of an interactive whiteboard with an Internet connection for her science classes:

> For me, I love SmartBoard—linked to the Internet—[it's] interactive and effective. I have United Streaming [an Internet-based multimedia curriculum resource] at my fingertips—the class can see it, practice their note-taking. I have video streaming and can use it to have great effective extensions for our lessons.

Math teachers also made extensive use of whiteboards for demonstrating problems and solutions, as well as for simulations "to show them what the law of large numbers is, what sampling distributions are, things like that" (Mr. Brown, 10th-grade math teacher). Teaching in a technology-rich classroom with 30 laptops and a broadband connection, this same teacher explained that he ran his entire class through

> computer-based, some web-based, some workstation-based presentations. . . . Every homework assignment and solutions to every homework assignment are out on [a class webpage]. That's also where I pull stuff off the Web. I pull a lot of stuff down off YouTube and show that.

Social studies/history teachers noted that they often used Power-Point presentations embedded with excerpts from films and print media. The beginning of an eighth-grade social studies class that we observed illustrates the melding of new technologies with a traditional emphasis on "test prep." Ms. Manning began the lesson, on reform movements in 19th-century America, with a PowerPoint display of a sample question from the Texas Assessment of Knowledge and Skills (TAKS) that, she said, students had gotten wrong when the test was administered. It showed a political cartoon—a western saloon with three horses tied outside the building. Each was wearing a blanket labeled in turn: "Poverty," "Crime," and "Family Breakup." Ms. Manning read the test prompt aloud from the PowerPoint, "This cartoon represents the point of view of which reform movement? A. child labor, B. temperance, C. abolition, D. women's rights." Such uses of technology may focus students' attention, but hardly represent a transformation of instruction.

Ms. Chen, another social studies teacher, described using a whiteboard every day with her 10th-grade students: "From the beginning of class I have the objectives and the agenda on the board from the LCD [projector]. I'll use movie clips from United Streaming or from YouTube or from CNN or from BBC." Her school also had photocopiers that could scan directly to the Internet:

I was doing something on the Industrial Revolution the other day, something on the domestic stuff, the background. I had a sheet that showed the different steps of the domestic system. It wasn't something I wanted to photocopy for everyone, but I wanted to show everyone. It took me two seconds to scan in.

Many English teachers also made regular use of interactive whiteboards, saying they had revolutionized their teaching. In addition to the ease of sharing materials with her students, Ms. Roderick, a sixth-grade language arts teacher, found it helpful in teaching basic word-processing skills:

A lot of kids . . . are just expected to know how to use the computer, but they don't have a class to teach them like I did. These children don't really get that. Part of using the SmartBoard is to help them do basic formatting and word processing like today, "Okay, you're going to push this button and you're going to get in the center of the page."

Ms. Clark, an eighth-grade English teacher, was similarly enthusiastic, citing as advantages the "great grammar" lessons available on the Internet, the power of the whiteboard in helping "kids who are used to screens" focus on the lesson, and the "efficiency" of using PowerPoints on a SmartBoard.

Internet Use

Students made extensive use of the Internet for background information for writing assignments in their science, social studies/history, and English classes. "The old encyclopedia days are gone," one teacher declared. "Now you can Google any term and find a vast array of material. It's so much faster and more in depth. . . . The Internet has become a basic resource."

Mr. Gregory, a high school principal in a school where technology was well integrated, talked about the transition that had taken place:

> The big thing is the technology, the integration of technology, the acceptance of technology by the teachers and obviously the students. The first time students are asked to do a paper online, you get some of the parents saying, "I don't know, I don't think that's fair, I don't have high-speed Internet." None of that is there anymore, it's all gone. It levels the playing field, and it's absolutely had a tremendous influence on research and writing.

Mark, a student in another school, described the transition to Internet-based research from the students' perspective:

> We have been given more privileges on the Web because we used to not get trusted with things like Google and YouTube and stuff. Now we have to find all kinds of information and that is better so we have better research skills. . . . We are using websites to create graphs, dig out maps, statistics, and stuff. (Grade 8, higher achieving)

Students' ventures on the Internet were not always successful. A student, Patrick (Grade 6, lower achieving), mentioned watching chemical reactions in film clips "like Bill Nye, the Science Guy" and then trying to re-create them with his chemistry set. "I almost burned up our shed. . . . Part of the wall is now black, but we've moved."

Teachers fluctuated between enthusiasm for the resources available on the Internet and a concern that students would simply cut and paste. Mr. Fisk, a 10th-grade English teacher, reported using Noodle notecards (www.noodletools.com) to deal with this problem:

> These kids have such a difficult time reading something, understanding it, and figuring out what is important in the article. It's a complicated, higher order skill and they struggle with it. They have a difficult time evaluating information and picking what's useful. . . . And this program really helps them do that.

The software also helped the teacher track what students were reading and taking from their reading, without having to read all of the articles herself.

New Formats for Presenting Writing

Even in schools where instruction was relatively traditional, students often were asked to present their ideas in some newer electronic formats: PowerPoint and (less often) blogs, wikis, or podcasts.

PowerPoint: A New School Genre. Unlike extended writing, which typically was meant to be read by the teacher, PowerPoints were usually meant to be shared with others in the class. A 10th-grade biology class reflected the typical approach. During the lesson we observed, the class was at the sharing stage of a short inquiry project on stem cells. Students had been given narrow topics and had chosen their own working groups. The groups shared their work through PowerPoint presentations offered in round-robin fashion to the class as a whole. The teacher offered clarifying comments and a brief lecture after all of the presentations were over, suggesting additional items for their notes in preparation for an upcoming test. As one of our field researchers commented at the end of the lesson summary, "The teacher's directions . . . were generally consistent with writing in a PowerPoint model: accuracy and completeness of information; simplicity of information; pictures to enhance understanding; no more than 20 words per slide."

At every grade level and in all subjects, students reported sharing key ideas through PowerPoint presentations; its use had become routine. Middle school students enjoyed not only preparing the wording but also using visuals to illustrate the ideas. Patrick (Grade 6, lower achieving) explained, "I like to use ClipArt because it gets me better grades. . . . I like to use WordArt to make the words colorful."

By Grade 12, students have had a great deal of experience with PowerPoint presentations, although it may not be their medium of choice. As Hannah (Grade 12, higher achieving) acknowledged,

> PowerPoint isn't my favorite thing to do, but it's what we use the most. . . . I don't think it's all that practical. You have to simplify in order to fit it on slides. I would rather use a poster board presentation and be able to move through points where everyone can see everything at the same time.

Hannah's comments reflect a sophisticated understanding of the limits as well as the powers of technology, and the need to be sure that the genre and media fit the audience and purpose of the task.

Blogs and Wikis: Encouraging Collaboration and Response. A few teachers in our studies also reported using wikis or blogs for student writing. Ms. Johnson, an eighth-grade earth science teacher, had set up a class blog using wikispaces.com. When we visited, her students were doing a library-based project: "It's interesting," Tania commented. "It's on a closed page on the Web that you can only access with a password. Everybody in the class created their own page, but we can access other people's pages and edit our own."

Similarly, Mr. Zhang, a 10th-grade chemistry teacher, was using a class blog, tying it directly to preparation for the state exam. Students worked in groups, each of which was to create a review page on one topic that might be on the exam. Mr. Zhang described the advantages:

> They work together using classroom materials and stuff they find online and they publish in Wikispaces. That way I can see what everyone is contributing, and what editing and changes they have made. They post by a certain date, and then they have to critique each other's pages. I have a rubric for that kind of critique, and then they can go back and revise those pages.

Students commented favorably on such activities. As Charla (Grade 12, higher achieving) put it, "I find it very helpful. We can just do it at home when it's convenient. We comment and give feedback to other people in class. . . . We've been doing blog entries on current issues such as genocide. It's been interesting to go and see what other people write."

Some teachers found that such technologies were particularly useful for teaching writing. Ms. Riordan, a 12th-grade English teacher, for example, reported using classjump.com for a classwide writing conference:

> [Students] are not only able to see what we are working on at the time, but they can see what the assignments are. They can make copies of the assignments in case they are absent for any reason. . . . There are also message boards so that they can reflect on what we've read, particular thematic statements, they can reflect on that. They can make comments like, "I'm having problems with a thesis statement, can someone help me?"

The discussion boards were open to all students in the class, and also their parents, allowing everyone to see the work being done and what was coming up.

When teachers did not make use of the available technology, some students simply took it into their own hands. Rebecca (Grade 12, higher achieving) explained that she was supposed to write "a page handwritten" in response to regular journal prompts for a health class. Instead, she did hers "on a blog. What I write is often more coherent when I'm typing. I type faster than I write, I can rearrange stuff, and it's organizationally easier."

Podcasts: Linking Spoken and Written Language. A few teachers in schools we studied had broadened student presentations to include podcasts. Ms. Tarro, a Grade 12 social studies teacher, for example, had her students create podcasts based on fictional but historically accurate characters that could have lived during the Civil War. Students created the podcasts by role playing the characters. They then shared the podcasts with one another—a new-technology version of a typical social studies task asking students to imagine life in another era (see Chapter 4).

Mr. Rupo, a 12th-grade journalism teacher in the same school, used podcasts to make the students' work more relevant to contemporary journalism. The final project was a portfolio, which included a podcast. He described the students' work in an interview:

> My class is responsible for some of the content on the news in the morning, too, for which we collaborate with the digital video editing class, as well. A lot of the information in the journalism class when I first took it over was a little outdated because the technology changes so fast, so I was trying to take one more opportunity for them to write in different formats. This will be the first year for the podcast program. [It is] a variation on the earlier portfolio project. They'll write it down—so there's a written component, but they'll also record.
>
> It is so important for kids to hear themselves. Students don't have opportunity to reflect on the way they speak, and this gives them a chance they don't usually have, and I think it's so important.

Creation of a Technology-Rich Environment

If teachers have largely adopted technologies that they found mostly on their own, Batavia High School in western New York is in a district that has made a concerted effort to make evolving technologies readily and easily available to students and teachers. The districtwide educational plan listed among the strengths of the system, "Integration of technology in all curricular areas to support students reaching the standards and to support teachers in procuring resources." Batavia also had a technology plan "focusing on increased accessibility to district resources for students and families, better use of technology to support best practice, and more classroom-based resources, i.e., laptop carts and presentation devices" (Batavia City Schools, 2009).

The district was selected by the National School Boards Association (NSBA) as a model of the successful embedding of technology into learner-centered classrooms. The district described their activities in a brochure prepared for the NSBA site visits as follows:

Teachers guide and motivate excited and enthusiastic learners using:

- Interactive white boards
- Student response systems
- Moodle online course management
- Distance learning
- Curricular software and other technology tools

These tools facilitate collaboration, critical thinking, and improve student achievement. (Batavia City Schools, 2008)

Getting to this point was the result of a consistent focus on technology-enriched school improvement, supported by a series of district technology plans dating back at least to a 1996 "vision" for districtwide adoption of technology to support all members of the district staff, students, and families. Through a series of 3-year plans that continue to the present day, the district developed a comprehensive technology infrastructure to support teaching and learning, as well as administrative functions, with consistent and easy-to-use interfaces and log-ins across all buildings in the district.

Once the basic infrastructure for voice, video, and data was in place throughout the district, later efforts focused on professional development and effective implementation of technology resources through a technology-enhanced, learner-centered classroom initiative, as well as continual updating of the technology itself (Batavia City Schools, 2012). Such efforts require the commitment of staff (in addition to school-based media specialists, there are seven members of a district technology support team for five schools and the district administration), and resources ($15 million districtwide by the time of the 2008 National School Boards Association site visits.)

As a result of these efforts, students and teachers had easy access to a wide variety of materials to aid teaching and learning. Readily available online resources ranged from traditional reference works to databases from ProQuest and other providers, including Noodle Bib, Culturegrams, and BrainPOP (animated curriculum resources and educational games). Moodle, an online course delivery system, was used both to supplement classroom-based learning and for stand-alone distance learning courses for students. (Moodle was also used for professional development for teachers.) Individual teachers used their webpages not only for course assignments and traditional supporting materials, but also for links to on-line demonstrations, interactive simulations and games, problem sets, test preparation sites, and resources for writing, revising, and editing.

Mr. Merton, the principal, provided his perspective on technology and writing in an interview with our visiting team:

> We want to create an environment where kids can express them-selves orally as well as through the written word. It's tied in not just to our core subjects, but to all subjects. . . . The kids can write even in math. We want the kids to be able to express themselves in a way that will make them marketable in the modern world, written as well as oral. . . . So our kids have tremendous access to computers, to technology to enhance that. . . . What's amazing to me is seeing what these students can do coming in younger and younger as far as presenting the material they have researched and the wonderful things they can do with the technology. They show us all the time different ways to research that our teachers are catching up on.

TECHNOLOGY AND THE COMMON CORE STANDARDS

The Common Core State Standards (CCSSO & NGA, 2010) seem likely to accelerate the adoption of technology to support the teaching of writing across grades and subject areas. The introduction to the Common Core clearly states that students who are ready for college and career "use tech-nology and digital media strategically and capably":

> Students employ technology thoughtfully to enhance their read-ing, writing, speaking, listening, and language use. They tailor their searches online to acquire useful information efficiently, and they integrate what they learn using technology with what they learn offline. They are familiar with the strengths and limitations of various technological tools and mediums and can select and use those best suited to their communication goals. (p. 7)

Given this emphasis, uses of technology are embedded in the stan-dards as early as kindergarten, where students are expected to "explore a variety of digital tools to produce and publish writing, including in collaboration with peers" (Standard 6, p. 19). By Grade 3, students also are expected to be gathering information from digital as well as print resources to support their writing (Standard 8, p. 21). The assessments being developed to accompany the Common Core provide yet additional impetus to the adoption of technology: Both assessment consortia, Partnership for Assessment of Readiness of College and Careers (PARCC) and Smarter Balanced Assessment Consortium, are committed to computer-based assessment.

Taken together, these features of the Common Core directly address some of the hesitations about technology use expressed by teachers and administrators in our studies: The assessments will be computer-based, removing the need to insist on handwritten responses to on-demand writing; the Internet is legitimated as a powerful resource for knowledge development, though also a resource that students need to use with care and discrimination; and collaboration and cooperation are an integral part of the composing process beginning in kindergarten. Coupled with changes in other assessment systems, including the shift by the National Assessment of Educational Progress (NCES, 2012) to a computer-based writing assessment, the Common Core may force schools to embrace technology much more fully than has been the case in the past.

THE BOTTOM LINE

It is clear that middle and high school students, with only a few exceptions, are comfortable with a wide range of technologies that can support writing and interaction; they are often more comfortable with technology than their teachers are. Resources drawn from the Internet are already playing a major role in student writing within each of the disciplines. Many students, particularly in the upper grades, make regular use of word-processing software, even if they have to do so at home rather than at school. Nevertheless, opportunities to write on the computer continue to be limited in many schools and classrooms.

In some cases, teachers require writing to be handwritten out of a concern that students will need to write by hand during high-stakes tests. In other cases, writing that is started in class has to be handwritten because there are not enough computers for everyone to use, even if the students then have to type up the draft later before handing it in.

As schools and districts place more emphasis on technology-enriched instruction, teachers are making use of a wide variety of resources to support their preferred modes of teaching. The majority, however, are most comfortable with a traditional presentational approach to instruction—replacing chalk-and-talk with PowerPoint and illustrative material projected from the Internet. Far fewer classrooms are utilizing technology to support students in the process of thinking about new material (beyond locating information on the Internet). We saw little of the collaboration and interaction that supports developing interpretations and more complex understandings. Blogs and wikis, as well as more complex platforms such as BlackBoard and Moodle, have the still largely untapped potential to engage students in intellectually challenging ways to think about and with the concepts they are studying as well as to interact conceptually with their teachers and peers.

Looking across all of the classrooms we studied, we find a number of practices that contribute to successful uses of technology to enrich teaching and learning:

Curriculum and Instruction

- Use online portfolios of student work as a way to encourage drafting, revising, and sharing of student writing.
- Expand the formats and genres of student written work to reflect the evolution of digital media, including such formats as blogs and wikis, podcasts, and other social media.
- Treat the Internet as a resource for students and teachers, building on its strengths.
- Exploit the potential of online databases for student research and inquiry.
- Incorporate technological tools that foster collaboration and inquiry, including online instructional platforms such as those included in BlackBoard and Moodle, as well as tools like wikis and blogs that promote interaction.

Assessment

- Ask students to complete assessment writing tasks using a full-featured word processor, including spell-check, dictionary, thesaurus, and other tools.
- Develop performance-based assessment tasks in which students access the Internet to find and evaluate the credibility of source material to incorporate in their responses.

Schoolwide Initatives

- Provide support for the development of expertise in technologies appropriate for producing and sharing text, making productive use of the Internet, engaging in collaborative inquiry and problem solving, and keeping up with conceptually supportive technological innovations.

FUTURE DIRECTIONS

When schools have the knowledge and resources to embrace technology, the effects can be impressive. The following notes are drawn from a field researcher's interview with a middle school humanities chair describing the effects of technology in a school with computers in every classroom, three technology labs, computers in the library, and laptop carts:

> Has influenced/created different kinds of writing . . . blogging, lots of writing, real audience. Book trailers (movie trailer for books). Students still had to be concise and choose their words. Use of wikis. Lots of PowerPoint presentations. E-mailing teachers is available. E-mail is modern-day letter writing but they are doing more of it. SmartBoards in every room makes technology accessible to the whole class. Can show a website without bringing entire class to a computer lab. . . . Some teachers use it for webquests, drafting, final drafts, research.

Nachowitz (2012) describes another approach using Knowledge Forum, an online platform designed especially to support written conversations about complex topics, with scaffolding to help students think about the material in more complex ways as they communicate through writing. Nachowitz studied Ms. Fleck, a sixth-grade language arts teacher, as she used Knowledge Forum to support her students' developing interpretations of literature. Rather than relying on a traditional, presentational pedagogy, Ms. Fleck sought to foster a collaborative, interactive, and engaging learning environment in which students contributed to one another's explorations of literature. Nachowitz summarized the results of using technology to support these goals, observing that the students in this classroom were learning a great deal:

> Learning how to participate in progressive dialogue that is going somewhere, that builds on shared understandings, learning how to challenge other's ideas without being hurtful, learning how creativity is itself not the result of one person's insight but collaborative, ongoing creations. (p. 224)

As a profession we have many other good models of what such engagement can look like (Burke, 2010; Langer, 2011a, b); the challenge still is to build from those models to transform teaching and learning in the majority of our schools and classrooms.

Reflect and Discuss

1. Think about how well technology is currently being integrated into curriculum and instruction in your school. Consider ways to strengthen the following uses of technology:
    a. Students' use of digital tools for producing and publishing writing
    b. Use of the Internet as a resource for research and inquiry
    c. Support for student inquiry and collaboration through interactive platforms that provide scaffolding for discussion and developing understanding
2. Internet-based resources for curriculum and instruction are proliferating almost daily. Working with others in your school, develop a plan for finding and sharing resources that seem particularly useful.
    a. Who will look for what sorts of resources?
    b. How will the results be shared, and at what level (schoolwide, within a department or team, teacher to teacher)?
3. What technologies would you like to have better access to, for yourself and for your students?
    a. Develop a rationale that highlights how these technologies could support conceptual rather than rote learning.
    b. Make a plan for obtaining the necessary resources. This might be through a districtwide technology initiative, through a commitment of resources at the building level, or by applying for external grants to provide new technologies for your classrooms.

CHAPTER 8

◇◇◇◇◇◇◇

English Language Learners

Kristen Campbell Wilcox

In this chapter we will examine how schools are dealing with the rising number of students whose native language (or language used outside of school) is not English. These students, referred to as English language learners (ELLs), represent over 10% of the kindergarten through 12th-grade student population nationally, and over half of these ELLs are adolescents between 10 and 17 years old (NCES, 2007). Unfortunately, many adolescent ELLs do not meet basic levels of achievement on a variety of measures correlated with college and career readiness, including writing. For example, at Grade 12 only 2% of ELLs (compared to 24% of native English speakers) scored at or above proficient in writing on the 2007 National Assessment of Educational Progress, indicating only partial mastery of knowledge and skills that are fundamental for the grade level (Graham & Hebert, 2010; Graham & Perin, 2007; Salahu-Din, Persky, & Miller, 2008).

Adolescent ELLs often have difficulties with a variety of writing skills and abilities necessary for the tasks expected by colleges or employers, such as producing clear and coherent texts appropriate to specific tasks, purposes, and audiences. These deficiencies will only become more apparent as schools implement the Common Core State Standards (CCSSO & NGA, 2010), with their emphasis on the need for all students to write effectively in each of the core content areas.

Approaches to content-area writing instruction for adolescent English language learners should be responsive to the students in an individual school's population. In particular, schools with larger populations of ELLs need to build teacher capacity to adapt instruction. Some schools and districts meet this need through professional development in sheltered instructional approaches or "specially designed academic instruction in English" (SDAIE) models of course delivery. These approaches are characterized by adapting content instruction and using literacy scaffolds to make content more comprehensible in mainstream classrooms (Echevarria, Richards-Tutor, Chinn, & Ratleff, 2011). Professional development for all teachers (rather than just language specialists) has a positive impact on student achievement on academic literacy (Echevarria et al., 2011).

Although, on average, adolescent ELLs continue to perform well below grade level on measures of literacy, there has been little research focused on how content-area writing instruction is best approached in different school contexts (Tardy, 2006). The first section of this chapter, therefore, presents a comparison between instructional emphases and professional development experiences reported by teachers whose classrooms include English language learners and those whose classes do not include ELLs. The second part of the chapter then takes a closer look at an example of typical practice in a high-diversity school, contrasting the instruction ELLs received with instruction received by native English speakers. The chapter concludes by highlighting writing pedagogies from schools with traditions of excellence in the teaching of writing, examining the implications these examples hold for the future of adolescent ELL writing instruction.

WRITING INSTRUCTION FOR ELLs AND NON-ELLs

In our national survey, 65% of teachers reported teaching English language learners in their classrooms. When ELLs were present, they comprised, on average, 27% of the students. We begin by contrasting responses from teachers who had ELLs in their classes to those from teachers who had no ELLs in terms of (1) the length and complexity of the writing they required, (2) the types of writing they felt were important, (3) the extent to which test preparation guided their instruction, and (4) the extent to which teachers felt responsible for writing instruction and had been supported by schoolwide initiatives related to the teaching of writing.

Expectations for Extended Writing

A variety of previous studies suggest that a student's identification as an ELL correlates with lower academic expectations, which may in turn render ELLs less able to succeed in advanced coursework, including writing (Callahan, Wilkinson, & Muller, 2010). Results in the present study were quite different: When teachers were asked about the types of writing they assigned, ranging from assignments that required very little writing (multiple-choice, fill-in-the-blank, or short-answer) to tasks requiring a page or two of writing, there were no large differences between the responses of teachers with ELLs and those with no ELLs in their classrooms. For instance, in our random sample of teachers across the country, 78% with ELLs in their classrooms and 74% with no ELLs reported having asked their students to complete a multiple-choice, fill-in-the-blank, or short-answer exercise in the past 5 days. When asked about longer writing assignments (a page or two in the past 5 days), there was still relatively little difference between teachers with ELLs (52%) and those with no ELLs (54%). This similarity in length of assignments paints a promising picture with regard to the value teachers with ELLs in their classes place on writing requiring some extent of composing, or at least it suggests that, on average, ELLs are on a par with non-ELLs in the amount of writing they are assigned.

Emphasis on Writing Tasks Requiring Analysis and Synthesis

In addition to benefiting from opportunities for extended writing, English language learners also benefit from opportunities to engage in complex writing tasks requiring analysis, synthesis, or related research (Janzen, 2008; Schleppegrell, Achugar, & Oteiza, 2004). When asked about such tasks, teachers with ELLs in their classrooms placed slightly less importance on these types of writing than teachers with no ELLs. For example, 34% of teachers with ELLs reported that writing requiring analysis or synthesis across multiple sources was very important, contrasted with 36% of teachers with no ELLs. There was a similar pattern with regard to writing requiring critical analysis of an issue or text, which 44% of teachers with ELLs reported was very important, in comparison to 50% of teachers with no ELLs in their classrooms. Finally, when teachers were asked about the importance of research papers or reports, the pattern repeated, with 22% of teachers with ELLs and 32% of teachers with no ELLs reporting such writing was very important.

These data are an encouraging result in that some teachers with ELLs in their classrooms reported valuing opportunities to engage in more complex writing, if not quite as often as their peers who had no ELLs in their classrooms.

The Role of Test Preparation

Research on the impact of state-mandated tests on ELL instruction indicates that many assessments typically used in schools do not adequately parse language proficiency and content knowledge (Abedi, 2004). This research suggests that schools with larger numbers of ELLs with lower baselines for student achievement may require greater gains in scores to meet their Annual Yearly Progress targets than schools with fewer ELLs. This in turn places extra pressure on educators with high numbers of ELLs to focus on the high-stakes tests, potentially narrowing what they teach to what is tested.

And, in fact, teachers who had ELLs in their classrooms reported doing more "test prep" than their counterparts who did not teach ELLs. Some 63% of teachers with ELLs compared with 52% of teachers with no ELLs reported practicing on old exams. Both groups reported providing practice on tasks that were similar to those on the exams (93% of teachers of ELLs, compared to 94% of with no ELLs). Teachers with ELLs were also more likely to provide their students with rubrics similar to those on the exams (74%), compared with 64% of teachers with no ELLs.

Teacher Beliefs About Responsibility for Writing Instruction

Some studies have pointed to a correlation between ELLs' performance on academic tasks and their content-area teachers' beliefs and schoolwide climate regarding linguistic diversity (Callahan, 2005). Encouragingly, in the present study teachers whose classrooms included English language learners were just as likely as their peers in classrooms without ELLs to believe that *all* teachers should be responsible for teaching disciplinary writing in their own subjects; 96% of those with ELLs compared with 97% of their peers with no ELLs agreed with this perspective. Responses were similar when teachers were asked about responsibilities for teaching general writing skills (as opposed to disciplinary writing), with 96% of both agreeing that this was a responsibility of all teachers. Since beliefs about responsibilities for instruction can be shaped by schoolwide climate and supports, it is interesting to note that slightly more teachers in classrooms with ELLs (78%) than in those with no ELLs (74%) reported that their schools had had schoolwide initiatives emphasizing writing across the curriculum in the past 3 years.

These contrasting responses—from teachers who have ELLs in their classrooms and those who do not—provide a complicated and incomplete picture of what might be happening in secondary content classrooms. Although there appears to be a relatively high value placed on complex and extended writing in classrooms with ELLs (similar to the value of these types of writing in classrooms with no ELLs), there is also more emphasis on test preparation, potentially limiting the variety and complexity of writing ELLs produce.

TYPICAL PRACTICE IN A HIGH-DIVERSITY SCHOOL DISTRICT

Our yearlong study of writing instruction in a high-diversity, high-poverty school district in New York highlighted some of the factors shaping the differences evident in teachers' survey responses. Although content-area teachers in this district valued writing as a tool for learning, they also felt they needed to place less emphasis on interdisciplinary writing projects and on opportunities for extended writing with ELLs and lower achieving native-English-speaking students. For these students, the teachers focused their instruction instead on the content knowledge needed to pass the high-stakes exams (Wilcox, 2011). Those exams placed little emphasis on extended writing overall, even though New York had higher expectations for extended writing on high-stakes exams than the other states we studied.

While the survey responses suggested many similarities in the writing expected by teachers of ELLs and by teachers with no ELLs in their classes, in this district, writing that went beyond that expected on high-stakes exams was more likely in classrooms dominated by native-English-speaking students. For example, ELLs were frequently given worksheets to record content likely to appear on high-stakes tests as preparation for responding to old test prompts. To guide their responses, students were then given model essays that they were taught to essentially fill in with the content they had recorded. The focus of instruction was on getting the facts and vocabulary right to achieve the highest score on the exam rubric.

Such tasks were also given to the higher tracked native English speakers, but native English speakers were given fewer of them. For the native speakers, these tasks were supplemented by requirements to produce more extended and complex writing than that expected on the high-stakes exam. Harvey, a native English speaker and higher tracked student, explained that he had completed numerous assignments for his eighth-grade science portfolio and contrasted this to the requirements in science classes for his lower tracked peers.

> We've done around 15 portfolios. We have to write complete sentences to answer questions. When the lower class had a worksheet we had an essay. We do more work—extra assignments and different portfolios.

Priscilla, an eighth grader for whom English was a second language (L2), explained that engaging in the more complex writing expected of her native-English-speaking peers was difficult in part because of a limited vocabulary, but also due to the disconnect between instruction in her pull-out ESL (English as a second-language) classroom and her science classroom:

> When you try to answer the questions—I sometimes don't get it. Sometimes I don't understand the words. Sometimes I don't know it because I'm not there because sometimes I have to take a test with the ESL teacher and then I miss out on some things.

Literacy initiatives at the middle school level were another factor that influenced the quality and quantity of writing instruction ELLs in this district received. Although the middle school had put a literacy initiative in place to improve ELLs' and other lower achieving students' performance in reading and writing, this initiative focused on the kinds of writing expected in English language arts. A veteran high school English language arts (ELA) teacher explained that, in her experience, such writing initiatives "have been directives with very little buy-in from staff and faculty. . . . They've focused on the ELA exam." Math, science, and social studies teachers reported shared concerns that focusing on the reading and writing skills needed to perform well on the high-stakes ELA exam makes "my exam scores suffer." As an eighth-grade social studies teacher asserted, "In other disciplines we end up teaching so much of the writing skills—it's our job too, but focusing on the writing skills leaves content wanting."

Typical practice as observed here and in the other parts of our study highlighted tensions between what teachers thought they should be doing to improve ELLs' writing performance and what they could do given the environment of high-stakes testing and what were perceived as conflicting priorities with regard to providing language and content instruction.

In the next section we turn to some examples of how writing instruction was approached in some of the schools identified for traditions of excellence in the teaching of writing.

PORTRAITS OF SUCCESS

In the schools with histories of exemplary writing instruction, we identified three dimensions of good practice that echo recommendations in the growing body of research on adolescent ELL writing. The features of each of these are displayed in Figure 8.1 and discussed in the following sections.

FIGURE 8.1. Features That Support ELL Writing

L2 Writing Assessment

- is formative and frequent
- allows formative language use
- crosses discipline

Schoolwide Initiatives

- provide a coherent focus on writing in the disciplines
- establish shared responsibility for L2 writing development
- are sustained by school leadership and professional development

L2 Instructional Strategies

- focus on building content vocabulary
- focus on academic language structures
- focus on cognitive strategies

Writing Assessment: Formative, Frequent, and Focused on Growth

Frequent and formative writing assessment that accounts for growth over time has long been recognized as a preferred method for monitoring ELL learning. One interesting example of such a practice came from the state of Kentucky where there was a tradition of portfolio assessment (since abandoned). In Bowling Green High School, where 10% of the school population was identified as ELL at the time of our study, writing development was monitored through the use of Program Service Plans (PSPs). PSPs, as shown in Figure 8.2, were not assessments, but rather a tool to encourage good ELL assessment practice. PSPs included a variety of components that emphasized a stance toward writing development that one 12th-grade social studies teacher characterized as "not stressed as a test-driven tool," but rather focused on writing "to promote learning." The PSPs, therefore, included information about recommended accommodations for writing tasks on required tests (e.g., reading text aloud, providing scribes), and specific suggestions for instruction (e.g., sheltering, reinforcing in native language, modeling task completion).

The PSP also records developing oral and written proficiencies based on the ACCESS for ELLs (Assessing Comprehension and Communication in English State-to-State for English Language Learners) tests developed in a partnership between World-Class Instructional Design and Assessment (WIDA) and the Center for Applied Linguistics (CAL). Kentucky is one of 31 states in the WIDA consortium. The ACCESS for ELLs assess-

FIGURE 8.2. ELL Program Service Plan

English Language Learner Individual Student Program Service Plan

Student Name   School   Gender   Date

Reason for Identification of English Language Learners Level of English Proficiency based on access from WIDA-ACCESS State ELL assessment		ACCOMMODATIONS/RECOMMENDATIONS TO ADDRESS EDUCATIONAL STRENGTHS, LEARNING NEEDS, AND ENGLISH ACQUISITION		
*SS –Scale Score *PL –Proficiency Level				
Listening	SS – PL–	Method of Instruction	Content Area	Teacher Responsible
Speaking	SS – PL–	----- reinforcement in Native Language		
Reading	SS – PL–	----- sheltered instruction ----- instruction in ELL class for __ hrs	Language Arts	
Writing	SS – PL–	----- paraphrase directions for tasks in English or in student's primary language		
Oral Languages (listening & speaking)	SS – PL–	----- translate text to student's native language ----- administer tests in small group settings ----- allow use of foreign language dictionary	Social Studies	
Literacy (reading & writing)	SS – PL–	----- allow use of word processor ----- use visual cues and graphic organizers in daily instruction	Science	
Comprehension (listening & reading)	SS – PL–	----- pair with a peer tutor ----- allow use of dictionary or thesaurus ----- shorten assignments	Math	
Overall score (comprehension)	SS – PL–	----- extended time ----- scaffold responses ----- model language and task completion ----- build background knowledge ----- link instruction to prior knowledge ----- provide content and language objectives ----- other		
ACCESS Assessment for ELLs Assessing Comprehension in English State to State		Read texts to students ----- all printed materials ----- grade level content materials ----- for reading completed under time constraints ----- for direct instruction in acquisition of reading skills and strategies	** Student will exit the ESL program when he/she reaches ACCESS Proficiency Level 5	_____ Student will participate in state achievement testing with accommodations
ACCESS Proficiency Levels 1 – Entering 2 – Beginning 3 – Developing 4 – Expanding 5 – Bridging 6 – Reaching		Scribe for the student ----- for prewriting activities while the students brainstorm ideas ----- for instructional activities/assessments completed under time constraints ----- for instructional activities/assessments requiring written responses in content areas ----- for all classroom assessment/activities requiring written responses		

ment along with WIDA's set of proficiency standards and other resources focus on "expanding students' academic language by building on the inherent resources of English language learners (ELLs) and accentuating the positive efforts of educators" (WIDA, 2011, para. 2).

The assessment practices that we saw at Bowling Green resonate with the results of other research. For example, researchers have pointed to the importance of frequent formative assessments (including the use of portfolios) as appropriate and supportive of ELLs' writing development (Hirvela & Sweetland, 2005; Leki, Cumming, & Silva, 2006). Recommended approaches from the research also include providing extended time for writing and encouraging students to draw on first-language knowledge both orally and in writing as they compose.

The PSPs at Bowling Green supported several of the features of second-language (L2) writing assessment recommended in the research. They provided (1) explicit directions for writing accommodations on content exams;

(2) objectives for writing across *all* content classes; and (3) measures of oral and written language proficiencies to inform instruction. Moreover, while plans for ESL instruction are typically shared with parents and legal guardians, the PSP is unusual in that it provided a mechanism for collaboration across disciplinary lines by requiring authorization of the plan after discussion with content classroom teachers, the ESL teacher, and the principal.

Schoolwide Initiatives: Shared and Sustained Focus on Writing

Schoolwide literacy initiatives have the potential to establish a climate of shared responsibility for ELL literacy development. We found an interesting example of such an initiative called "bundled skills" at Port Chester Middle School in New York (see also Chapter 4). Bundled skills was an interdisciplinary literacy initiative that included as one objective incorporating writing instruction into content classrooms; the program was developed in partnership with an outside consultant. As a large suburban school on the fringe of New York City with 12% of the students identified as ELLs at the time of our study, Port Chester's educators understood the importance of this effort.

Teachers and administrators at Port Chester described bundled skills as a set of essential literacy skills that, in the words of one sixth-grade social studies teacher, provided "a great deal of emphasis on writing." As this teacher explained, "We are all ELA [English language arts] teachers and need to incorporate reading and writing skills."

Although bundled skills set explicit expectations for writing instruction in content classrooms, teachers also adapted their focus based on what they felt was important in their disciplines. For Port Chester science teachers, for example, the focus of bundled skills was primarily on paragraph-length compositions requiring students to compare, contrast, or summarize. When evaluating students' writing, science teachers focused on the expression of content knowledge but also provided feedback to ELLs on control of mechanics and spelling. Math teachers also described a continual, yearly revisiting of bundled skills as a team with responsiveness to "what the ELA teachers were feeling needed to be targeted." For example, at the time of our visit, math teachers were explicitly encouraging students to underline questions and highlight key words while reading, in an effort to build content vocabulary that students could then use when they wrote word problems.

The bundled skills initiative exemplifies recommended features of schoolwide literacy initiatives found in the research including (1) providing a coherent focus on writing in the disciplines; (2) making explicit shared responsibility for L2 writing development; and (3) giving sustained support from school leadership and ongoing professional development.

Indeed, the research on such literacy initiatives indicates that their success is associated with sustained support through professional development opportunities, sometimes provided by organizations outside the school system (Echevarria et al., 2011; Echevarria, Short, & Powers, 2006; Olson, Kim, et al., 2012). Those initiatives that are interdisciplinary in nature and model specific strategies for the development of ELL content-area writing are also recommended (Fu, Houser, & Huang, 2007; Janzen, 2008).

L2 Instructional Strategies: Structures, Vocabulary, and Cognitive Strategies

To help adolescent second-language writers engage successfully in the advanced disciplinary tasks of the secondary school, classroom instruction must build from what is known about how all writers (whether writing in their first or second language) develop, but must also be responsive to the unique needs of second-language (L2) writers. We found the strategies being used by content-area teachers at Amadon High School (see Chapters 3, 6) provided abundant examples of effective practice. Amadon was one of the largest and most linguistically diverse schools in our five-state study, with approximately one third of the students classified as English language learners, almost all of whom spoke Spanish as a first language. In this context, teachers and administrators placed a great deal of emphasis on adapting instruction to individual needs.

Through schoolwide use of Small Learning Communities (SLCs) (see Chapter 3) that encouraged interdisciplinary collaboration, teachers at Amadon had learned to use writing as a thinking tool for content learning in every unit in every classroom. Grade-level teams planned their units backwards, beginning by naming the culminating essays that would be required. Teachers approached writing collaboratively, with more than one teacher providing assistance through the stages of completing any writing assignment. Teachers also integrated the students' reading and writing tasks. As the social studies department chair explained, "We do writing as warm-ups. We take a textbook question, and turn it into a writing prompt and we do full blown essays. Writing is an integral part of our performance. . . . Every unit ends with a writing component." The writing that resulted was also evaluated with consistent rubrics across content classes.

In addition, teachers drew on professional development experiences focused on "inquiry, hands-on writing—not read-and-answer questions," as a science chair explained. A 10th-grade teacher, for example, described how she combined the 5E (Engagement, Exploration, Explanation, Extension, and Evaluation) inquiry model (see Chapter 6) with the Specially Designed Academic Instruction in English (SDAIE) skills she had learned through professional development:

> Everyone is an English learner in this class, so I use all my SDAIE skills. I try to follow the 5E model for science instruction using demonstrations, cartoons—something to capture their interest. Then I get them to wonder aloud and formulate questions and start investigating. As we go along I introduce vocabulary words and ask students to repeat after me because they are terrified of sounding stupid. Every day everyone talks to a classmate—"think, pair, share" begins the day. Everyone writes every day and thinks every day.

Other examples of discipline-specific approaches to writing adapted for ELLs included "graffiti walls" (drawings of key historic figures with writing that pinpointed their essential thinking) in social studies and "think-alouds" (rephrasing problem solving orally and then in writing) in math.

Some research has indicated that content teachers often take a reductionist view of writing with ELLs—focusing on surface features such as spelling, conventions, and mechanics in shorter and simpler writing tasks rather than offering opportunities for ELLs to engage in longer and more complex disciplinary writing (Enright, 2011; Wilcox, 2011; Wilcox & Angelis, 2009, 2011). However, some studies indicate that an alternative approach that provides ELLs with explicit instruction on content vocabulary and academic language structures is preferable (Coxhead & Byrd, 2007; Schleppegrell, 2012) and this is what we found in Amadon. For example, in their research, Schleppegrell, Achugar, and Oteiza (2004) focused on the use of content-based instructional techniques in content-area classrooms, such as highlighting the role of discipline-specific language in constructing content-area knowledge. Olson's studies also have indicated the benefits of ELL instruction that integrates the activities of interpretive reading and analytic writing and incorporates explicit teaching of cognitive strategies: e.g., planning and goal setting, constructing the gist, revising meaning, analyzing author's craft, evaluating/assessing quality (Olson, Kim, et al., 2012; Olson, Land, Anselmi, & AuBuchon, 2010). Findings from these studies suggest positive impacts on ELL writing when the "thinking tools" (Olson, Kim, et al., 2012, p. 348) and specialized structures of disciplinary writing are explicitly taught and used in composing texts.

The educators at Amadon showed a deep understanding of how writing can propel thinking and promote content learning, and of how to assess writing across content areas. Teachers drew on a wide repertoire of approaches and strategies, adapting them to help ELLs develop their writing while echoing many of the recommendations from recent research. These instructional strategies included the following:

- Explicit focus on specialized structures of disciplinary writing through analysis of models in texts they read
- Extra support for increasing content-specific vocabulary (particularly the use of that vocabulary in one's own speech and texts)
- A focus on cognitive strategies for understanding and crafting texts of different lengths and complexity across content classrooms

What all of these examples of practice have in common is an acknowledgment of the benefits of building off the literacies ELLs already have developed in their first language in order to help them develop their writing in English. These examples also share acknowledgment of both the responsibility and the opportunity content teachers have for opening pathways for adolescent ELLs to engage in disciplinary discourse. Finally, they all position writing prominently in the service of both content and language learning. Used in these ways, disciplinary writing has an important role in developing ELLs' cognitive abilities and content knowledge as the complexity of the texts they read and need to write in secondary school increases.

ELLs AND THE COMMON CORE STANDARDS

The Common Core State Standards Initiative (2012) has a document on its website discussing the application of the Common Core for ELLs. It reminds teachers that "it is possible to achieve the standards . . . without manifesting native-like control of the conventions or vocabulary," and we have seen examples of this in our studies. It goes on to state that

> The Common Core Standards for English Language Arts (ELA) articulate rigorous grade-level expectations in the areas of speaking, listening, reading and writing to prepare all students to be college and career ready, including English Language Learners. (para. 3)

Thus teachers of ELLs are expected to integrate the standards into their coursework, and can do so in ways suggested in Chapters 3–6, where possible, as well as through practices discussed in this chapter.

The discussion of the standards and ELLs also highlights the importance of integrating speaking, listening, and reading with writing as ELLs develop both foundational skills in English and engage in discipline-specific classroom writing activities. In mathematics, the standards document encourages teachers to allow for verbal code-switching as students work through word problems, and it focuses teachers' attention on the discourse of explanation and argument. Whether in mathematics, science, social studies, English, or any other content classroom, the advice provided focuses teachers' attention on creating abundant and rich opportunities to engage in a variety of disciplinary writing tasks that require ELLs to fully participate in negotiating meaning. Frequent and varied opportunities for writing different kinds of texts for different purposes guide teaching and can address multiple standards at the same time—these characteristics were evident in our five-state study. In addition, the use of ELL proficiency standards and assessment tools (note the use of ACCESS for ELLs published by WIDA exemplified in the PSPs at Bowling Green) in combination with the Common Core will help teachers appropriately scaffold and use writing not only for assessment of content, but also to encourage ELL language and cognitive development.

THE BOTTOM LINE

As discussed in Chapter 2, students in U.S. secondary schools are doing more writing in their content-area classrooms and receiving more instruction focused on their writing than students did 3 decades ago. Moreover, as we have shown in this chapter, our studies provide an encouraging picture of similar expectations in terms of length and complexity of writing in classrooms with ELLs and those with no ELLs. This is good news with regard to the potential for meeting 21st-century content literacy demands among linguistically diverse secondary school populations. However, we also have seen that teachers in classrooms with ELLs tend to spend more time on test preparation that potentially limits the range of opportunities ELLs might have to engage in a variety of complex disciplinary writing tasks. Unfortunately, there has been little empirical research pulling together a coherent model for L2 writing that would support adolescent ELLs in meeting the kinds of writing demands embedded in the Common Core (Harklau, 2011; Ortmeier-Hooper & Enright, 2011).

The most recent research looking at promising approaches to L2 content-area writing, however, suggests that cognitive strategy instruction (see Olson, Land, et al., 2010; Olson & Matuchniak, 2012) within school contexts where what Langer (2004) refers to as "high literacy" is valued in assessment and instruction can positively impact ELLs' academic achievement, including their achievement in writing. In these studies, strategy instruction includes, for example, planning and goal setting, tapping prior knowledge, and revising meanings, while the focus on high literacy emphasizes thoughtful reading, writing, and discussion activities through which students gain the knowledge and skills to perform well in a variety of new situations.

The examples from schools with histories of successful writing instruction discussed in this chapter provide insight into different approaches toward L2 writing assessment, schoolwide initiatives, and L2 instruction that may prove beneficial for ELLs. These include a systematic approach to formative assessment that can facilitate close monitoring of L2 writing growth in and across disciplines in the form of Program Service Plans, a schoolwide bundled skills literacy initiative that can provide a model for a sustained and supported focus on writing in content classes, and discipline-specific writing strategies melded with content-sheltering techniques.

There is a variety of ways educators might use these ideas to meet the Common Core and improve ELLs' performance:

Curriculum and Instruction

- Build content vocabulary through the integration of reading, writing, speaking, and listening in the context of meaningful tasks.
- Focus explicitly on academic language structures through the analysis of models.
- Provide explicit instruction in the use of cognitive strategies as ELLs are reading and writing in their content classes.
- Give ELLs extra time to compose their writing with sufficient scaffolds to move beyond simple writing tasks to more complex extended writing.

Assessment

- Ensure writing assessment is formative and frequent in each content area.
- Allow for native language use orally and in writing during the composing process.
- Share rubrics that account for "foundational skills" (e.g., conventions) while also providing feedback on how well the writing

fulfills the requirements of the task type (e.g., argument; informative/explanatory; narrative) across disciplines.

- Provide explicit directions for writing accommodations on content exams per students' language proficiencies.

Schoolwide Initiatives

- Establish shared responsibility for L2 writing development through a schoolwide literacy-rich environment that incorporates writing instruction adapted for students with different language proficiencies.

FUTURE DIRECTIONS

Across the United States, demographic shifts the likes of which have not been seen in recent U.S. history are changing the ways we might understand "mainstream" content classrooms (Enright, 2011). While there are still many U.S. secondary school classrooms with no ELLs in attendance, there are also increasing numbers of ELLs of different proficiencies integrated into content classrooms. It is clear from writing achievement data that what is happening in the teaching of writing with adolescent ELLs is not sufficient to prepare them to successfully engage in writing tasks at the secondary level and beyond. With the increased emphasis on writing in the Common Core the bar is raised even higher. These changes require thinking differently about disciplinary boundaries and differently about what is needed to propel L2 writing achievement at the secondary level beyond "basic" levels (Batalova, Fix, & Murray, 2005). As was evidenced in the examples described in this chapter, an interdisciplinary and schoolwide approach utilizing assessment and instructional strategies adapted to promote L2 writers' growth are both possible and necessary.

The findings from our studies suggest the need to incorporate strategies for assessment and L2 writing instruction into schoolwide and districtwide initiatives and professional development. Since the Common Core has put new emphasis on the professional development of all teachers, this is an opportune time to provide professional support, including an emphasis on writing for ELLs, in all subjects. The examples of second-language writing assessment, schoolwide initiatives, and instructional strategies from the schools with traditions of success in writing instruction provide glimpses of what could be developed into a systemic and successful approach to L2 writing in secondary schools—one that is deeply connected to the writing and content goals within each particular discipline, while also providing the critical levels of support needed to meet the special needs of those for whom English is not the mother tongue.

Reflect and Discuss

1. Look back at the section on Portraits of Success. In these examples, students are identifying and practicing strategies for writing to learn and learning to write, which they can use across many writing contexts.
   a. With colleagues, identify your students' writing needs.
   b. Develop a chart that you can use as a reminder about particular writing strategies that you can teach to address those needs.
   c. In addition to listening and speaking activities, develop specific writing activities that provide opportunities to teach these strategies and monitor growth.
2. What are some of the big ideas or major concepts you want students to learn from their lessons this year? Invite colleagues in each subject area to choose one big idea and plan specific writing activities around it.
   a. Develop a range of problem-solving, hands-on, and inquiry-based activities that invite frequent writing about these big ideas throughout the year.
   b. Use the writing to help students explore the concepts, make connections, extend connections, and generate new connections to the subject area and life. Because the focus is on the content, allow for native language use when they are composing. Provide models of each writing type.
3. With your colleagues, develop rubrics for students and teachers to use in evaluating writing.
   a. Include separate sections for Content, Organization, Language, and Conventions.
   b. Collect a set of writing samples for students to analyze that highlight the features of more and less successful writing of various types required in different subject areas.

CHAPTER 9

◇◇◇◇◇◇◇

Students in Poverty

Children under the age of 18 represent a disproportionate share of the poor in the United States; they make up 24% of the total population and 36% of the poor population. Citing Census Bureau statistics, the National Poverty Center (2012) reports that in 2010, some 16.4 million children were living in poverty. This is an astounding number, representing 22% of all children. In our goals to help these children succeed, educators at all levels must be alert to their particular needs.

Poverty is clearly a major factor that prevents many children from doing well in school, or even graduating. For example, the National Center for Education Statistics (NCES, 2010, Figure CL-11) reported that while about 91% of 12th graders in low-poverty schools earned high school diplomas, only about 68% of 12th graders in high-poverty schools did so. (Designations of "high" or "low" poverty impose contrasts between extremes on a continuum of family income. For this analysis, NCES contrasted schools with 25% or fewer students eligible for free or reduced price lunch with schools in which 76% or more were eligible.) Yet, as Darling-Hammond (2010b) points out, too often educational output (e.g., in the form of test results) receives more attention than the educational input related to features that have been found to support students' academic growth and success.

In her book *The Flat World and Education* (2010a), Darling-Hammond argues that declines on international tests such as PISA (Programme for International Student Assessment) occurred at a time when high-stakes state tests took hold across the United States. While the international tests demanded more advanced analysis, requiring students to weigh and balance evidence, apply what they know to new problems, and explain and defend their answers, the high-stakes state tests in the United States focused more on the content and less on the higher order skills involved in reasoning about the content. This underscores our need to reconsider the cognitive demands of the curricular goals, teaching activities, and testing tasks we devise as yardsticks of success, especially as they apply to the learning needs of students in poverty.

THE BACKGROUND FOR WRITING IN HIGH-POVERTY SCHOOLS

There is a substantial and continuing gap in writing achievement between high- and low-poverty students as measured by eligibility for federal lunch programs. For example, in 1998 at Grade 8, 32% of low-poverty students (those not eligible for free or reduced-price lunch) but only 10% of those who were eligible scored at or above proficient on the NAEP writing assessment—a gap of 22 percentage points. By 2007 both groups had improved somewhat but the gap remained substantially unchanged: 40% of low-poverty students scored at the proficient level or above, compared to 17% of high-poverty students—a gap of 23 percentage points. (Data are calculated for public school students using the NAEP Data Explorer [NCES, n.d.].) At Grade 12, fewer students scored at the proficient level than at Grade 8, and the gains over time were lower: 23% of low-poverty students scored at the proficient level in 1998, rising to 27% in 2007, compared with only 8% of high-poverty students, rising to 11%. Results in 2011 on a new version of the assessment using a full-featured word processor were similar, with a 25-percentage-point gap between high- and low-poverty students at Grade 8, and a 21-percentage-point gap at Grade 12.

Let's explore this further. *The Condition of Education 2011* (National Center for Education Statistics, 2011), reports that in 2008–09 a greater percentage of Black, Hispanic, and American Indian/Alaskan Native students across the grades attended high-poverty public schools than did White or Asian/Pacific Islander students. In an article published by *The Nation*, a major national policy magazine, Linda Darling-Hammond (2010b) writes that

> inequality has an enormous influence on U.S. performance [on the international assessment, PISA]. White and Asian students score just above the average for the European OECD nations in each subject area, but African American and Hispanic students score so much lower that the national average plummets to the bottom tier. The United States is also among the nations where socioeconomic background most affects student outcomes. (para. 5)

Surely, students in poverty are at risk, and the various state and national education initiatives designed to help them have not made a substantial impact on their performance.

What's to be done? Langer's "beating the odds" studies (Langer, 2004) and "envisionment-building" studies (Langer, 2011a, b; Applebee et al.,

2003) as well as those of others (e.g., Knapp & Associates, 1995; Needels & Knapp, 1994) make a strong case that what teachers do, and how they carry out instruction, makes all the difference. Across subject areas, when students in high-poverty schools are taught in a deeply engaging manner, with challenging material appropriate for the subject, they do better than similar students in schools with more traditional approaches to curriculum and instruction. In the most successful classrooms, writing becomes a useful vehicle for inviting students to think through, reason, and reflect on, about, and with the material as students move to increasingly more advanced understandings. In such classrooms, writing is used throughout the day to engage students in "minds-on" (Langer, 2004) and discipline-appropriate activities that teach for deep and connected understandings.

Approaches to instruction, the high-stakes tests, and the professional environment within a school and district all contribute to the ways in which writing gets conceptualized and used. When these factors all support using writing as a way to come to understand, to learn more fully, and to make new connections, students learn to become better writers, as well as to understand the material more fully.

This is a far cry from the more typical classrooms where writing is given little time or space, and does not require much cognitive manipulation of the content on the part of the students. In the discussion to follow, we can see evidence of such narrowness in response to high-stakes state assessment systems.

THE STATE OF WRITING IN HIGHER POVERTY SCHOOLS

With some notable exceptions, schools with large numbers of students living in poverty tend to do poorly on high-stakes assessments, with sometimes dire consequences for teachers and administrators as well as for students. This in turn can lead to an even greater emphasis on the tests and the content reflected in them, reducing attention to writing in favor of reading and math. For this reason, we have taken a special look at the ways in which writing was used and taught in higher poverty schools, across the four core subject areas. We feared that the focus on testing and raising test scores, and the reduction of writing within the tests themselves, might have overshadowed the benefits of writing and learning discussed in earlier chapters. In order to examine this, we contrasted schools with 40% or more of their students eligible for free or reduced-price lunch (higher poverty) with schools with 20% or fewer eligible (lower poverty) in both the national sample and the five-state study of schools with local reputations for excellence. This also allowed us to compare what teachers said they did with what we actually observed in their classrooms.

Overall, there is good news and bad as we examine the effect of high-stakes tests, the kinds of writing students do, the instruction they receive, and the professional context in which writing instruction is embedded.

The Effect of High-Stakes Tests

By far the greatest differences between the higher poverty and lower poverty schools we studied stemmed from the importance that teachers and administrators placed on the high-stakes tests that students faced. In the higher poverty schools, fully 83% of teachers across subject areas reported state exams were important in shaping curriculum and instruction, compared with 64% of their colleagues in lower poverty schools. They were also less likely than their peers to feel that the majority of their students were proficient writers (38% compared with 58% in lower poverty schools).

These teacher beliefs in turn seemed to lead to an even greater emphasis on a wide variety of different approaches to test preparation. For example, fully 96% percent of teachers in higher poverty schools said they frequently had their students practice on tasks similar to those on the tests themselves, in comparison to 61% of their colleagues in lower poverty schools. Eighty percent of the teachers in higher poverty schools reported using old exams for classroom exercises, in comparison to 55% in lower poverty schools. Some 80% of teachers in higher poverty settings also incorporated scoring rubrics from the exams into their teaching, compared with 62% of the teachers in lower poverty schools.

In addition to instruction directly geared toward "test prep," 86% of teachers in higher poverty schools reported incorporating exam-related tasks into their broader curriculum, compared with 66% in the lower poverty schools. Clearly, high-stakes testing affects both groups of teachers in the writing they assign and the instruction they offer. However, it affects the teachers and their students in higher poverty schools even more dramatically.

The Writing Students Do

Teachers' concerns with high-stakes tests also had some impact on the kinds and amount of writing they assigned in higher poverty schools. In general, these teachers were more likely than their peers to attribute more importance to all types of activities and types of writing. They reported more emphasis on multiple-choice or short-answer assignments (reportedly used in 88% of classes during the past 5 days, versus 78% in lower poverty schools), as well as a page or two of writing (55% versus 51%) and writing of three or more pages (13% of classes versus 9%).

(Such teacher reports, of course, may be as much a reflection of what they feel they *should* do as they are a measure of what they are actually able to do given the constraints on their teaching.)

The Instruction Students Receive

Teachers' concern with student performance on high-stakes tests also carried over to their responses about instruction. When asked about their approaches to writing instruction in a specific class, a greater percent of teachers in higher poverty than lower poverty schools reported they taught specific strategies for planning, drafting, revising, and organizing written work (50% versus 41%), organized a workshop environment (25% versus 13%), and asked students to work together to plan, edit, or revise their work (52% versus 37%).

Teachers' responses in the higher poverty schools seem to reflect a heightened awareness of the kinds of instructional approaches that have been shown to be effective in the teaching of writing: process-oriented instruction in a collaborative environment involving frequent writing in a variety of formats, coupled with direct instruction in appropriate writing strategies.

However, a somewhat different picture emerged when we observed ongoing instruction during the five-state study of schools with reputations for excellence. Across all schools, students had pencil-on-paper 48% of the time, but this was dominated by note-taking or copying (26% of class time) and short-answer exercises of various sorts (20% of time). In the lessons we observed in the higher poverty schools, students were somewhat less likely to be engaged in either short-answer exercises (40% of observed lesson time versus 49% in lower poverty schools) or paragraph-length writing (4% versus 6%). Teachers in both groups were rarely engaged in strategy-oriented instruction (5% of time for both groups). Somewhat less time was spent with the teacher lecturing or leading a question-and-answer recitation in the higher poverty than in the lower poverty classes (40% versus 50%), and more time was spent on group or pair work (24% versus 16%). Overall, although there were some differences in writing instruction between teachers in the higher and lower poverty schools, those differences were small. More interesting is that, based on what they reported, both groups of teachers seemed to know what they should be doing (based on research cited earlier) to a greater extent than they were actually carrying out when we observed them.

There were also some differences between groups in the availability of technology to support instruction, though the gaps were not large. In the higher poverty schools, 78% of the teachers reported they had access to most of the technology they needed, compared with 85% in the lower poverty schools. Student access to technology to support their writing also seemed slightly more constrained in the higher poverty schools: Teacher reports indicated that, when they had the option of submitting their work either typed or handwritten, 50% of students in higher poverty schools submitted typed final drafts, compared with 56% in lower poverty schools.

The Professional Context for Writing

Reflecting their overall concern to improve writing achievement, teachers in the higher poverty schools were more likely to report that there had been a schoolwide initiative emphasizing writing across the curriculum within the past school year (35%) than were their peers in lower poverty schools (19%). Reflecting the national emphasis in high-stakes testing, they were even more likely to report a schoolwide initiative in reading across the curriculum (39% of higher poverty schools, 25% of lower poverty schools). Such initiatives usually involve in-service programs of one sort or another, and teachers in the higher poverty schools considered such programs particularly important. For example, 84% of English teachers in higher poverty schools considered in-service programs to be an important influence on their teaching, compared with 72% of their peers in lower poverty schools. This pattern was reflected across all four core subjects, even in math where writing in general received the least emphasis (39% considering in-service programs to be important in higher poverty schools versus 32% in lower poverty schools). A number of schools we observed had developed strong affiliations with local universities or professional programs such as the National Writing Project to provide this in-service professional development.

Thus we are faced with both the good news and the bad. Teachers across all subjects think writing is important, but not a lot of extended writing gets done in any of the subjects, and much of the writing that does occur involves exercises requiring low-level responses. Nor does much actual writing instruction occur in most classes. However, teachers of students in poverty are more likely to say they provide instruction in specific writing strategies, within a supportive process-oriented environment. They seem to recognize the qualities of effective writing instruction, even if they do not often carry them out. As we have discussed in previous chapters with regard to the general student population, the high-stakes tests may well carry a share of responsibility. High-stakes tests count for everyone, but especially so in the higher poverty schools. Teachers in these schools focus largely on "test prep," and this seems to limit the kind of writing instruction they do.

But even with these limitations, students in both higher and lower poverty schools in our five-state study of schools with reputations for excellence in writing instruction were scoring better on their high-stakes tests than their classmates in demographically similar schools.

PORTRAITS OF SUCCESS

Now, let us step into some classrooms in these higher poverty schools, to see examples of instruction going right. In each case we will focus on the professional environment for teachers, the cognitive level of the tasks students engaged in, the ways teachers helped students understand what these tasks required, and how teachers supported their students throughout these processes.

A Schoolwide Focus on Writing

John Adams Middle School, or JAMS as it is called (see also Chapter 3), is as a parent wrote on the school website, "incredibly multicultural, a great reflection of our world today" (http://www.adams.smmusd.org). Compared with schools with similar demographics, JAMS was one of the strongest performing schools on the California English Language Arts exam. Its mission statement emphasizes diversity, the maximizing of student potential and shared decision making with all stakeholders: "interested community members, parents, teachers, counselors and administrators." We chose John Adams for the study in the hope that we could identify features that contributed to its success.

At the conclusion of their visit to John Adams, the field researchers described its strengths:

> JAMS strength includes its diversity, its teachers, and its administration. The school also has a strong science magnet, a Spanish/English immersion program and a highly acclaimed music program. . . . It has a stable and dedicated teaching staff for reasons described by teachers as "the magic of John Adams, everyone is willing to help, we want to help the kids." Teachers work with students during lunchtime and at Saturday Scholars, when they focus on math and English language arts. Parent/school relations are excellent.

Administrative Support for Writing. Ms. Bridges, the principal at JAMS, was the driving force behind a schoolwide emphasis on writing in all subject areas. As a former English teacher with a strong background in writing and literacy, her conviction that writing had a critical role to play in all subjects was clear in faculty meetings, in her memos, and in the instructional innovations she supported. At her monthly professional development workshops, she expected each teacher to write in a reflective journal. She also responded personally to each one. In keeping with her schoolwide focus, all departments (including art and physical education) had been asked to integrate writing into their instructional activities. This included reflective writing, analytical writing, and discipline-specific writing tasks. Ms. Bridges also distributed articles about writing to her staff to discuss, and supported ongoing professional development and conference attendance. Teachers who attended conferences were expected to share new strategies and research with others in the school.

A sixth-grade science teacher described the principal's impact on her teaching: "I don't think I would have come to it [writing] on my own. She [Ms. Bridges] convinced me of the benefits. The way she put it, writing is an orchestra of the mind, and that has really stuck." This teacher went on to say, "It's safe to say that every staff meeting we've had, there has been something about writing."

Since teachers of each grade level had a common prep period, they were encouraged to work collaboratively on writing instruction. They also met monthly with an on-site writing coach who focused on particular kinds of instructional supports (e.g., modeling) and helped them see that the key elements of instruction were helpful in all disciplines, although the actual activities would differ across subjects and also from teacher to teacher. Students who were having difficulty could go to a resource teacher for extra help, based on the student's request or a teacher's recommendation.

Although John Adams had begun to integrate technology into its programs, the teachers and principal were dissatisfied with the resources available and were working to augment them. At the time of our visit, the school had two computer labs and two COWS (Computers on Wheels), computer carts with 30 laptops each that a teacher could use in the classroom. Ms. Bridges said she wanted to bring laptops into all classrooms; she felt they had the potential to transform writing instruction and content learning. Each class already had one laptop and an LCD projector, and the principal wanted them to also have a document reader. Rather than wait for resources to become available through the district, some departments had augmented their technology by winning grants. The math department, for example, received SmartBoards, ELMOs, and computers from an Education Through Technology grant, using the SmartBoards to engage students in solving, refining, and rethinking math problems. The science department received document readers and LCD projectors.

Let us look at what the administrators, teachers, and students said about writing in each of the core subjects in this successful higher poverty school.

Writing for Social Studies. Social studies teachers at John Adams focused primarily on three types of writing: historical narrative, summarization of content presented, and analytical essays developing an argument. They used quick writes to help stimulate thinking about the content, graphic organizers as a way to organize and relate the ideas students were learning, and Cornell notes to help students take cogent notes, from which they could craft summaries. The teachers met during a common prep time to develop assignments and common rubrics, to share what worked, and to plan new ways to integrate writing into their instruction. As the chair told us,

> Our principal requires that once a week, during prep period, we collaborate. We meet with our partner and decide on a writing assignment/prompt/project, let's say an analytical piece on Manifest Destiny. It's hard to coordinate after that, because one of us is always ahead of the other. We focus on good content and good writing. It's quality, not quantity. I also am an AVID teacher, so we've introduced Cornell notes. . . . Students take notes, then write a summary of their notes in 3–5 sentences. In the AVID program, we focus on note-taking, how to be a good student, how students can advocate for themselves, and good reading and writing strategies. They take notes in their various classes, take their notes to AVID, convert them to Cornell notes, and with texts or anything else they remember, add information, come up with questions, and highlight the information. Next day, they write a summary.

The AVID program referred to here is an academic elective, Advancement Via Individual Determination, focused on college readiness through an emphasis on strategies for effective learning across the disciplines (see http://www.avid.org).

When asked about his writing activities in social studies class, Ramon, a lower achieving eighth grader, said:

> Sometimes we write summaries. They give us a quote, like when we were working on Native Americans, and write about what the quote

says. We use RAP: read, analyze, predict. We also do reading [Cornell] notes. We read and then take notes, then we summarize on a piece of paper.

And Sonia, an ELL student, said,

My teacher told me that she's so proud . . . and says I'm doing really well. Each month we did current events, where we found about what's new and explained what happened. We used mostly Obama's election and the debates. And the last paragraph we do is about how we can connect it to what we're doing in social studies class. For one, I compared it to the U.S. Presidents. For the last essay we did, we had to choose different groups to show challenges in Westward Expansion. It helped me a lot, because I learned a lot about the expansion and helped me explain it.

Writing for Mathematics. Mathematics teachers at John Adams had their students use writing as a way to explain their thought processes as well as the steps they used in solving math problems. As a department, the math teachers agreed to use writing as a way to help the students understand underlying concepts, not merely procedures. They also had the students compare and contrast concepts. Overall, students were expected to arrive at an answer and then explain how they got there. The open-endedness of this kind of writing activity helped students understand that there is more than one way to solve a math problem.

The math teachers used writing as a way to help students access and think about the concepts being learned. To foster this, a teacher would sometimes paraphrase a student response or ask students to paraphrase each other's responses. This process of restatement and rethinking was continued in reflection journals that all students kept. For the journal, students might be prompted to consider, "How might you do this problem differently if you had to do it again, perhaps to make it easier?" The math department was working with the UCLA Math Project and Center X faculty about teaching math concepts instead of focusing primarily on the algorithms (see http://centerx.gseis.ucla.edu/math-project). The collaboration helped them focus on project-based writing and long-term writing assignments to make math relevant to students' daily lives and to become aware of how larger math concepts connect.

The math chair described the role of writing in mathematics instruction:

I feel it's very important to explain in words what they are thinking. . . . They write reflections on every homework assignment, a reflection on if they did well, and how they might improve it—to turn math into words and vice versa. The principal . . . really believes that if the students can write what they are thinking, they can do it in every subject. . . . Not only do they have to show their math content, they also have to explain in words what they did. She feels the technology . . . allows the students to write more and to interact more about the math concepts.

The math chair also used math department meetings to develop a sense of good student writing and how to support it. She explained,

Teachers also bring student work to department meetings. They discuss what the student writing showed as to content (using the department rubric), discuss whether it was a good question/prompt to ask and whether it covered what the teacher(s) wanted the students to know.

In general, such discussions focused on teachers jointly improving the wording of their prompts in terms of the content they wanted their students to focus on, the connections they wanted them to make, and the level of complexity they wanted them to grapple with.

Writing for Science. Writing was also central to science instruction at John Adams. One of the eighth-grade science teachers described the ways in which the schedule was arranged to allow ongoing professional development to support this work:

On Fridays the students have a late start, 9:15. Teachers have some type of meeting between 8 and 9:15 when the assistant principal or someone from the district will lead a workshop on something dealing with writing and reading. I got the idea for my science brochure from one of these workshops, as well as ideas for other types of research for my students to do. Also, our principal finds ways to support science and writing, and block scheduling gives me opportunity for more writing.

Science teachers at John Adams used writing in a variety of ways to help students extend their understandings of science concepts. Students were expected to be able to describe their procedures and analyses clearly and to explain their findings in relation to the concepts they were studying. The teachers also used narrative writing and role play to connect scientific concepts to events and conditions in students' lives and the world. Mr. Boyd, for example, asked his students to act as weather forecasters and to predict weather problems, while an eighth-grade teacher had students use WebMD (see http://www.webmd.com) to diagnose Patient X when presented with the patient's symptoms. Like the social studies department, science teachers collaborated in creating grade-level rubrics and assignments.

Another science teacher, Ms. Jones, had her students write up experiments in such a way that elementary grade students could understand them. She explained the project to our visiting team:

> My environmental project took four weeks. . . . The project involves teaching the content to an elementary class. My students considered "What If?" questions, then tested out their experiment and wrote it up so younger children could understand. Three or four students collaborate, write a first draft, then they will present to children in grades K–5.

A sixth-grade science teacher, Ms. Sosa, explained the role of writing in her classes:

> Whenever they complete lab activities, there is usually a culminating writing activity, for example, "Imagine you are going to the center of the earth. Describe how you got there, what you would find, and what might be some problems in getting there." . . . Sometimes it's technical, like "Tell me how this works." . . . Eventually, I'd like to give them writing samples.

Ramon, the eighth-grade lower achieving student quoted in the social studies/history section, also reflected on the work he was asked to do for science:

> In science we do projects, sometimes poster boards like on the environment. Not too long ago, we did a project on drugs. We did a project on what it's like on the moon. She also gives us a PowerPoint and we'll have to write the most important details.

Writing for English. English teachers at John Adams engaged their students in a wide range of genres, including short stories, biography, nonfiction, essays, and poetry. They also focused on particular tasks, such as character analysis and narrative which, along with essay writing, were often included in the district writing assessment. English teachers used writing as a way to help their students engage more deeply in the nuances of language and style underlying the range of genres their students addressed, taking a workshop approach designed to support writing and revision over time. Sixth-grade English was taught as part of a humanities program, which allowed teachers to integrate various writing genres and literature into social studies.

A sixth-grade English teacher, Mr. Montana, provided a good overview of the general philosophy and approach to writing within the English department:

> Writing is thinking on paper. It demonstrates an ability to think clearly and express thoughts clearly. We focus on essay writing the first half of the year, especially literature analysis. Students read, think critically, respond to a [thought-provoking] prompt, organize thoughts in a logical way—a clear and even eloquent way. Now, we're doing a creative unit, a short story. This exercises the creative part of the brain. First students need to understand the story structure, then create their own. . . .
>
> Students do more than one draft for most of the major assignments. All peer edit first, then the teacher looks and makes notes, and sometimes has writers' conferences. I do a lot of modeling, too. Our principal is also a great proponent of this. . . . I start with a grammar warm-up every day. Sometimes we do isolated grammar activities. We plan lessons with other teachers and watch each other teach the lesson. . . . This year I use a laptop and LCD projector when I model writing. It works out well. I'm toying with starting a blog with response to literature.

Mr. Montana went on to comment about the school as a whole:

> The school definitely values writing. Our principal is a huge advocate of writing. She's the one who pushed for writing across the curriculum, involving teachers in all disciplines, including phys ed and music. Eighth-grade ELA includes a writer's and reader's workshop; they read some material, then write. . . . ELLs and special education students will have a resource class too. The resource teacher will support what I am doing [in ELA].

As to his writing in English language arts class, Ramon said, "We do themes, predicting the text, what do you think about the book and why—but mostly themes. Basically we are doing lots of different types of writing."

Summing Up. Across the various subjects and grades, we can see a consistent schoolwide pattern of an array of purposes for writing that

students experienced from class to class each day and throughout their
3 years at JAMS. Clearly, writing was highly valued. Ms. Bridges shaped
her school as a writing community, where everyone wrote to learn,
including the teachers. In turn, the administrators and teachers viewed
writing as a way to enhance subject-area learning, and this value was
echoed across the subjects and grades. The field researchers, in summarizing their visit to the school, wrote, "It was clear throughout this middle school the emphasis was not on test prep, getting the right answer,
or low-level skills. . . . There really is impressive thinking and action
across the disciplines at JAMS." Moreover, students appeared actively
engaged in the ideas being discussed; they participated, conversed, and
collaborated.

Writing in Action

Let's look now at the student work that is produced in higher poverty
schools where writing has a firm place in each of the academic disciplines. Here we will turn to King Drew Medical Magnet High School. As
you will see from the examples below, students were helped to explore
new learning and refine their understandings as well as to "show what
they know" in their writing. The examples illustrate the range of uses of
writing, from structured note-taking through an elaborated and carefully
scaffolded writing process.

Writing for Note-Taking and Summarization. Let us look at Ms. Garr's Advanced Placement Environmental Science class. During a unit on global
warming, she asked her students to take Cornell notes while viewing a
related film. Figure 9.1 displays a segment of the notes taken by Roberto
(Grade 12, higher achieving) in response to the film.

In the right-hand column, Roberto has written what he judged to be
key ideas in the film. He was clearly an ELL student, who wrote some of
the ideas in Spanish. Likely this was a quicker way to record his thoughts
with his intended meaning, available to translate into English when he
had time. We also see that these are notes for himself. Roberto did not
write in full sentences (as the assignment requests but difficult in response
to a film) because it would have slowed down his thinking. However, he
got a lot of the ideas on paper, for future use. In the left-hand column,
he also included drawings, perhaps to help him connect concepts that he
thought were important to understand and remember.

Afterward, the students were asked to answer seven questions, based
on their viewing of the film and the notes that they had taken. Roberto's
response, transcribed in Figure 9.2, shows that he had already acquired

FIGURE 9.1. Roberto's Notes on a Global Warming Film

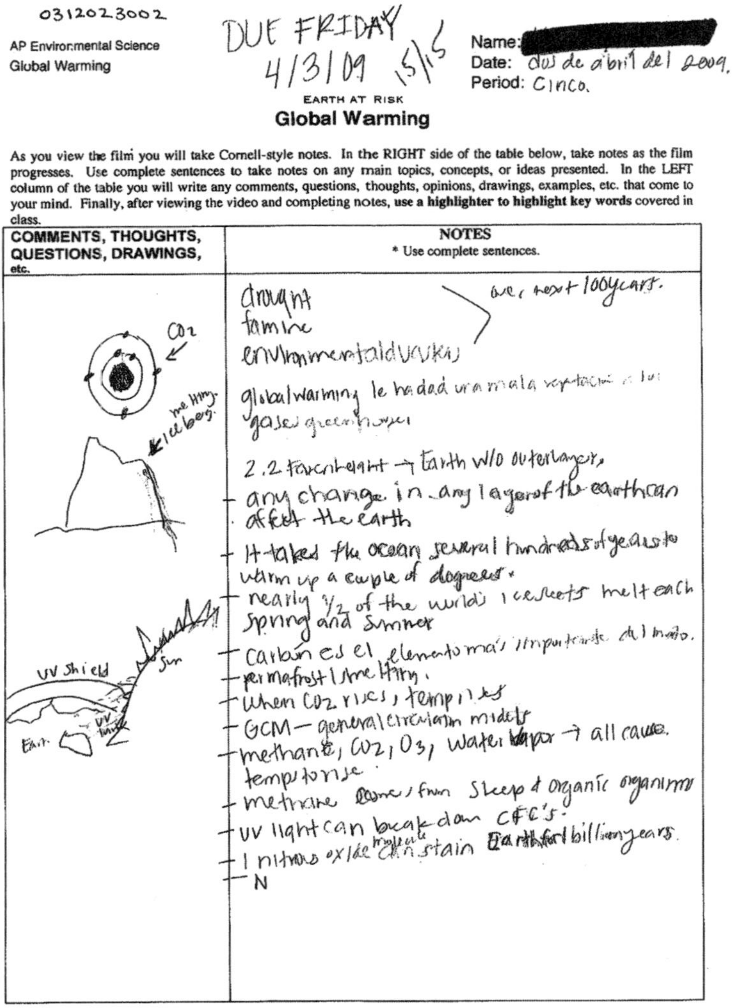

an appropriate technical vocabulary, and also demonstrates an understanding of the scientific concepts and related content discussed in the film. Because he had more time to complete this activity, we see it is completely in English.

Writing to Make Connections. A few weeks later, the students in Ms. Garr's class were asked, based on their readings, videos, class discussions, and

FIGURE 9.2. Roberto's Global Warming Short Constructed Responses

After viewing the film, answer the following questions.

1. Describe the cycling of carbon through the environment (refer to biogeochemical cycles):

   Carbon comes from plants. It exits the plants through photosynthesis. The plants are eaten by animals. When the animals die, the carbon goes back into the soil and air.

2. The absorption of CO_2 in the ocean is an important component in cycling of carbon in the environment.

   a. Discuss some conditions that could limit the absorption of CO_2 in the ocean:

   If oceans heat up, then the amount of CO_2 absorbed will be a lot lower; instead, the CO_2 will be released into the atmosphere.

   b. Discuss the impact of limited oceanic CO_2 absorption to the environment:

   Removes approximately ½ of the CO_2 currently in the atmosphere; will kill animals.

3. Describe two strategies that address each of the following:

   a. Decreasing atmospheric carbon production.

   Stop buying cars   release CO_2
   Stop burning fossil fuels   releases large amounts of CO_2

   b. Increasing carbon absorption.

   Increase already exists in forests.
   Highly developed countries should help lesser developed countries.

4. Computer modeling often generates varying, and sometimes conflicting, outcomes for future global warming trends.

   a. Explain why such varying predictions exist.
   The world is too large & there are different scenarios. Scenarios where CO_2 rises show that the world will get hotter while the scenarios where the models do not have CO_2 changing levels. Show no change in global warming.

   b. Discuss why we then continue to use computer modeling.

   You can't get an answer like it from anywhere else. Everything is represented by it and it simulates the real world closer than any other representation can simulate it. Tells us what we will be like in the future.

7. Explain why international laws are needed to address global warming, and yet why it is difficult to get universal agreement and adherence:

   Laws will regulate how many greenhouses gases are emitted into the atmosphere. It is difficult to get universal agreement and adherence because not all countries agree on the existence of global warming and some cannot afford to regulate it.

a recently completed lab experiment, to answer a set of questions about water pollution and water treatment. Figure 9.3 transcribes Roberto's responses to five of the nine questions. Instead of the usual lab report, some of the questions required students to explain in greater depth what happened—what worked or did not work in various stages of the experiment. Other questions asked them to relate what they learned in the experiment to concepts that they had been developing across the entire unit of study preceding the experiment.

In these examples, we see the teacher using writing to support understanding of content, while at the same time requiring the students to express themselves in scientifically appropriate ways.

Scaffolding an Extended-Writing Process. Mr. Moore, a 12th-grade English teacher at King Drew, combined writing with reading to support his students' developing interpretations of difficult works of literature. During their study of Shakespeare, for example, Mr. Moore led his students individually and in groups through an extended exploration of two plays, *Macbeth* and *Hamlet*. Mr. Moore used a variety of instructional techniques to help students approach the plays, including literature circles with assigned roles (e.g., summarizer, discussion director, connector; see Daniels, 1994). These roles provided a structure to small-group discussion of each of the plays, with the groups feeding their questions and interpretations in turn back to the class as a whole.

As students completed their readings and moved toward the major writing—a character analysis with references in MLA format—they were introduced to professional literary criticism drawn from an online database. Mr. Moore gave students selected essays relevant to the issues they intended to explore in their own writing, calling particular attention both to the interpretations that were being offered and to the ways the essays were structured.

From early in the process, Mr. Moore provided his students with an Analytical Response to Literature Rubric with three dimensions: Thesis and Content (e.g., uses a unique and convincing thesis; provides accurate and insightful analysis); Organization, Structure, and Style (e.g., crafts an inviting introduction and satisfying conclusion; uses vivid and precise language to create satisfying tone and structure); and Conventions and Syntax (e.g., uses an abundance of varied sentence types and grammatical structures).

Selections from the work of Paris, a lower achieving 12th-grade student, will illustrate his developing understanding of the plays. During the initial reading, Paris was given a variety of roles in their literature circles—roles that helped him focus on the significance of specific details

FIGURE 9.3. Roberto's Water Pollution and Waste Water Treatment Questions

1. Our polluted water had only organic compounds while real polluted water tends to have both organic and inorganic compounds. The solids in our polluted water came from fruit and vegetables only, while real polluted water may contain both fruits and vegetables, but also other material such as dead animals, human waste, or other compounds. . . .

3. Having the water go through the carbon filter reduced the odor of the garlic. When the water was poured through the carbon filter the odor particles may have been mixed with the carbon odor and caused the water sample to smell more like carbon instead of garlic. Adding chlorine to the sample, however fully removed the odor. Adding the chlorine made the water smell like chlorine, fully removed the smell of garlic. . . .

6. The sand filter was a lot like primary treatment because it removed the large suspended particles by filtering the water, but hazardous materials still remained. The carbon filter was like secondary treatment because it took away bacteria and some particles were removed. Adding the chlorine served as [illegible] *treatment because it removed the remaining pollutants with a chemical. . . .*

8. You can use the rich organic solids that remained in the jug after removing the liquid for composting and create rich soil out of them. If we feed it to the worm then when they pump it out, it will be rich soil for plants and the plants will grow better.

9. Wetlands have plants that have their roots wet at all times and this allows them to purify water. Also, their soils are deficient in oxygen/meaning that they allow there to be slow decomposition of dead plant material. Wetlands slow down runoff because of the roots of the plants. They help to get rid of pathogens and reduce contamination. Water is purified through the hydrology of the plants. Also, this removes 20–60% of metals in the water and traps and retain 80–90% of sediment from runoff.

---

of the text. While reading *Macbeth,* for example, in the role of connector, Paris completed a role sheet with a column for what he found in the text, and a second column to explain the connections he was making. After highlighting Banquo's comments to Macbeth about the fulfillment of the witches' prophecy, Paris made a connection to a contemporary sports story:

Here Banquo basically calls MacBeth out on his decietful deeds committed to be king and put truth behind the phrophecy this is similar to the character Jason . . . who has what seems to be the perfect marriage, family, and career. for he just won a NFL championship ring. But he knows it all a façade because his marriage is flawed because he took steroids and cheated in the game (similar to professional athletes).

A second entry from the same literature circle activity again quotes Banquo, "It will be rain tonight," and connects this time to another of Shakespeare's plays:

This is suggesting the motif/symbol of weather and "rain" brings a bad mood like the beginning of Julius Ceasar when the conspiracy meets in a storm which ultimately foreshadows Julius Ceasar's death.

For his character analysis essay, Paris focused on whether or not Hamlet was psychologically sound. He used this to focus his reading of the critical essays on *Hamlet* drawn from the Internet. His copies of the three essays that the teacher had provided were heavily marked up, with highlighter, circles, underlines, and marginal comments focusing on Hamlet's character and motivations. After circling "reason and emotion" and "man as victim of fate versus man as the controller of his destiny" in one essay, for example, Paris added the comment, "focus." On another essay, he bracketed seven short paragraphs refuting the notion that Hamlet's fate was determined by external events, adding the comment, "Supporting the theory."

Mr. Moore led his students through a careful sequence of steps in the actual writing of the paper, with feedback and suggestions after each step. Figure 9.4 presents Paris's prewrite, with an initial thesis ("Hamlet is the price of self-pity; he loves to dwell on emotions and the past") and Figure 9.5 shows his notes on how he will support this character analysis, and a set of quotes drawn from the scholarly essays.

After completing their general outlines and possible quotations, the students had a formal "conference and sharing" session with a partner that generated the marginal annotations on Figures 9.4 and 9.5, including the advice to find more examples and more support. With that advice in hand, Paris produced a new and more detailed outline, with a thesis that had evolved into "Indeed Hamlet is psychologically incoherent because. . . ." When he reviewed this outline, Mr. Moore cautioned Paris, "Don't forget to add quotes from scholarly journal #2 and #3—3 each," as well as adding some comments about which parts of the outline should become the body paragraphs and topic sentences of the paper itself.

After these preparatory activities, students began their first drafts in class and typed them up at home. During this transition Paris's "psychologically incoherent" became part of his topic sentence and the draft gained a new title, "Victim of Insanities." The paper went through two additional drafts, each shared in a formal "conference and sharing" with a classmate. Peer feedback ranged from suggestions for how to include additional evidence to correcting substantive errors (e.g., Claudius was

FIGURE 9.4. Paris's Prewrite for Hamlet Essay

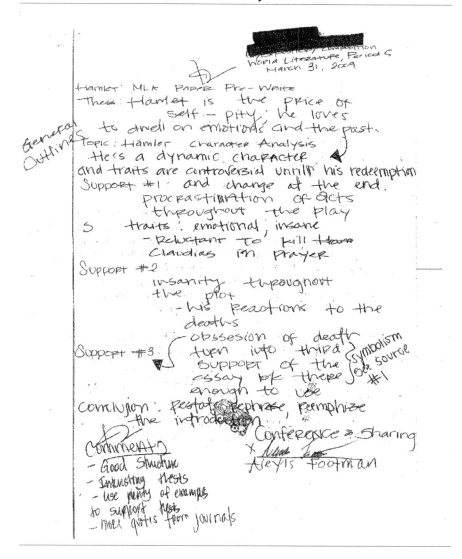

Hamlet's uncle, not his brother) and minor errors in spelling or syntax.

The opening paragraph of the final four-page essay, with Mr. Moore's questions and edits, is reproduced in Figure 9.6. His final comment on the paper was, "Overall I really enjoyed your paper—your product is evidence of your effort." He gave Paris 39 out of a possible 55 points for the project.

FIGURE 9.5. Paris's Quotes from Research for Hamlet Essay

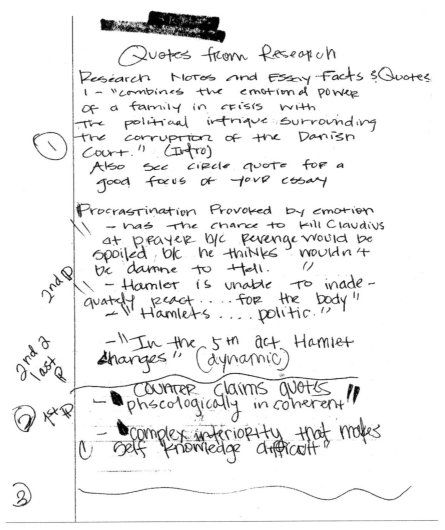

The unit as a whole included deep reading and discussion in which students learned to develop and defend their interpretations of the two plays, after which they read three academic and well-argued critiques relevant to their readings. With Mr. Moore's guidance, their study of literary criticism not only gave the students deeper insights into the plays, but also familiarized them with the genre of academic criticism itself as a

FIGURE 9.6. Paris's Hamlet Essay, Page One

World Literature
3 April, 2009

Victim of Insanities

"Psychologically incoherent" is a common description of the protagonist of

Shakespeare's 1603 play *Hamlet*. The tragedy of Hamlet captures a character who

struggles with rational thoughts and feelings, or as Shakespearean critic Lynn M. Zott

puts it, "conflicts between reason and emotion and between man as a victim of fate versus

man as the controller of his destiny." Zott contends that Hamlet, a nephew to Claudius

who is also his father's murderer, is in constant toil with his emotions, judgment, and

resulting actions, or perhaps, delayed actions. Moreover, there are also counter claims

that are strong enough to bring debate to the matter of Hamlet's state of mind, but the

argument that Hamlet is definitely frenzied is evidently more convincing. For this reason,

Hamlet's insanity makes for a satisfyingly controversial critical discussion. Initiating

such incoherence, Hamlet reacts to his father's (King Hamlet, or known as 'The Ghost of

Hamlet's father) homicide in a ludicrous and unusual manner that leaves the reader

questioning his sanity. Hamlet's unstable mind results in a series of delayed actions that,

over the course of the play, confirm his insanity. Hence, Shakespeare's tragedy of Hamlet

is a mere story of a man who proves indeed that he is "psychologically incoherent." (Zott,

2003)

The tragedy begins with Hamlet's extreme sorrow over his father's murder, only

to be confronted by a ghost resembling that of his deceased father, King Hamlet. The

ghost assures Prince Hamlet that Claudius, his brother is guilty for the murder of King

Hamlet. Hamlet presents false insanity because his mother fails to mourn from King

Hamlet's death, and within a month she marries King Hamlet's brother, Claudius. Prince

model for their own writing. The students also were expected to reflect on and evaluate their own and their classmates' work. As in the writing in Ms. Garr's environmental science class discussed earlier, Mr. Moore's students were learning to write about English content in conceptually more complex and literate ways.

STUDENTS IN POVERTY AND THE COMMON CORE STANDARDS

The documents associated with the Common Core provide some discussion of how the standards relate to English language learners and to students with disabilities. They are silent, however, about the long-standing problem of educating students who come from families living in poverty. Instead, the standards make it clear that the goals for college and career readiness apply to all students, with schools and teachers left to develop the curriculum and instruction necessary to achieve those goals:

> The Standards set grade-specific standards but do not define the intervention methods or materials necessary to support students who are well below or well above grade-level expectations. No set of grade-specific standards can fully reflect the great variety in abilities, needs, learning rates, and achievement levels of students in any given classroom. However, the Standards do provide clear signposts along the way to the goal of college and career readiness for all students. (CCSSO & NGA, 2010, p. 6)

The Common Core can be seen as offering a vision of regular and rigorous writing within subject areas. It also can be interpreted narrowly, leading, as we have seen with other standards and assessments, to narrow and formulaic approaches to curriculum and instruction. Such approaches result from a too-narrow interpretation of the goals and intent of the standards as well as a too-narrow understanding of disciplinary thinking and literacy. Although the goals of the Common Core are set high, the examples discussed in this chapter show schools and classrooms that are well on their way to achieving them, while also focusing on learning to write and writing to learn within the academic disciplines. It is important that teachers and administrators in high-poverty schools do not lose sight of the high-level goals of the Common Core and of these examples of aiming high and getting there.

THE BOTTOM LINE

We must remember that both John Adams Middle School and King Drew Medical Magnet High School were higher poverty schools, with 44% and 60% of their students eligible for free or reduced-price lunch, and had very diverse student populations. Although they differed in school organization and approaches to writing, the teachers in both schools were highly professional, highly motivated, had high expectations, and assumed their students could succeed—which, in fact, they did. John Adams and King Drew students, on average, did better on their state tests than their peers in similar schools.

As a whole, the success of John Adams Middle School was influenced by the principal's philosophy that strong teaching in minds-on classrooms will prepare students to do well, not only on assessments, but at school and beyond. This included a focus on multiple approaches to skills and concept instruction, the teaching of enabling strategies, reasoning beyond the given, and an emphasis on activities requiring collaborative problem solving. The principal also believed that writing with and about the content, in all courses, is an essential ingredient for success. Clearly, the teachers agreed; they used writing in engaging ways that invited students to think deeply about what they were learning and to develop literacy appropriate to each discipline.

At King Drew, all the professionals, including the principal and administrative staff, had similarly high expectations for their students. Because it was affiliated with the King Drew Medical Center next door, an atmosphere of professionalism and courtesy permeated the academic program, and the students (who wore uniforms) were part of this environment. Both schools, in their own ways, had created strong, supportive, and successful learning environments that had integrated writing into their everyday instructional plans because it assisted their students in thinking about and learning the course material. Teachers and administrators recognized writing as an instructional tool for content learning and used it regularly.

Looking across all of the classrooms we studied, we find a number of practices that contribute to successful teaching of writing across subject areas in higher poverty schools:

Curriculum and Instruction

- Explicitly teach the discipline-based strategies for generating ideas, drafting, revising, and editing that students will need in order to be successful in each subject area.
- Teach students strategies that will help them develop deeper understandings (e.g., Cornell notes, "What if" questions, RAP [read, analyze, predict]).
- Across the year, ensure that students will be engaged in a wide variety of writing tasks for varied audiences and purposes, including systematic attention to the argument, informative/expository, and narrative tasks of the Common Core.

- Develop minds-on writing activities around big ideas in the curriculum.

Assessment

- Provide students with rubrics that clarify the differing expectations for their writing within each of the academic disciplines.

Schoolwide Initiatives

- Make writing a schoolwide priority in curriculum and instruction, with a consistent emphasis across the core academic subjects.
- Provide time for shared planning meetings and participation in professional learning communities committed to continual improvement of writing instruction. These may be school- or department-based or rely on external networks such as the National Writing Project, individual subject-area associations, or school-university collaboratives.

FUTURE DIRECTIONS

Unfortunately, in most higher poverty schools we studied the focus was more often on the material the students must learn to pass high-stakes tests then on the activities that would help them better understand the disciplinary content and develop disciplinary literacy. Teaching to the test turns out to be shortsighted, because as we have seen in past studies (Langer, 2004), when instruction is geared to the tests and the test focus changes, traditionally low-performing students fare poorly. Test-driven instruction focuses attention on specific content rather than on ways such content relates to larger concepts within the discipline. Appropriate writing tasks can help students develop a growing network of interconnected ideas and concepts that provides them with the disciplinary understandings necessary to deal with new content and solve new problems.

We have evidence from this study and others (Applebee et al., 2003; Langer, 2001) that schools in poverty can outperform others with similar demographics, when teachers have high academic expectations, when they believe their students can succeed at school, and when instruction engages students in writing activities that are related to the central issues and problems of the discipline. John Adams and King Drew can serve as models of what is possible if, in fact, such conceptual understanding, disciplinary literacy, and preparedness for college and career are the goals.

Reflect and Discuss

1. Look back at the section on Portraits of Success. In these examples,
    students are identifying and practicing strategies for writing to learn
    and learning to write, which they can use across many writing con-
    texts.
    a. With colleagues, identify your students' writing needs and de-
        velop a chart to use as a reminder about particular writing strat-
        egies that you can teach to address those needs.
    b. Develop writing activities that provide opportunities to teach
        these strategies and to monitor growth.
2. What are some of the big ideas or major concepts you want students
    to learn from their lessons this year? Invite colleagues in each sub-
    ject area to choose one big idea and plan specific writing activities
    around it.
    a. Develop a range of problem-solving, hands-on, and inquiry-
        based activities that invite frequent writing about these big ideas
        throughout the year.
    b. Use writing to help students explore what they know, make
        connections, consolidate new understandings, and reformulate
        what they know about the subject area and life.
3. With your colleagues, develop rubrics for students and teachers to
    use in discussing and evaluating writing.
    a. Include separate sections for Content, Organization, Language,
        and Conventions.
    b. Collect a set of writing samples for students to analyze that
        highlight the features of more and less successful writing of
        various types required in different subject areas, including the
        argument, informative/explanatory, and narrative writing of the
        Common Core.

CHAPTER 10

◇◇◇◇◇◇◇◇

Reclaiming Writing in the Academic Disciplines

If we take a broad look at the role of writing and writing instruction in the core academic subjects in middle and high schools in the United States, the results are discouraging. Though students spend a great deal of time on written assignments, around 80% of the work they do requires very little composing. Instead, they are being asked to copy notes, fill in short answers, or complete multiple-choice questions focusing on what they have learned. Only occasionally are students engaged in activities that harness the power of writing as a tool for learning, engaging students in the exploration of new concepts and developing interpretations through the process of writing itself. Equally rare is the focus on writing within a particular discipline, with an emphasis on the forms of argument and evidence, as well as the vocabulary and norms for presenting ideas, that are most appropriate for that discipline.

Although simple averages mask important variations in the appropriate length and frequency of different tasks in different disciplines, they highlight the problem: On average, teachers' reports in our national survey suggest that students are writing only a little over a page and a half for English in a typical week, and just over two more pages for their other core academic subjects combined (science, social studies/history, and math). Although the length of thoughtful writing differs from discipline to discipline, by teachers' own reports as many as 9% of middle and high school students may be doing almost no writing at all, even for English (Applebee & Langer, 2006).

Yet the previous chapters also contain some good news about the uses to which writing is put as well as the kinds of writing instruction all students receive, including those in poverty and English language learners. Compared with teachers 30 years ago (Applebee, 1981), teachers today have a much better understanding of the value of writing as a tool for learning, and a much wider repertoire of research-based approaches to instruction (Graham & Perrin, 2007; Hillocks, 1986). Favored approaches to instruction vary somewhat by subject area, but include an emphasis on what are considered as appropriate ways of expressing ideas, as well as a focus on the content itself, in particular types of writing assignments. This instruction includes a clear specification of the parts required by the assignment, analysis and imitation of models of effective responses, and the use of rubrics that highlight the characteristics of good writing in each discipline. Process-oriented approaches to instruction are also popular, particularly in English and social studies, but in science and mathematics as well. These approaches include spending class time on generating and organizing ideas before writing, and teaching specific strategies for planning, drafting, revising, and organizing. Collaborative work does take place in some classes, and worked well when we saw it, but having students work together is less common than teacher-led activities.

The best news is that a great majority of teachers in English, social studies/history, science, and mathematics recognize that there are discipline-specific genres or types of writing, as well as discipline-specific vocabulary, that are important for success in their classes. And they accept that it is their responsibility to teach students these discipline-specific forms.

THE TEACHING OF WRITING FOR THE 21ST CENTURY

As we look across the previous chapters, five broad features of policy and practice stand out as making a difference in the teaching of writing:

1. The recognition that writing is an integral part of the disciplinary knowledge base in each of the core disciplines
2. The broad-based initiatives that encourage a department, the faculty within a school, or a subject-area team to work together to improve the teaching of writing within and across disciplines
3. The embrace of opportunities new technologies offer to broaden the tools available for students to write to learn and to learn to write within each discipline, as well as the venues and forms they can use to write regularly
4. The emphasis on extended writing of various types and lengths on examinations at classroom, school, district, and state levels
5. The uptake of opportunities offered by the Common Core State Standards (CCSSO & NGA, 2010) to enrich students' content learning through writing

Writing in the Disciplines

As we have discussed in earlier chapters, American schools have experienced several generations of reform movements emphasizing writing (and reading) across the curriculum. Championed by English teachers eager to broaden students' opportunities to write, such movements have inevitably failed as teachers of other subjects fretted about the amount of time and attention such writing was taking away from their own subject matter. Scholarship over the past 20 years, however, has clarified the extent to which each discipline has unique forms of argument and evidence that are at the heart of disciplinary knowledge. Such knowledge about how and what to write can only be taught by teachers who are specialists within each particular discipline. Whether it is learning to read and write like a historian or exploring scientific phenomena in lab notes, explorations, and explanations, these kinds of writing activities can and should be central to teaching and learning within each of the school subjects.

As we explored instruction in each of the core subject areas, we saw clear examples of writing activities that reflected two traditions: teaching writing as a way to learn the content, and teaching the forms and conventions of ways to write within the discipline. Thus many of the teachers we studied embraced writing as a powerful tool for supporting students' developing understandings of new concepts. This was evident in activities as diverse as tasks asking them to explain their problem-solving processes in math or science, or to write a stump speech from the perspective of a Senate candidate in Oklahoma during the Great Depression. What such tasks have in common is that they require students to reconfigure what they are learning, in the process of making their new ideas more explicit and weaving new connections within what they are learning.

At the same time, in each of the subject areas, we saw teachers introducing students to norms and practices that are unique to writing within the discipline. Again, these tasks ranged widely, from the development of a character analysis that draws appropriately on published literary criticism, to analysis and synthesis across multiple sources in history, to answering questions like "Why should we care?" that lead science students to relate their emerging findings in their laboratory notebooks to broader issues in science and the world. Although such activities are relatively rare in today's classrooms, they represent the leading edge of instruction for the 21st century.

Broadly Based Initiatives

Teachers from our studies of schools with reputations for excellence in the teaching of writing (see Appendix B) pointed again and again to particular initiatives that had contributed to the improvement of writing and writing instruction in their classrooms. Some of these were discipline-based initiatives, like the regional math and science collaboratives that were shaping instruction in Grisham Middle School (Chapter 6); some were cross-disciplinary such as the long-lasting impact of the National Writing Project cited by teachers in Amadon High School (Chapters 3, 6, 8), as well as many other schools we studied; some were schoolwide initiatives focused on writing in particular or literacy more generally, as in Amadon High School (Chapters 3, 6, 8), College View Middle School (Chapters 3, 5, 6), and Port Chester Middle School (Chapters 4, 8); some had a particularly supportive administrator who provided strong leadership as well as a supportive context for writing across the curriculum, as in John Adams Middle School (Chapters 3, 9); and some, such as in Bowling Green High School (Chapters 5, 8), provided teachers with the agency via schoolwide support to grow and share professionally.

More often than not, several of these features coexisted to create a strong professional environment for writing within the subject areas. What these initiatives shared was an emphasis on building teaching capacity by engaging teachers in long-term study and reflection, experiment, and resource development within a professional learning community that supported risk taking and change. These schools recognized that improvements in student achievement come from concerted effort within a larger community of practice, not from the single teacher, however extraordinary, working alone.

Embracing Technology

Our examination of the role of technology in the teaching of writing offers a mixed picture. On the one hand, students in many schools are very comfortable using computers for word processing; in fact many complain about the amount of writing that they still have to do by hand. Research into the use of computers for writing has quite consistently shown positive effects on student writing achievement (Bangert-Drowns, 1993; Graham & Perrin, 2007), particularly so for lower achieving students, so the widespread comfort students have is very positive. On the other hand, very few of the schools we studied had computers so widely available that students could use one whenever they were asked to write. More commonly, work was begun by hand in class and transferred to a computer later, either at home or in the library or computer lab. In some cases this pattern was also reinforced by the teachers' belief that too much work on the computer would put students at a disadvantage when they were faced with high-stakes assessments that had to be handwritten.

Instructional uses of technology also present a mixed picture. What seems to have happened is that as technology has become quite widely available in schools and classrooms, teachers have used it to reinforce their traditional patterns of teaching. The Internet as a resource for print-ed materials and video demonstrations, interactive whiteboards to dis-play PowerPoint presentations, ELMOs and document projectors to share samples of student work with the whole class—these are the kinds of uses of technology that currently prevail. Technology use is dominated by teachers rather than students, and functions primarily as a presentational medium supporting or illustrating teacher lecture.

Much less common even in our studies of schools with reputations for excellence in the teaching of writing are uses of technology that might transform rather than reinforce traditional approaches to instruction. In fact, we saw little evidence that teachers were taking advantage of the ways many students already use technology at home (e.g., uploading videos, participating in social networks, or becoming members of specific online communities). There was also little use of technology to support the kinds of collaboration and interaction that fosters developing interpretations and more complex understandings. Blogs and wikis, as well as more complex platforms such as Edmodo, Moodle, and BlackBoard, have the still largely untapped potential to engage students in intellectually challenging ways to think about and with the concepts they are studying as well as to engage in interactive knowledge building with their teachers and peers.

The only major effects of technology that we saw in student work were (1) the use of the Internet as a major source of material for writing, replacing to a large extent library work and encyclopedias, and (2) the emergence of PowerPoint as a major writing genre, though again as a medium of presentation rather than interaction.

The bright spots were surprisingly few, but when schools and teachers embrace technology and make it easily available, its effects can be trans-formative (e.g., see Burke, 2013). Clearly, however, the technology itself is not driving a reform of instruction: Until schools and teachers decide that collaboration and interaction are important elements of effective in-struction, the power of technology to support such ways of learning will be sharply limited. Also, until schools and teachers embrace technology as a medium that can engage students in an array of activities that serve new purposes, rather than solely as replacements for old ones (e.g., word processing and the search for source materials, the ways technology is currently being used), a breakthrough in the kinds of learning demanded in the 21st century will be slow in coming.

Writing as Part of the Examination System

When we began our series of studies, we thought we understood how powerful high-stakes examinations had become in shaping curriculum and instruction. We were wrong. The examination system in all of its variability and complexity is having an even larger impact than we had imagined. When writing had a role in assessments that mattered, writing found a place within the classroom (whatever the subject area). When writing had no place in assessing what students know and can do, it tended to be crowded out in favor of other instructional activities. As Hillocks (2002) noted, even exams that include writing can distort instruction, and we found such effects were widespread. Typical practice nationally focuses writing instruction on tasks that mirror assessment items, often emphasizing simple, formulaic approaches to responding to such tasks. In those rare cases when extended writing continued to be used, it often required students to present expected content rather than to develop and defend their own interpretations. Most state tests use multiple-choice and short-response formats, but do not require students either to write at some length about what they know in relation to a given topic or to use what they have learned to explore, analyze, or reach conclusions about new situations. When high-stakes tests do include writing, the long-vilified five-paragraph theme (Emig, 1971) is typically transcendent, though it is not a genre that is anchored in any discipline nor is it used in any forum for professional writing.

Encouragingly, however, when we turned to schools that provided a supportive environment for writing instruction, we found teachers who had a much better chance of developing a rich, supportive curriculum for writing. These teachers tended to co-opt the high-stakes tests for their own purposes, helping students to understand the rhetorical purposes and task demands inherent in the examination questions as part of a broader curriculum embedded within the discipline they were studying. Like the schools in Langer's (2001, 2004) previous studies of schools that "beat the odds," these schools kept the high-stakes tests in the background of their planning. They used them as a kind of checklist to be sure that necessary knowledge and skills were embedded in highly challenging curriculum and highly engaging instruction, without succumbing to the temptation to reduce their curriculum and instruction to a decontextualized emphasis on test preparation.

Because the current examination system is so complex, we also found that it impacted different schools and classrooms in different ways. In schools where many students were performing poorly, state and district exams were usually of paramount importance and tended to strongly shape curriculum and instruction. We were told that if it was not on the test it did not get taught. And in most states, that meant an emphasis on multiple-choice or short-answer activities even in English. In schools where students tended to be higher achieving, including those with high student diversity and high-poverty, programs like the Advanced Placement examinations and the International Baccalaureate tended to receive more emphasis, with a corresponding greater emphasis on writing and writing instruction in the core subject areas, including science and mathematics as well as English and social studies/history. Often, systems of tracking students by achievement level brought these forces into play within the same school, limiting the curriculum for students in lower tracked classes even as they enriched the writing experiences of higher achievers.

THE CHALLENGE AND OPPORTUNITY OF THE COMMON CORE

As we write, the nation's schools are facing a new set of challenges posed by the Common Core State Standards (CCSSO & NGA, 2010), as well as by the formative and summative evaluation and assessment systems being developed to accompany them. Developed in response to the uneven emphases and levels of difficulty in state standards in literacy and mathematics that had been developed over the past 2 decades, the Common Core gives a new prominence to the role of writing in English and other school subjects. Rejecting the primary focus on reading achievement enshrined in the No Child Left Behind legislation, the Common Core gives writing equal attention to reading across the grades. Both reading and writing are represented by ten "anchor standards" describing the expected accomplishments of college and career ready students by the end of high school. Equally important, there are separate reading and writing standards for literacy in history/social studies, science, and technical subjects. In this, the Common Core makes a clean break from earlier emphases on writing and reading across the curriculum, emphasizing instead the centrality of literacy within the disciplines themselves.

The Common Core has been accompanied by an unprecedented effort to redevelop the system of high-stakes examinations, supported by federal funding for the two state consortia, the Partnership for Assessment of Readiness for College and Careers (PARCC) and the Smarter Balanced Assessment Consortium. Both groups are committed to having new systems ready for implementation in the 2014–2015 academic year. Whether or not they make this ambitious deadline, our studies make clear that these new assessments, even more than the standards themselves, are likely to have a profound effect on curriculum and instruction in each of the subject areas. Both consortia plan to utilize a variety of items, ranging from multiple-choice (selected-response) items to extended-response items and performance tasks. The goal is to tap deeper understandings that will, at least some of the time, be expressed in writing. The consortia claim that their tasks will be engaging and thought-provoking, getting at students' understanding and application of concepts rather than simple memory of content, but our studies suggest that multiple-choice and short-response formats will lead to similar emphases in instruction.

The constraints on these assessments are similar to those on the state assessments they are meant to replace. The tasks that are being developed are tied to the standards, not to the curriculum. As such, any writing that is required will likely be based on material contained in the test situation itself, rather than drawing on subject-area knowledge developed over the course of a semester or year (as in portfolio-based assessments, for example, or the kinds of curriculum-based writing called for in some Advanced Placement classes and the International Baccalaureate program).

With stakes high, as they will be, our studies also highlight some of the other challenges that are likely to unfold. These challenges include the following:

1. Maintaining a rich and broad curriculum
2. Avoiding formulaic approaches to the teaching of writing
3. Teaching argument well
4. Embedding literacy in work appropriate to the discipline

Maintaining a Rich and Broad Curriculum

Schools and districts faced with high-stakes standards and assessments have tended to narrow curriculum and instruction to focus more specifically on what is being assessed. At one level, this is a natural response, and one that echoes the emphasis in systemic school reform (Smith & O'Day, 1991) on alignment among the various components of the educational system, including curriculum and assessment. The studies described in previous chapters also indicate that it has disastrous implications for student learning. No set of examinations is able to cover everything that is important for students to learn, but what is not covered by assessments tends not to be taught. Over the past decade, for example, writing (as well as other subjects) has been deemphasized in response to the focus on reading and mathematics in No Child Left Behind (Applebee

& Langer, 2009). In comments captured in particular in Chapter 2, teachers across subject areas described how they have modified their teaching of writing in response to the exams, leaving out research papers, for example, and personal or creative writing in favor of tasks that would be directly assessed. And as discussed in Chapters 8 and 9, this tendency is exacerbated in classrooms with high poverty and linguistic diversity.

The Common Core is very explicit that the standards do not describe a full and rich curriculum:

> While the Standards focus on what is most essential, they do not describe all that can or should be taught. A great deal is left to the discretion of teachers and curriculum developers. The aim of the Standards is to articulate the fundamentals, not to set out an exhaustive list or a set of restrictions that limits what can be taught beyond what is specified herein. . . . While the ELA and content area literacy components described herein are critical to college and career readiness, they do not define the whole of such readiness. Students require a wide-ranging, rigorous academic preparation. (CCSSO & NGA, 2010, p. 6)

This caveat aside, our studies suggest schools and teachers may have a great deal of difficulty keeping these broader goals in mind, particularly if their students are struggling. They need support in keeping their focus on offering the best curriculum and instruction in every subject, or once again students' opportunities to learn will be diminished.

Avoiding Formulaic Approaches to the Teaching of Writing

The impulse to limit the curriculum applies not only to topics to be covered, but also to the definitions of good writing implicit in curriculum and instruction. Our discussions about the teaching of writing in each of the core subject areas have highlighted the tendency to provide students with clear guidelines and simple routines for responding to writing tasks, even seemingly complex tasks like those posed by document-based questions in history and social studies. Such routines can easily strip writing tasks of their power to become cognitively engaging—to support disciplinary interpretation and understanding—turning them instead into lengthy fill-in-the-blank exercises where the content of every paragraph has been laid out in advance. Although we have presented examples of classrooms that avoided such oversimplification, in the present high-stakes environment such classrooms are still the exception rather than the rule.

Unfortunately, some aspects of the Common Core reinforce this tendency toward simplistic characterizations of effective writing. This occurs in particular when the anchor standards describing the accomplishments of college and career ready students are expanded into the extensive set of grade-by-grade standards, K–12. Here, the broad goals that give power to the anchor standards are in danger of being trivialized in an attempt to specify poorly conceptualized differences across the grades. This leads to an emphasis on formal characteristics of types of texts. For example, consider Writing Standard 1 for Grade 6:

> Write arguments to support claims with clear reasons and relevant evidence.
>
> a. Introduce claim(s) and organize the reasons and evidence clearly.
> b. Support claim(s) with clear reasons and relevant evidence, using credible sources and demonstrating an understanding of the topic or text.
> c. Use words, phrases, and clauses to clarify the relationships among claim(s) and reasons.
> d. Establish and maintain a formal style.
> e. Provide a concluding statement or section that follows from the argument presented. (CCSSO & NGA, 2010, p. 42)

The subheads in this description address a variety of features of language use, organization, and development—features that in an assessment context would usually be addressed through a writing rubric and examples of responses that reflect the score points in the rubric. The problem in the Common Core is that laying these features out in this way suggests a specific set of emphases for curriculum and instruction at each grade. And unfortunately, the emphases suggested tend toward the formulaic and perfunctory, rather than supporting the development of a flexible array of strategies for addressing a wide variety of audiences and specific purposes. In fact, Writing Standard 1 for Grade 6 looks very much like a specification for a five-paragraph theme, which as Emig (1971) noted, is not a form that exists outside of school.

The challenge for teachers, then, will be to provide students with a rich understanding of the rhetorical context implicit in such writing, and of strategies for addressing such tasks effectively without reducing them to a formula. We have presented good examples of such approaches in our discussions in this book, but such examples at present are far from the norm across the core academic subject areas.

Anchoring Argument in Disciplinary Ways of Knowing

The Common Core places a special emphasis on the building of effective arguments (Writing Standard 1), using a vocabulary of claims, reasons, and evidence that derives from Toulmin's *The Uses of Argument*

(1958). In this book, a seminal work in the more general literature on the philosophy of language, Toulmin attacks a conception of argument that idealizes mathematical reasoning and symbolic logic. Instead, he argues for an applied logic that is rooted in disciplinary differences, the history of science, and the social processes of the scientific community. Toulmin's work has often been taken as the justification for teaching a formalized and artificial argument structure based on the stating of claims and evidence, and the warrants and backing that bind them together. This, however, is actually a misreading of Toulmin.

In fact, Toulmin's analysis of the structure of argument was a tool for building his theoretical case within the philosophy of language. His analysis was not intended as a teaching tool, nor as a model for the development of new texts. In his other writings, Toulmin is quite explicit about the ways in which novices move from apprenticeship to mastery by being immersed in disciplinary tasks appropriate to a particular time and place in the evolution of a discipline. Like others who have studied writing in science, he recognizes the difference between the process of inquiry and the process of presenting the results of that inquiry. As he explains in *The Philosophy of Science* (1953),

> A scientist . . . gradually becomes accustomed to using the novel technical terms and the everyday-sounding phrases in the way required; but he may only be half-aware of what is happening— . . . the building of the language of the sciences is not entirely a conscious process (p. 13)

Rather than using a template of claims and evidence, Toulmin recognizes that arguments and explanations within a discipline are built up out of the context of ongoing scholarship, or conceptual learning. As he explains in *Foresight and Understanding* (1961),

> To this task of interpretation we bring principles of regularity, conceptions of natural order, paradigms, ideals, or what-you-will: intellectual patterns which define the range of things we can accept (in Copernicus' phrase) as "sufficiently absolute and pleasing to the mind." An explanation, to be acceptable, must demonstrate that the happenings under investigation are special cases, or complex combinations of our fundamental intelligible types. (p. 81)

Toulmin's point that the ability to participate effectively in scientific discourse develops through a process of enculturation supports other analyses of how argument is learned. Moje (2007), for example, in an extended review of research on disciplinary literacy, points out that studies of expert readers or writers have consistently found that they have "little conscious awareness of their ways of knowing." (Langer, 1992, reported similar findings in a study of high school and university teachers talking about writing in their disciplines.) Moje goes on to say that "it could be argued that such learning requires apprenticeship in the text practices of the disciplines, over time" (2007, p. 23). In their own studies of middle grade science, Moje, Ciechanowski, Ellis, Carrillo, and Collazo (2004) argue for a perspective that includes the knowledge and discourse competencies students bring with them, creating a "third space" at the intersection of disciplinary knowledge and student competencies. This third space becomes even more nuanced and important for students for whom English is but one of their language resources.

The processes of apprenticeship and immersion in disciplinary activity that both Moje and Toulmin describe reflect the models of good writing instruction discussed in this book. They are also compatible with the anchor standards for the Common Core. The danger is that the way Writing Standard 1 is elaborated at individual grade levels (as in the example for Grade 6 presented earlier in this chapter) foregrounds individual parts of the task (claims, reasons, evidence, counterclaims) at the expense of the larger context. Because these descriptions are not anchored in disciplinary ways of knowing, they can easily be translated into curriculum and test items that prompt formulaic approaches to argument that never get at the essential disciplinary experiences Toulmin (1961), Langer (2011a), and Moje et al. (2004) describe.

Embedding Literacy in Work Appropriate to the Discipline

The final challenge posed by the Common Core is one of relating the literacy standards to the larger curriculum in each subject area. The writing, reading, and oral language tasks implied by the standards are meant to be tasks that are embedded in work appropriate to the discipline. An effective curriculum for any of the school subjects will need to begin, as it has in the past, with subject matter that is central to the discipline or, put another way, with the disciplinary conversations (Applebee, 1996) in which members of the disciplinary community are engaged. The reading, writing, and language abilities reflected in the standards will need to be developed as students learn to engage appropriately in the disciplinary conversations that shape their classroom experiences. (We are taking "conversation" in the broad sense here, to include reading, writing, and discussion, including the voices of students, teachers, and others working in the discipline.)

We have already discussed some of the threats to such disciplinary conversations, in particular the impetus to transform the curriculum in any subject into a series of activities that mimic the examinations students will face rather than that teach them to work within the disciplinary norms of history (Wineberg, 2007) or science (Singer et al., 2006).

Although the detailed standards for subject-area literacy acknowledge the importance of disciplinary content and disciplinary norms (CCSSO & NGA, 2010, pp. 64–66), they suffer from the same trivialization at the grade-by-grade level as in the example above for Writing Standard 1 for Grade 6. Embedding such activities in history and science curricula runs a real risk of creating another era of generic writing across the curriculum: activities that reflect an abstract notion of what good writing entails, rather than activities that, in fact, do embody disciplinary norms of argument and evidence.

The issues here may be particularly salient for teachers of English. Because the standards are presented as standards for English language arts, they are easily misconstrued as a new set of standards for the curriculum as a whole—that is, a new definition of the subject matter of English. And though "What is English?" has a long history as an essential question about curriculum and instruction, the standards in their current form are not an answer to that question.

The standards document itself makes the point that "the ELA classroom must focus on literature (stories, drama, and poetry) as well as literary nonfiction" (CCSSO & NGA, 2010, p. 5), and literature has a long history as the central disciplinary content of English (Applebee, 1974). The Common Core goes on to elaborate a bit further on this point in a later section:

> Furthermore, while the Standards make references to some particular forms of content, including mythology, foundational U.S. documents, and Shakespeare, they do not—indeed, cannot—enumerate all or even most of the content that students should learn. The Standards must therefore be complemented by a well-developed, content-rich curriculum consistent with the expectations laid out in this document. (CCSSO & NGA, 2010, p. 6)

While we would not take any of these statements as encompassing a comprehensive or well-conceived definition of the disciplines of English (including language and composition as well as literature), they do make clear that the standards do not provide such a definition, and are not meant to.

Nonetheless, our studies of how schools and districts are responding to the current emphasis on high-stakes tests suggest that teachers of English will be under considerable pressure to redefine their curriculum in these terms—as a version of reading instruction with supporting writing, extended throughout the high school English language arts curriculum. Such a curriculum would not be a disciplinary curriculum at all, but a trivialization of the contributions that literature, composition, and language study can make to the development of the individual and to society at large (Applebee, 1974; Langer, 2011a, 2011b).

WRITING IN THE 21ST CENTURY

Overall, we have discussed many problems in the state of writing instruction in American schools. At the same time, we have presented examples of the kinds of thoughtful and engaged instruction that are found in the more successful schools and districts. We have seen a wide variety of writing activities used for a wide variety of appropriate purposes. In presenting our findings, we have focused primarily on uses of writing to learn subject-area content, and on uses of writing to learn to write in meaningful ways within each discipline.

In an environment of high-stakes testing, we also found examples of ways in which teachers have co-opted the demands of the assessments they face, providing rich writing instruction that goes well beyond the formulaic writing or short-answer response that the tests might require. A new generation of tests is in the process of being developed to accompany the Common Core. But as we have seen, when the stakes are high, as they will be with the Common Core, the pressures to limit the curriculum around formulaic approaches to typical assessment tasks may be difficult to avoid.

If rich writing tasks that support developing understandings and interpretations over extended periods of time become a central part of the assessment systems surrounding the Common Core, this will be a big step in moving us toward providing substantive college and career readiness for all students, while also preparing them for the cognitive and social demands of the 21st-century workplace—all through the uses of writing. These workplaces call not only for critical thinking abilities, but also for knowledge generation, production, and transformation. Mix these with students' independence to control their own learning and the ability to collaborate effectively, drawing on extended networks of colleagues and peers, and students will be well prepared for the work environments that have come to define the successful 21st-century workplace.

Elements of all of these accomplishments have run through our examples of successful writing instruction, even if at present such instruction seems to succeed in spite of, rather than because of, the emphasis on high-stakes tests. If the goals of instruction shift more toward success at complex tasks extending over time, during which students develop and enrich their understandings, uses of technology may also change from presentational techniques supporting traditional instruction toward tech-

nologies that engage students in discussion and dialogue, thereby supporting their collaborative knowledge development. As the Common Core and
other assessment systems shift from paper-and-pencil to computer-based
assessments, this may be a further impetus for teachers to begin using
forms of technology that support knowledge building activities as students
engage in writing to learn as well as to writing to share their understandings with others.

Our studies indicate that we are still a long way from seeing these as
typical goals or activities in most schools. But the time is right; nationwide, the goals have changed and the tests are changing as well. The call
for educators at all levels, in all contexts, in all disciplines is undeniable: It
is time for writing instruction that works.

The Project Team

Center on English Learning and Achievement, University at Albany

Arthur N. Applebee
Judith A. Langer
Kristen Campbell Wilcox
Marc Nachowitz
Michael P. Mastroianni
Christine Dawson
Linda Baker
Renee Banzhaf
Ae Lee Lee
Chin Ee Loh
David Manarel
Jason Vickers
Sharon Wiles

National Writing Project, University of California, Berkeley

Paul LeMahieu
Linda Friedrich
Carisa Lubeck

Eastern Kentucky Writing Project

Lee Ann Hager*
Sally Martin*

Western Kentucky Writing Project

John Hagaman*

Note. *Field researchers, Year 3. All affiliations are as of the time of participation in NSWI.

Oakland (MI) Writing Project

Laura Roop
Linda Denstaedt*

Red Cedar (MI) Writing Project

Janet Swenson
Toby Kahn-Loftus*

Capital District Writing Project (NY)

Robert Yagelski
Carol Forman-Pemberton
Molly Fanning*
Pat Lynch*
Dan McBride*
Brigid Schmidt*
Aaron Thiell*
Alicia Wein*

UCLA Writing Project

Faye Peitzman*
Carrie Usui*
Robyn Wisinski*

Central Texas Writing Project

Liz Campbell Stephens*
Cynthia Vetter*

Characteristics of Participating Schools (Year 3)

School name	State	Size	Grades	% Lunch-Program Eligible	% ELL	% African American	% His-panic	% White
Montebello	CA	1,664	5–8	83	28	<1	97	2
King Drew	CA	1,680	9–12	66	3	60	38	<1
Amadon*	CA	4,000	9–12	80	33	<1	99	<1
John Adams	CA	977	6–8	44	16	10	50	33
College View	KY	843	6–8	30	1	2	<1	94
Bowling Green	KY	1,111	7–12	45	10	22	8	65
Highland	KY	1,036	6–8	51	4	32	1	63
Oldham	KY	1,330	9–12	16	2	4	2	92
Grand Blanc	MI	2,528	9–12	16	1	13	<1	80
Abbott	MI	764	6–8	12	7	15	2	71
Evart High	MI	340	5–8	54	0	<1	4	93
Evart Middle	MI	367	9–12	46	0	2	2	94
New Paltz	NY	803	9–12	14	0	7	6	84
Albert Leonard	NY	1,195	6–8	25	1	29	22	45
Port Chester	NY	794	6–8	43	12	9	72	18
Batavia	NY	763	9–12	34	0	8	2	87
Moak*	TX	763	6–8	20	3	2.2	25	71

Note. *School name is a pseudonym

School name	State	Size	Grades	% Lunch-Program Eligible	% ELL	% African American	% His-panic	% White
Palladium*	TX	1,718	9–12	35	5	22	30	46
Sonata*	TX	2,648	9–12	24	5	11	27	57
Grisham	TX	657	6–8	19	4	7	18	59

◇◇◇◇◇◇◇

References

Abedi, J. (2004). The No Child Left Behind Act and English language learners: Assessment and accountability issues in the teaching of English. *Educational Researcher, 33*, 4–14.

Applebee, A. N. (1974). *Tradition and reform in the teaching of English: A history.* Urbana, IL: National Council of Teachers of English.

Applebee, A. N. (1981). *Writing in the secondary school: English and the content areas.* Urbana, IL: National Council of Teachers of English.

Applebee, A. N. (1986). Problems in process approaches: Toward a reconceptualization of process instruction. In A. R. Petrosky & D. Bartholomae (Eds.), *The teaching of writing* (pp. 95–113). Chicago, IL: National Society for the Study of Education.

Applebee, A. N. (1996). *Curriculum as conversation: Transforming traditions of teaching and learning.* Chicago, IL: University of Chicago Press.

Applebee, A. N., & Langer, J. A. (2006). *The state of writing instruction in America's schools: What existing data tell us.* Albany: Center on English Learning and Achievement, University at Albany, State University of New York.

Applebee, A. N., & Langer, J. A. (2009). What is happening in the teaching of writing? *English Journal, 98*(5), 18–28.

Applebee, A. N., & Langer, J. A. (2011a). *The national study of writing instruction: Methods and procedures.* Albany: Center on English Learning and Achievement, University at Albany, State University of New York. http://www.albany.edu/cela/reports.html

Applebee, A. N., & Langer, J. A. (2011b). A snapshot of writing instruction in middle schools and high schools. *English Journal, 100*(6), 14–27.

Applebee, A. N., Langer, J. A., Nystrand, M., & Gamoran, A. (2003). Discussion-based approaches to developing understanding: Classroom instruction and student performance in middle and high school English. *American Educational Research Journal, 40*(3), 685–730.

Atwell, N. (1998). *In the middle: New understandings about writing, reading and learning* (2nd ed.). Portsmouth, NH: Boynton/Cook.

Bangert-Drowns, R. L. (1993). The word processor as an instructional tool: A meta-analysis of word processing in writing instruction. *Review of Educational Research, 63*(1), 69–93.

Batalova, J., Fix, M., & Murray, J. (2005). *English language learner adolescents: Demographics and literacy achievements.* Washington, DC: Migration Policy Institute.

Batavia City Schools. (2008). *Small city/big technology: Embedding technology into learner-centered classrooms.* Batavia, NY.

Batavia City Schools. (2009). *Comprehensive district education plan, July 1, 2009–June 30, 2012.* Retrieved July 14, 2012, from http://www.bataviacsd.org/district.cfm

Batavia City Schools. (2012). *About our technology.* Retrieved from http://www.bataviacsd.org/district.cfm?subpage=1789

Bazerman, C. (1988). *Shaping written knowledge: The genre and activity of the experimental article in science.* Madison: University of Wisconsin Press.

Bazerman, C., & Paradis, J. (Eds.). (1991). *Textual dynamics of the professions: Historical and contemporary studies of writing in professional communities.* Madison: University of Wisconsin Press.

Biancarosa, G., & Snow, C. E. (2006). *Reading next: A vision for action and research in middle and high school literacy:* (2nd ed.). Washington, DC: Alliance for Excellent Education.

Black, R. W., & Steinkuehler, C. (2009). Literacy in virtual worlds. In L. Christenbury, R. Bomer, & P. Smagorinsky (Eds.), *Handbook of adolescent literacy research* (pp. 271–286). New York: Guilford Press.

Braddock, R., Lloyd-Jones, R., & Schoer, L. (1963). *Research in written composition.* Champaign, IL: National Council of Teachers of English.

Brenner, J. (2012). Pew Internet: Teens. *Pew Internet & American Life Project.* Retrieved from http://pewinternet.org/Commentary/2012/April/Pew-Internet-Teens.aspx

Britton, J.N. (1970) *Language and learning.* London: Penguin Press.

Britton, J., Burgess, T., Martin, N., McLeod, A., & Rosen, H. (1975). *The development of writing abilities* (pp. 11–18). London: Macmillan Education.

Brown, M. W. (1990). *The important book.* New York: Harper Collins. (Original work published 1949)

Burke, J. (2010). *What's the big idea? Question-driven units to motivate reading, writing, and thinking.* Portsmouth, NH: Heinemann.

Burke, J. (2013). *The English teacher's companion* (4th ed.) Portsmouth, NH: Heinemann.

Burton, L., & Morgan, C. (2000). Mathematicians writing. *Journal for Research in Mathematics Education, 31*(4), 429–453.

Bybee, R. W., Taylor, J. A., Gardner, A., Scotter, P. V., Powell, J. C., Westbrook, A., & Landes, N. (2006). *The BSCS 5E instructional model: Origins and effectiveness: A report prepared for the Office of Science Education, National Institutes of Health.* Colorado Springs, CO: BSCS.

Calkins, L. M. (1986). *The art of teaching writing.* Portsmouth, NH: Heinemann.

Callahan, R. M. (2005). Tracking and high school English learners: Limiting opportunity to learn. *American Educational Research Journal, 42*(2), 305–328.

Callahan, R. M., Wilkinson, L., & Muller, C. (2010). Academic achievement and course taking among language minority youth in U.S. schools: Effects of ESL placement. *Educational Evaluation and Policy Analysis, 32*(1), 84–117.

Common Core State Standards Initiative. (2012). *Application of Common Core State Standards for English language learners.* Retrieved from http://www.corestandards.org/assets/application-for-english-learners.pdf

Connolly, P. (1989). Writing and the ecology of learning. In P. Connolly & T. Vilardi (Eds.), *Writing to learn mathematics and science* (pp. 1–14). New York: Teachers College Press.

Connolly, P., & Vilardi, T. (Eds.). (1989). *Writing to learn mathematics and science.* New York: Teachers College Press.

Cope, B., & Kalantzis, M. (Eds.). (1993). *The powers of literacy: A genre approach to teaching writing.* Pittsburgh, PA: University of Pittsburgh Press.

Council of Chief State School Officers (CCSSO) & the National Governors Association (NGA). (2010). *Common core state standards for mathematics and for English language arts and for literacy in history/social studies, science, and technical subjects.* Washington, DC: National Governors Association. Available at http://www.corestandards.org/the-standards

Coxhead, A., & Byrd, P. (2007). Preparing writing teachers to teach the vocabulary and grammar of academic prose. *Journal of Second Language Writing, 16*(3), 129–147.

Cross, D. I. (2009). Creating optimal mathematics learning environments: Combining argumentation and writing to enhance achievement. *International Journal of Science and Mathematics Education, 7*(5), 905–930.

Daniels, H. (1994). *Literature circles: Voice and choice in the student-centered classroom.* Portland, ME: Stenhouse.

Darling-Hammond, L. (2010a). *The flat world and education: How America's commitment to equity will determine our future.* New York: Teachers College Press.

Darling-Hammond, L. (2010b). Restoring our schools. *The Nation.* Retrieved from http://www.thenation.com/print/article/restoring-our-schools

Dawson, C. (2009). Beyond checklists and rubrics: Engaging students in authentic conversations about their writing. *English Journal, 98*(5), 66–71.

Drouin, M., & Davis, C. (2009). R u txting? Is the use of text speak hurting your literacy? *Journal of Literacy Research, 41*(1), 46–67.

Echevarria, J., Richards-Tutor, C., Chinn, V. P., & Ratleff, P. A. (2011). Did they get it? The role of fidelity in teaching English learners. *Journal of Adolescent and Adult Literacy, 54*(6), 425–434.

Echevarria, J., Short, D., & Powers, K. (2006). School reform and standards-based education: A model for English language learners. *Journal of Educational Research, 99*(4), 195–210.

Echevarria, J., Vogt, M. E., & Short, D. J. (2004). *Making content comprehensible for English learners: The SIOP model.* Boston: Pearson Education, Inc.

Educational Testing Service. (2012). *Criterion*. Retrieved from http://www.ets.org/criterion.

Eisenkraft, A. (2003). Expanding the 5E model. *Science Teacher, 70*(6), 56–59.

Emig, J. (1971). *The composing processes of twelfth graders* (Research Monograph No. 13). Urbana, IL: National Council of Teachers of English.

Enright, K. A. (2011). Language and literacy for a new mainstream. *American Educational Research Journal, 48*(1), 80–118.

Fu, D., Houser, R., & Huang, A. (2007). A collaboration between ESL and regular classroom teachers for ELL students' literacy development. *Changing English: Studies in Culture and Education, 14*(3), 325–342.

Gee, J., & Hayes, E. R. (2011). *Language and learning in the digital age*. New York: Routledge.

Giroux, H. A. (1978). Writing and critical thinking in social studies. *Curriculum Inquiry, 8*(4), 291–310.

Graham, S., & Hebert, M. (2010). *Writing to read: Evidence for how writing can improve reading*. Washington, DC: Alliance for Excellent Education.

Graham, S., & Perin, D. (2007). *Writing next: Effective strategies to improve writing of adolescents in middle and high school*. Washington, DC: Alliance for Excellent Education.

Gregg, L., & Steinberg, E. (Eds.). (1980). *Cognitive processes in writing*. Hillsdale, NJ: Erlbaum.

Guthrie, J. T., & Alvermann, D. E. (Eds.). (1998). *Engaged reading: Processes, practices, and policy implications*. New York: Teachers College Press.

Hairston, M. (1982). The winds of change: Thomas Kuhn and the revolution in the teaching of writing. *College Composition and Communication, 33*(1), 76–88.

Halliday, M. A. K., & Martin, J. R. (1993). *Writing science: Literacy and discursive power*. Pittsburgh, PA: University of Pittsburgh Press.

Hand, B., Wallace, C. W., & Yang, E.-M. (2004). Using a science writing heuristic to enhance learning outcomes from laboratory activities in seventh-grade science: Quantitative and qualitative aspects. *International Journal of Science Education, 26*(2), 131–149.

Harklau, L. (2011). Commentary: Adolescent L2 writing research as an emerging field. *Journal of Second Language Writing, 20*(3), 227–230.

Hillocks, G., Jr. (1986). *Research on written composition*. Urbana, IL: National Conference on Research in English.

Hillocks, G., Jr. (1995). *Teaching writing as reflective practice*. New York: Teachers College Press.

Hillocks, G., Jr. (2002). *The testing trap: How state writing assessments control learning*. New York: Teachers College Press.

Hirvela, A., & Sweetland, Y. L. (2005). Two case studies of L2 writers' experiences across learning-directed portfolio contexts. *Assessing Writing, 10*(3), 192–213.

Janzen, J. (2008). Teaching English language learners in the content areas. *Review of Educational Research, 78*(4), 1010–1038.

Kentucky Department of Education. (1999). Spring1999 Release Item: Grade 8 Mathematics. Retrieved August 1, 2012, from http://www.education. ky.gov/KDE/Instructional+Resources/Curriculum+Documents+and+Resou rces/Released+Test+Items/1999+Release+Forms+Open+Response+Comme ntaries.htm

Keys, C. W. (2000). Investigating the thinking processes of eighth grade writers during the composition of a scientific laboratory report. *Journal of Research in Science Teaching, 37*(7), 676–690.

Kinneavy, J. (1980). *A theory of discourse: The aims of discourse.* New York: Norton.

Klentschy, M., & Thompson, L. (2008). *Scaffolding science inquiry through lesson design.* Portsmouth, NH: Heinemann.

Knapp, M. S., & Associates. (1995). *Teaching for meaning in high-poverty classrooms.* New York: Teachers College Press.

Lane, B. (1993). *After the end: Teaching and learning creative revision.* Portsmouth, NH: Heinemann.

Langenberg, D. N. (2000). *Report of the National Reading Panel: Teaching children to read.* Washington, DC: National Institute of Child Health and Human Development.

Langer, J. A. (1986). Learning through writing: Study skills in the content areas. *Journal of Reading, 29*(5), 401–406.

Langer, J. A. (1992). Speaking of knowing: Conceptions of knowing in the academic disciplines. In A. Herrington & C. Moran (Eds.), *Writing, teaching, and learning in the disciplines* (pp. 69–85). New York: Modern Language Association.

Langer, J. A. (2000). Excellence in English in middle and high school: How teachers' professional lives support student achievement. *American Educational Research Journal, 37*(2), 397–439.

Langer, J. A. (2001). Beating the odds: Teaching middle and high school students to read and write well. *American Educational Research Journal, 38*(4), 837–880.

Langer, J. A. (2004). *Getting to excellent: How to create better schools.* New York: Teachers College Press.

Langer, J. A. (2011a). *Envisioning knowledge: Building literacy in the academic disciplines.* New York: Teachers College Press.

Langer, J. A. (2011b). *Envisioning literature: Literary understanding and literature instruction* (2nd ed.). New York: Teachers College Press.

Langer, J. A., & Applebee, A. N. (1987). *How writing shapes thinking: A study of teaching and learning.* Urbana, IL: National Council of Teachers of English.

Leki, I., Cumming, A., & Silva, T. (2006). Second-language composition teaching and learning. In P. Smagorinsky (Ed.), *Research on composition.* New York: Teachers College Press.

Lenhart, A. (2012). Teens, smartphones & texting. *Pew Internet & American Life Project*. Retrieved from http://www.pewinternet.org/Reports/2012/Teens-and-smartphones.aspx

Lenhart, A., Arafeh, S., Smith, A., & Macgill, A. R. (2008). Writing, technology and teens. *Pew Internet & American Life Project*. Retrieved from http://www.pewinternet.org/~/media//Files/Reports/2008/PIP_Writing_Report_FINAL3.pdf

Lenhart, A., Purcell, K., Smith, A., & Zickuhr, K. (2010). Social media and young adults. *Pew Internet & American Life Project*. Retrieved from http://pewinternet.org/~/media//Files/Reports/2010/PIP_Social_Media_and_Young_Adults_Report_Final_with_toplines.pdf

Lewis, C., & Fabos, B. (2005). Instant messaging, literacies, and social identities. *Reading Research Quarterly, 40*(4), 470–501.

Marshall, J. D. (1984). Process and product: Case studies of writing in two content areas. In A. N. Applebee (Ed.), *Contexts for learning to write: Studies of secondary school instruction* (pp. 149–168). Norwood, NJ: Ablex.

Mathematical Sciences Education Board. (1990). *Reshaping school mathematics: A philosophy and framework for curriculum*. Washington, DC: National Academy Press.

Metz, S. (2012). Reading, writing, and science. *Science Teacher, 79*(1), 6.

Miller, C. R. (1984). Genre as social action. *Quarterly Journal of Speech, 70*, 151–167.

Moffett, J. (1968). *Teaching the universe of discourse*. Boston: Houghton Mifflin.

Moje, E. B. (2007). Developing socially just subject-matter instruction: A review of the literature on disciplinary literacy teaching. *Review of Research in Education, 31*, 1–44.

Moje, E. B., Ciechanowski, K. M., Ellis, L., Carrillo, R., & Collazo, T. (2004). Working toward third space in content area literacy: An examination of everyday funds of knowledge and discourse. *Reading Research Quarterly, 39*(1), 38–70.

Morgan, C. (1998). *Writing mathematically: The discourse of investigation*. London: Taylor & Francis.

Nachowitz, M. (2012). *Reading for deep understanding: Knowledge building and conceptual artifacts in secondary English* (Unpublished doctoral dissertation). University at Albany, State University of New York.

National Center for Education Statistics (NCES). (2007). *The condition of education* (NCES 2007-064). Washington, DC: U.S. Department of Education, Institute for Education Sciences, National Center for Education Statistics.

National Center for Education Statistics (NCES). (2010). *The condition of education:Closer look 2010: High-poverty public schools*. Washington, DC: U.S. Department of Education, Institute of Education Sciences, National Center for Education Statistics. Retrieved from http://nces.ed.gov/programs/coe/analysis/2010-index.asp

National Center for Education Statistics (NCES). (2011). *The condition of education 2011*. Washington, DC: U.S. Department of Education, Institute of Education

Sciences, National Center for Education Statistics.

National Center for Education Statistics (NCES). (2012). *The nation's report card: Writing 2011: National Assessment of Educational Progress at grades 8 and 12* (NCES 2012-470). Washington, DC: U.S. Department of Education, Institute of Education Sciences, National Center for Education Statistics.

National Center for Education Statistics (NCES). (n.d.). *NAEP Data Explorer* [Database]. Washington, DC: U.S. Department of Education, Institute of Education Sciences, National Center for Education Statistics. Retrieved from http://nces.ed.gov/nationsreportcard/naepdata

National Commission on Writing in America's Schools and Colleges. (2003). *The neglected "r": The need for a writing revolution.* New York: College Entrance Examination Board.

National Committee on Science Education Standards and Assessment, & National Research Council. (1996). *National science education standards.* Washington, DC: National Academies Press.

National Council for the Social Studies (NCSS). (2008). *A vision of powerful teaching and learning in the social studies: Building social understanding and civic efficacy.* Retrieved from http://www.socialstudies.org/print/121

National Council for the Social Studies (NCSS). (2010a). *National curriculum standards for social studies: A framework for teaching, learning and assessment.* Silver Spring, MD: National Council for the Social Studies.

National Council for the Social Studies (NCSS). (2010b). *Principles for learning: A foundation for transforming K-12 education.* http://www.socialstudies.org/principlesfor learning.

National Council of Teachers of English, & International Reading Association. (1996). *Standards for the English language arts.* Urbana, IL: National Council of Teachers of English; Newark, DE: International Reading Association.

National Council of Teachers of Mathematics (NCTM). (2000). *Principles and standards for school mathematics.* Reston, VA: National Council of Teachers of Mathematics.

National Poverty Center (NPC). (2012). *Poverty in the United States: Frequently asked questions.* Retrieved from http://www.npc.umich.edu/poverty

National Research Council. (2011). *A framework for K–12 science education: Practices, cross-cutting concepts, and core ideas.* Washington, DC: National Academies Press.

Needels, M. C., & Knapp, M. S. (1994). Teaching writing to children who are underserved. *Journal of Educational Psychology, 86*(3), 339–349.

New York State Education Department (NYSED), Office of State Assessment. (2007). Appendix B. Revised document-based essay generic scoring rubric (February 2004). In *Revised generic scoring rubric for the Regents examinations in global history and geography and United States history and government.* Retrieved from http://www.p12.nysed.gov/assessment/ss/hs/rubrics/revisedrubrichssocst.pdf

Nystrand, M. (1997). *Opening dialogue: Understanding the dynamics of language and learning in the English classroom.* New York: Teachers College Press.

Olson, C. B., Kim, J. S., Scarcella, R., Kramer, J., Pearson, M., van Dyk, D. A., . . . Land, R. E. (2012). Enhancing the interpretive reading and analytical writing of mainstreamed English learners in secondary school. *American Educational Research Journal, 49*(2), 323–355.

Olson, C. B., Land, R., Anselmi, T., & AuBuchon, C. (2010). Teaching secondary English learners to understand, analyze, and write interpretive essays about theme. *Journal of Adolescent and Adult Literacy, 54*(4), 245–256.

Olson, C. B., & Matuchniak, T. (2012, April). A cognitive strategies approach to connecting reading and writing instruction for English language learners in grades 6–12. In R. E. Bennett (Chair), *Reading/Writing strategies: Supporting intertextuality in 21st century literacy.* Symposium conducted at the annual meeting of the American Educational Research Association, Vancouver, BC, Canada.

Ortmeier-Hooper, C., & Enright, K. A. (2011). Mapping new territory: Toward an understanding of adolescent L2 writers and writing in US contexts. *Journal of Second Language Writing, 20*(3), 167–181.

Pearson Education. (2010). Intelligent essay assessor (IEA) fact sheet. Retrieved from http://kt.pearsonassessments.com/download/IEA-FactSheet-20100401. pdf

Porter, M. K., & Masingila, J. O. (2000). Examining the effects of writing on conceptual and procedural knowledge in calculus. *Educational Studies in Mathematics, 42*(2), 165–177.

Prensky, M. (2001). Digital natives, digital immigrants. *On the Horizon, 9*(5), 1–6. Retrieved from http://www.marcprensky.com/writing/prensky%20-%20 digital%20natives,%20digital%20immigrants%20-%20part1.pdf

Pressley, M., Allington, R. L., Wharton-McDonald, R., Block, C. C., & Morrow, L. M. (2001). *Learning to read: Lessons from exemplary first-grade classrooms.* New York: Guilford Press.

Prior, P. (2004). Tracing process: How texts come into being. In C. Bazerman & P. Prior (Eds.), *What writing does and how it does it: An introduction to analyzing texts and textual practices* (pp. 167–200). Mahwah, NJ: Erlbaum.

Pritchard, R. J., & Honeycutt, R. L. (2006). The process approach to writing instruction: Examining its effectiveness. In C. A. MacArthur, S. Graham, & J. Fitzgerald (Eds.), *Handbook of Writing Research* (pp. 275–290). New York: Guilford Press.

Quinn, R. J., & Wilson, M. M. (1997). Writing in the mathematics classroom: Teacher beliefs and practices. *The Clearing House: A Journal of Educational Strategies, Issues and Ideas, 71*(1), 14–20.

Ray, K. W. (2006). *Study driven: A framework for planning units of study in the writing workshop.* Portsmouth, NH: Heinemann.

Ray, K. W., & Laminack, L. L. (2001). *The writing workshop: Working through the hard parts (and they're all hard parts)*. Urbana, IL: National Council of Teachers of English.

Rhodes, J. A., & Robnolt, V. J. (2009). Digital literacies in the classroom. In L. Christenbury, R. Bomer, & P. Smagorinsky (Eds.), *Handbook of adolescent literacy research* (pp. 153–169). New York: Guilford Press.

Russell, D. R. (1991). *Writing in the academic disciplines, 1870–1990: A curricular history*. Carbondale, IL: Southern Illinois University Press.

Russell, M., & Abrams, L. (2004). Instructional use of computers for writing: The effect of state testing programs. *Teachers College Record, 106*(6), 1332–1357.

Salahu-Din, D., Persky, H., & Miller, J. (2008). *The Nation's Report Card: Writing 2007: National Assessment of Educational Progress at grades 8 and 12* (NCES 2008-468): U.S. Department of Education, Institute of Education Sciences, National Center for Education Statistics.

Santa, C. (1988). *Content reading including study systems*. Dubuque, IA: Kendall/Hunt.

Scardamalia, M., & Bereiter, C. (2006). Knowledge building: Theory, pedagogy, and technology. In K. Sawyer (Ed.), *The Cambridge handbook of the learning sciences* (pp. 97–115). New York: Cambridge University Press.

Schleppegrell, M. J. (2012). Academic language in teaching and learning. *The Elementary School Journal, 112*(3), 409–418.

Schleppegrell, M. J., Achugar, M., & Oteiza, T. (2004). The grammar of history: Enhancing content-based instruction through a functional focus on language. *TESOL Quarterly, 38*(1), 67–93.

Shermis, M. D., & Hamner, B. (2012, April). *Contrasting state-of-the-art automatic scoring of essays: Analysis*. Paper presented at the annual meeting of the National Council of Measurement in Education, Vancouver, BC, Canada.

Singer, S. R., Hilton, M. L., & Schweingruber, H. A. (Eds.). (2006). *America's lab report: Investigations in high school science*. Washington, DC: National Academies Press.

Smagorinsky, P. (2008). *Teaching English by design: How to create and carry out instructional units*. Portsmouth, NH: Heinemann.

Smagorinsky, P., Johannessen, L. R., Kahn, E. A., & McCann, T. M. (2010). *The dynamics of writing instruction: A structured process approach for middle and high school writing*. Portsmouth, NH: Heinemann.

Smith, A., & Brenner, J. (2012). Twitter use 2012. *Pew Internet & American Life Project*. Retrieved from http://pewinternet.org/Reports/2012/Twitter-Use-2012.aspx

Smith, M., & O'Day, J. (1991). Systemic school reform. In S. H. Fuhrman & B. Malem (Eds.), *The politics of curriculum and testing: The 1990 yearbook of the Politics of Education Association* (pp. 233–267). Philadelphia: Falmer Press.

Stanford History Education Group. (2012). *Reading like a historian*. Retrieved from http://sheg.stanford.edu/?q=node/45

Steele, D. (2005). Using writing to access students' schemata knowledge for algebraic thinking. *School Science and Mathematics, 105*(3), 142–154.

Steffens, H. J., Dickerson, M. J., Fulweiler, T., & Biddle, A. (Eds.). (1986). *Writers guide to history*. Stamford, CT: Wadsworth.

Tagliamonte, S. A., & Denis, D. (2008). Linguistic ruin? LOL! Instant messaging and teen language. *American Speech, 83*(1), 3–34.

Tardy, C. (2006). Researching first and second language genre learning: A comparative review and a look ahead. *Journal of Second Language Writing, 15,* 79–101.

Torgesen, J., Houston, D. D., Rissman, L. M., Decker, S. M., Roberts, G., Vaughn, S., . . . Lesaux, N. (2007). *Academic literacy instruction for adolescents*. Portsmouth, NH: RMC Research Corporation, Center on Instruction.

Toulmin, S. E. (1953). *The philosophy of science*. New York: Hutchinson.

Toulmin, S. E. (1958). *The uses of argument*. Cambridge, UK: Cambridge University Press.

Toulmin, S. E. (1961). *Foresight and understanding*. Bloomington: Indiana University Press.

Wilcox, K. C. (2011). Writing across the curriculum for secondary English language learners: A case study. *Writing & Pedagogy, 3*(1), 79–112.

Wilcox, K. C., & Angelis, J. I. (2009). *Best practices in high performing middle schools*. New York: Teachers College Press.

Wilcox, K. C., & Angelis, J. I. (2011). *Best practices in high performing high schools*. New York: Teachers College Press.

Wineberg, S. (2007, December). Unnatural and essential: The nature of historical thinking. *Teaching History, 129,* 6–11.

Wineberg, S., Martin, D., & Monte-Sano, C. (2011). *Reading like a historian*. New York: Teachers College Press.

Wolff, T. (1989). *This boy's life: A memoir*. New York: Grove Press.

World-Class Instructional Design and Assessment (WIDA). (2011). *Academic language*. Madison: University of Wisconsin, Madison, School of Education, Wisconsin Center for Education Research. Retrieved from http://www.wida.us/aboutus/academiclanguage

Zickuhr, K., & Smith, A. (2012). Digital differences. *Pew Internet & American Life Project*. Retrieved from http://pewinternet.org/Reports/2012/Digital-differences/Main-Report/Internet-adoption-over-time.aspx

Index

◇◇◇◇◇◇

About the Authors

Arthur N. Applebee is a Distinguished Professor in the School of Education, University at Albany, State University of New York, the chair of the Department of Educational Theory & Practice, and the director of the Center on English Learning and Achievement. He advises at international, national, state, and local levels on effective approaches to language and literacy education, and was a member of the Validation Committee for the Common Core State Standards. Applebee is a past president of the National Conference on Research in Language and Literacy and has been recognized for the cumulative contribution of his work by election to the International Reading Hall of Fame and by the David H. Russell Award for Distinguished Research in the Teaching of English.

Judith A. Langer, an internationally known scholar in literacy learning, is Vincent O'Leary Distinguished Professor at the University at Albany, State University of New York. She is founder of the Albany Institute for Research in Education and director of the Center on English Learning and Achievement. Her most recent book, *Envisioning Knowledge: Gaining Literacy in the Academic Disciplines,* received the David H. Russell Award for Distinguished Research in the Teaching of English. Langer has received several other notable awards including: Honorary Doctorate from the University of Uppsala, Sweden; Imaginative Scientists award from Lund University, Sweden; induction into the Reading Hall of Fame; and the Albert J. Harris award for research on teaching students with reading difficulties.

Kristen Campbell Wilcox is an assistant professor in the Department of Educational Theory & Practice of the University at Albany, State University of New York. Her areas of research interest are in the intersections of language, culture, and cognition in ethnically, linguistically, and culturally diverse educational contexts. She is coauthor of *Best Practices from High-Performing Middle Schools* and *Best Practices from High-Performing High Schools,* in addition to publishing articles in such journals as *Cultural Studies: Critical Methodologies; Critical Inquiry in Language Studies; Critical Educa-*

tion; Education and Urban Society; Writing & Pedagogy; The Middle School Journal; The High School Journal; Phi Delta Kappan; and *Principal Leadership.*

Marc Nachowitz is an assistant professor of Teacher Education at Miami University (Ohio) where he teaches courses in content-area literacy, secondary ELA methods, and foundations of literacy and language. Nachowitz's research focuses on the development of effective teaching and learning strategies for improving students' deep understanding of literature and improving literacy strategies for content-area learning. He earned a B.S. and M.A. in English Education from the University of Connecticut and taught high school English in suburban and urban settings. He completed his doctoral studies in Curriculum and Instruction at the University at Albany, State University of New York, and was a recipient of the State Farm Foundation Doctoral Dissertation Award.

Michael P. Mastroianni is a doctoral student in the Department of Educational Theory & Practice at the University at Albany, State University of New York. In addition to his work with the National Study of Writing Instruction, his research has focused on both physics education and elementary science instruction, which he has presented at various conferences and colloquia. He participated in the Sandra K. Abell Research Institute for Doctoral Students sponsored by the National Association for Research in Science Teaching, and was the recipient of the 2012 Dr. H. Craig Sipe Science Education Award from the University at Albany. Recently, Mastroianni interned at the New York State Education Department in the Office of College and University Evaluation.

Christine Dawson is a Lecturer in Education at Siena College (New York), where she teaches literacy, curriculum, and methods courses. She earned her doctorate in Curriculum, Instruction, and Teacher Education from Michigan State University, where she was awarded a University Distinguished Fellowship. She is a postdoctoral visiting research associate at the University at Albany, State University of New York. She earned her MA (Curriculum and Teaching) from Columbia University Teachers College and her BA from the University of Virginia. Her research focuses on writing pedagogy, English teacher preparation, and curriculum design. She presents regularly at national conferences and has published in *English Journal* and *Research in the Teaching of English.*